Uninvited Guests

Uninvited Guests

The Intimate Secrets
of Television and Radio

Laurie Taylor and Bob Mullan
Photographs by Nigel Inglis
Qualitative Research
by The Research Business

Chatto & Windus . London

Published in 1986 by
Chatto & Windus
40 William IV Street
London WC2N 4DF

British Library Cataloguing in Publication Data
Taylor, Laurie
    Uninvited guests: the intimate secrets of television
    and radio.
    1. Broadcasting – Social aspects – Great Britain
    I. Title   II. Mullan, Bob
    791.44'0941   PN1990.6.G7

    ISBN 0-7011-2973-5

Photoset by Rowland Phototypesetting Ltd
Bury St Edmunds, Suffolk
Printed in Great Britain by
Redwood Burn Ltd
Trowbridge, Wiltshire

Contents

Acknowledgements

We must first thank all the people who took part in the discussion groups reported in this book. On the research side we are greatly indebted to Bob Towler and Michael Svennevig of the IBA's Research Department, Pam Mills, head of Special Projects in BBC's Research Department, Special Projects, and Rebecca Wynberg of *The Research Business*. The enthusiasm of these people was particularly sustaining on those days when we felt we might disappear without trace under piles of unanalysed transcripts. Our thanks also to Jan Dalley, Bill Podmore, Phil Redmond, Mary Hickman, Marian Dudman, Michèle Allen, Guislaine Morland, Helen Moroney, Jill Schostak and 'Keith Little'.

The following newspapers were kind enough to allow us to use extracts from their television reporting: the *Daily Star*, *Daily Mail*, *Sun*, *Sunday Express Magazine*, *Mirror* and *Sunday Mirror*.

We acknowledge with thanks the permission of BARB (Broadcasters' Audience Research Board) to reproduce the audience figures and Audience Reaction Survey data which appear throughout this book.

We should also like to thank the IBA for kind permission to quote from some research reports and from *Television Programme Guidelines*.

We are grateful to the following for permission to reproduce the photographs: BBC Hulton Picture Library for pages 2, 41, 99, 170; BBC for page 107; and Associated Newspapers, BBC, *Marketing Week*, *Options*, Robin Hanbury-Tenison and the *Times Higher Education Supplement* for pages 116 and 117.

All other photographs are by Nigel Inglis.

Finally, we must thank the IBA for a research grant which enabled us to extend the scope of this study.

Preface

Every day, several hundred thousand people throughout the country settle down over breakfast, lunch, dinner, tea or supper to chat in loving, gossiping, sometimes downright scurrilous terms about their favourite or least favourite personalities and programmes.

They talk about *Wogan* and *Dallas* and *Dynasty* and 'the *Street*', about Benny and Mac, Quincy and Alexis, Sue Lawley and Ian McCaskill, about all those programmes and people which regularly capture the attention of nearly a quarter of the population of this country. Everyone present is likely to be an expert on the topic: not only to have seen last night's episode of *Coronation Street* or *This is Your Life* but several hundred of the episodes which have preceded it. What's more, all the participants will have additional background information to bring to bear on the topic: personal details about presenters and stars, news of sudden rises or falls in their popularity, details of the forthcoming death, marriage or disablement of the characters in soap operas. (The popular press now employs considerably more reporters on television news than it does on foreign affairs.)

Our everyday talk about television does not stick slavishly to the subject. When we talk about J.R. and Pam (from *Dallas*), Arthur and Terry (from *Minder*), Del Boy and Rodney (in *Only Fools and Horses*), we also talk about ourselves, about what is important to us, what makes us laugh and cry and feel fearful. The affair between Mike and Deirdre (in *Coronation Street*) can quickly turn into a debate on marital fidelity, the quarrel between Gail and Brian (also in the *Street*) into a discussion on whether a woman's proper place is in the home.

Little of this talk gets back to those who make television, or write about it. Studies of the television audience are few and far between and often rely upon nothing much more intimate or personal than long statistical tables of viewing figures or the coding of responses to questionnaires.

We became interested in the possibility of remedying this situation when we read a number of BBC research reports on viewers' and listeners' reactions to specific programmes which had employed 'discussion groups'. These reports, on such subjects as *Songs of Praise* and *That's Life!*, did at least seem to contain some bits of conversation which sounded as though they came from normal discussions.

'Discussion groups' usually contain nine or ten people who are recruited on the basis of their age, sex, social class and particular interest in the topic. They get together at a private house, where, after a drink together, they are led into the discussion by a 'moderator' who gradually introduces a variety of open-ended and 'projective' questions. ('What picture do you have in your mind of the typical Radio Three announcer?' 'What are the things you least like about Radio Four?')

At the end of a two-hour session, all participants are paid for their time, and a recording of their discussion is sent off for transcription and subsequent analysis, in which names and some personal details are changed to ensure their anonymity.

We had no expertise ourselves in this technique, but early in 1985 we persuaded one of the leading qualitative research firms in this country – *The Research Business* – to cooperate with us in setting up a wide range of discussion groups. The group members were chosen according to their social class, sex, age and also their devotion to particular types of programme: American Soaps, British Soaps, Wildlife Programmes, News and Current Affairs, Sport, Religion, Royalty, Cops-and-Robbers, Popular Music, Chat Shows, Quizzes and Game Shows, Documentaries.

We asked *The Research Business* (TRB) to hold these groups in urban, suburban and rural locations, and as far as possible to make sure that each group contained people who were typical viewers of the programmes under discussion. So, for example, game and quiz shows were principally discussed by groups of people over forty from social categories C_2 and D (skilled and semi-skilled), while the groups for natural history were mainly recruited from social categories B and C_1 (managerial and clerical).

Discussion groups did not stick to only one type of programme. After about an hour the members went on to debate a common set of questions about personalities, programmes and attitudes to television.

Whereas the BBC research was chiefly interested in gathering information which would help producers and programme planners, we asked *The Research Business* to promote conversation about *any* aspect of programmes, performers and television itself, and we provided a range of open-ended questions to assist the moderators in their task. These were questions such as:

- What characters on television are most like themselves in real life?
- What is so special about news readers? What can they do? Why do they become famous?
- Is there any resemblance between your family and the Ewings [from *Dallas*]?
- Can you imagine any of the royal family as characters in one of the soap operas?
- Which popular characters would you like to kill off, and which would you like to live for ever?

- What kind of person is your television set – male? female? warm? cold? a friend? a critic?
- In what ways is the Crossroads motel [in the soap opera *Crossroads*] unlike a real motel?
- Have you ever cried real tears during a television programme?

Altogether, twenty discussion groups were held, involving 193 people. In addition, we were fortunate in being allowed to draw upon the material gathered by BBC researchers from approximately thirty other groups, and to have access to other studies of the television audience conducted by the Research Department of the Independent Broadcasting Authority (IBA).

To supplement all this information the IBA undertook research on our behalf using the Audience Reaction Service of BARB to conduct a national enquiry. A representative sample of 3000 television viewers in the UK aged 12 or over were asked for their opinions on a number of statements which we also raised in the discussion groups, such as:

- I sometimes wish that violence in programmes like *The Sweeney* was more realistic.
- I sometimes feel that I could be a better actor than those in *Crossroads*.
- I hope to watch more television in future than I do at present.

In a book about popular television, it is essential to know exactly which programmes are popular, and with whom. We are therefore very grateful to the IBA, the BBC and BARB for allowing us access to the audience composition figures for all the programmes which are discussed or quoted in these pages.

From the beginning we also realised that it was impossible to talk about popular television without also referring to the coverage of the topic in the popular press. So we carried out a small survey on the subject, which drew upon Fleet Street files and upon extensive interviews with one serving general in that small army of reporters who now spend their lives ferreting out such matters as the exact way in which the scriptwriters of *Dynasty* will resurrect Fallon. (We agreed with some reluctance to protect him from the wrath of his colleagues by allowing a pseudonym – 'Keith Little'.)

We have moved some way from the days when television was regarded as positively dangerous to the viewer as 'a box of cathode-ray guns which are literally aimed at us . . . guns powered by 25,000 volts', or the times when it was thought likely that the box would empty us of all personal interests and hopes and ambition, transform us into 'a blob of plastic matter modelled after the moving images'. (Jerry Mander, *Four Arguments for the Elimination of Television*, 1977.) 'Nowadays,' as Clive James observes, 'it is much less common for educated people to scorn television. Even some of the Cambridge dons now have television sets standing bare-faced in the living room instead of hidden behind an antimacassar. General statements about the culturally deleterious effects of television are nowadays less likely to go unchallenged.' (*Glued to the Box*, 1983.)

This account of how the audience itself regards its nightly viewing provides some support for those who do the challenging. The viewers who talk in these pages are anything but passive and accepting. Far from being 'culturally deleterious', television often seems culturally productive – providing an occasion for the display of opinions, attitudes and sentiments about the world which might otherwise have remained unspoken.

But perhaps, more importantly, the strain of irreverence which runs round and about all the expressions of enthusiasm and delight and concern about the television suggests that its hosts and hostesses, presenters and performers, characters and stars, should remain on their best behaviour, aware that despite the attention and even devotion they routinely receive in our homes, they are nevertheless – uninvited guests.

I

Dallas without Arabs: Television and Reality

'They actually mix up things in the programme with reality. In *Dynasty* [the glamorous American soap opera set in Denver] the other day, they went to this dinner party and who should walk along but ex-President Ford. "Oh, good afternoon, Mr President. How are you?" And there he is. In the programme.'

Part-Time Work

Some writers would hardly think it worthwhile for viewers to fret so much about reality. Whatever pretensions television may occasionally have about opening up a window on the world – and how frequently that image recurs in its publicity – it is primarily an escape from reality, an invitation to the viewers to enter an artificial paradise, to live on the screen a life they will never live in fact.

Yet we seem intensely interested in making distinctions between what is real and what is unreal on our screens: not usually with reference to any grand notions about the meaning of all television, but in relation to particular events and episodes and characters which we encounter nightly.

> DEREK (40): Now take that Quincy [pathologist hero of an American 'detective' series]. He is hilarious, because the guy does autopsies but he also solves every single crime in Los Angeles. He's never got a scalpel in his hand. *He's always down the street solving crime.*

Of course, the trouble with *work*, as far as television is concerned, is that most of it is not intrinsically interesting. This means that in *Dallas* and *Dynasty*:

> MARGARET (37): Those offices – they're never like real offices. You never see paper on the secretary's desk; you see one sheet of paper in the typewriter and that's it. There's never a mess in the office, no waste-paper bins full of rubbish.
> TRB: Do you ever see them working?
> MARGARET: The main thing they seem to do is make appointments.

Certainly they do make appointments: the long round of official and unofficial appointments which constitute the plot. Indeed, as long as 'work' can be shown as some sort of interaction between people, rather than as a sheer physical activity, then it can be harnessed to the story. At Mike Baldwin's factory in *Coronation Street*, we may know all about the relations between those who work there and their employer, but we are left completely puzzled about how the actual production targets are ever reached:

> WENDY (33): There aren't enough machinists, to start with. There are only four of them, and they're making jeans for half the population of England.

Perhaps the problem is that we don't see the whole factory – perhaps there are other parts where unknown machinists labour away to supplement the output of those who chatter before the camera. But this is at odds with other 'realistic' features of the *Street*, the front doors of the houses and shops and pub, and the evident fact that you can walk through these doors into actual interiors.

> TRB: How many people do you think work in that factory?
> CAROL (35): Well, you only see those you see. You don't see anybody else.
> LOUISE (29): You don't go downstairs to where all the material is kept.
> CAROL: No, you don't see any other part of the factory.
> LOUISE: No place where the cutting is done.
> WENDY: It's only a small part of a large factory: it's just to give you a rough idea of Mike Baldwin's place. It's not like *Gems* [a British soap opera based on the rag trade] for instance, where the factory area is a lot bigger.
> MICHELE (31): They do say there's a downstairs though, don't they? You see Emily Bishop coming up from downstairs, don't you?
> CAROL: She does the VAT and all that sort of thing. Her husband died, didn't he? Got shot.

Even if the mysteries of Baldwin's factory concerning production targets, concealed machinists, and what exactly goes on downstairs are not readily resolved, *Coronation Street* can still score marks for reality – especially when a direct comparison comes so readily to the mind of a member of an all-male discussion group:

> GEOFF (32): I think some of the scenes recently with Brian [Brian Tilsley, married to Gail] in the garage have been pretty true to life. At least he's got oil on his hands. The mechanics in *Crossroads* never have.
> MARTIN (37): Make a good mechanic cry, wouldn't they?
> GEORGE (31): The only guy in *Crossroads* who's ever got any black on his hands is the black guy.

In television's quiz and game shows, the funnier and more idiosyncratic the jobs, the better life is for the presenter. Back in 1951, the BBC first broadcast *What's My Line?*, a panel game in which the eccentric nature of the contestant's occupation provides the panel with every opportunity for disingenuous questions such as 'Could I do it?' or 'Could you do it to me?' Rosalind Brunt (in *Television Mythologies*, 1984) collected the job titles from six programmes in the present (revived by ITV) series:

> *Women*
> traffic warden, corsetière, bus driver, belt-and-braces maker, ERNIE
> operator, Easter-egg maker, turkey stuffer, crab fisher, sleeping-bag stuffer,
> 'she makes Boy George's collar jackets', pyjama corder, flower seller.
> *Men*
> Saddler, Forth Rail Bridge painter, Morris dancer, sporran maker, butterfly
> farmer, pheasant plucker, bosun's mate, bottle washer, fish-cake maker,
> billiard-table leveller, sundial designer.

All in all, it's whimsical enough to make *Coronation Street* seem like part of our industrial heartland. Baldwin may be unrealistically short-staffed, but at least his meagre quota of machinists produce something rather more substantial than a weekly load of double entendres.

Extra, Extra

Not everything, though, seems quite right in other parts of the *Street*. There are the peculiarities of Alf Roberts's corner shop where 'absolutely everybody has the right change for every single product' and the very strange goings-on at the Rovers Return pub where Pat (47) observed:

> They have the most brilliant bar service ever. They actually read the
> customers' minds. 'Give us a pint, Bet,' they say. Never mind a pint of
> what. And it always comes up right.

And in the Rovers the problem of extras once again raises doubts about the reality of the setting. In Mike Baldwin's factory you can just about assume that there are other workers out of sight, but in the open-plan Rovers this is hardly an option. If the place is left half empty, you diminish the sense of community upon which the series depends, but if you fill it up with protagonists – Brian, Gail, Bet, Hilda, Ken, Deirdre, Ivy, Vera, Jack, Betty, Alf, Curly and Mike – you immediately provide the opportunity for the resolution of most of the conflicts and estrangements which make up the plot. The only solution is to bring in a few strangers who are somehow separate from the *dramatis personae*. Helen (47) has been studying them for some time:

> I always watch them. People sitting around. Playing darts. But you never
> hear them.
> JOAN (51): They talk, though. You can see their mouths moving.
> HELEN: I'd like to know what they're saying.
> JANET (51): They must just move their lips.
> HELEN: Well, they mustn't talk, must they? If they talk they've got to be
> paid.

Helen had extended her study of background figures to *Dallas*:

> In that, even the passers-by are handsome. And the women are all wonderful. You look.

But Janet had spotted that even if the extras in American soaps were always good-looking, economies were still being made:

> Whenever they go into La Mirage [La Mirage hotel, *Dynasty*] there are always these two people, the same two people walking across the set. And that annoys me. My little girl always notices it. She says, it's exactly the same car there and exactly the same two people as last week.

Others, back in Britain again, remarked on the peculiar absence of crisps and nuts from the Rovers because of the efforts that are made not to show branded goods. In *EastEnders* (the BBC soap opera set in an East London square) you can see, for example, Skol and Guinness behind the bar, but they still order pints of fictional 'Churchill'. And Newton and Ridley's beer in the Rovers not only bears a made-up name but is now known by some – thanks to frank speaking by reformed drinker Len Fairclough (actor Peter Adamson) in the tabloids – to be merely coloured water.

Such acuity has practical uses. For Miss S. Ogden of Warleigh Road, Hull (who makes clear that there is no hint of nepotism in her request) it provides a chance to procure a present for her boyfriend.

Dear Sirs,

My boyfriend collects model and toy Land Rovers.

I have noticed, on the shelves of "The Cabin", two toy Land Rovers. There are surprisingly few Land Rover toys in the shops and I wonder if you could consider selling the two that you have to me.

I realise that you must constantly get requests of this sort and would not have the time to deal with them all but I would be extremely grateful if you could make an exception in this case

If this is possible please notify me of the price and any postage/packageing costs

Thanking you in anticipation.

Yours Sincerely

S. Ogden
MISS. S. OGDEN
(No relation)

P.s. Love the programme. Don't change the formula.

Street Credibility

Not all the peculiarities of settings like the Rovers Return need to be attributed to the exigencies of filming or to production lapses; some can be seen not so much as departures from reality as evidence of the existence of another reality. When we rather ruthlessly asked why jukeboxes and fruit machines were conspicuous by their absence, Martin (37) managed to find an answer which lay somewhere between fact and fiction. The Rovers Return wasn't that sort of pub. It wouldn't be that sort of pub.

> MARTIN: If they brought jukeboxes and fruit machines into it, it wouldn't be the Rovers Return. It is just an ordinary little pub in a street, a close community, people can just pop in. And when you think of the North, there's a lot of hardship. They have enough money to go for a pint at the end of the day but they wouldn't be putting money into machines.

When Andy (25) joined in to support Martin he was quite happy to draw on his experience of the North to confirm the accuracy of the *Street*'s portrayal.

> ANDY: They are twenty years behind London and the southeast. Maybe even twenty-five: A man up there goes out and has a pint, the woman goes out and has half of a bitter and sits in the corner and natters with the girls. It's very much a different way of life. It is quite a way behind. I find it quite alien when I go up there.

But there are consequences involved if you believe in the reality of this world – believe that it is at least a faithful record of how life is for some people. After all, the *Street* may have some laughs from time to time but the relentless pressure of the plot (not to mention the background rhythm of the ratings) means that misfortunes have periodically to descend upon its residents. Jill (21) captured the dilemma of knowing all this and still believing in the reality of the *Street*:

> The people in it are believable. [*Pause.*] *It's very tragic.*

The Missing Arabs

When it came to *Crossroads*, nobody appeared to feel the same need to get hold of reality and knock it into a shape which fitted its fictional image. The fact that the entire layout of the motel seemed to have changed without the intervention of a single carpenter, bricklayer or plumber, and without much comment from the staff, suggested the presence of a powerful nonfictional *deus ex machina*: someone, in fact, who, according to news leaked to the press, was anxious to improve the status of the motel, to make it more classy: more in the style of La Mirage, Denver (once run by Fallon but now by the pensive, beautiful, and once insane Claudia), and less like the Newton Pagnell service centre.

> Bowman [producer Phillip Bowman] has taken *Crossroads* upmarket . . .

more boardroom and bedroom, less kitchen and wheelchairs. He's bringing in younger characters and a faster pace, 'more thrills and spills' like the American soaps which are 'all plot, plot, plot, coming at you all the time'. (David Housham, *Broadcast*, 21 June 1985.)

Regular viewers were alert to at least some of the changes:

DOT (37): Now they seem to have the office downstairs behind the reception, where the door used to go into the kitchen.

VAL (51): They've changed the bar as well.

LORNA (50): Even the restaurant is somehow not as it was before.

TRB: Do you think it's a set or is it real?

VAL: No, it's an actual motel now, isn't it?

TRB: Is it?

LORNA: There are motels called Crossroads, as it happens . . .

TRB: If you were driving along the M6 and you came across the Crossroads motel, would you go in?

DOT: Oh, I would, yes.

MARY (38): Oh, yes.

DOT: See Jill Harvey standing behind the desk [*laughing*], lovely.

We decided to check in all our soap-opera groups on the extent to which Crossroads motel's new up-market image was reflected in the estimated price for an overnight stay:

TRB: How much does it cost for a room with bathroom and continental breakfast for one night at the Crossroads motel?

The lowest estimate was £20 and the average £35.60. Not quite La Mirage prices, perhaps, but then certain of the Denver facilities are still absent: wall-to-ceiling carpeting, outdoor cocktail lounge, and a black millionaire cabaret star as a permanent guest (Blake's half-sister Dominique Devereaux).

When it comes to reality slips, however, there is little to distinguish the high-priced and glossy American soaps from their English counterparts. Nothing, for example, fascinated some viewers so much as the peculiar behaviour which occurs on the patio in *Dallas*, particularly in the early morning. (The extraordinary numbers of advertisements on television and in the press for 'patio' doors and 'patio' furniture means that we may be dealing here with a genuine British obsession.)

PAT (47): They're always eating on that patio, aren't they?

JUDITH (40): Breakfast, yes.

PAT: No one comes down for breakfast looking like that. Already shaved. Not like us.

JUDITH: But then some people don't look like we do, do they? I don't suppose the Queen does, does she?

JANET (32): Even the Queen doesn't come down to breakfast fully made up with her hair all perfect.

But the patio has even more significance at Southfork ranch (the home of the Ewing family in *Dallas*):

> JANET: There isn't a front door. A great big place like that and no front door. You wouldn't invite people in through the patio door, would you?
> JUDITH: And also there's always a great load of stuff for breakfast, and yet none of them ever eat it.
> JANET: It must be freezing on that patio. [*Laughs.*]

Much of the talk about the reality of *Dallas* or *Dynasty* concentrated on background details: the breakfast going cold, the lack of a front door, the same passers-by appearing in the background. Questions about the reality of the social relations in, say, *Dallas*, or about the economic infrastructure of the place, the relationship between the dealings which go on there and events in the real world of trade and commerce, are only raised by a minority:

> CALVIN (40): I don't think I've ever once seen an Arab in *Dallas*. I know America has got its own oil industry but they must have to collaborate with the Arabs from time to time. I don't think I've ever seen an Arab negotiating.

In fact part of the delight of *Dallas* and *Dynasty* seems to come from the almost comic irrelevance of such matters. It's as though we enjoy the notion that the writers and actors in *Dallas* and *Dynasty* are 'camping up' the fantasy: making it more and more irreconcilable with any known reality. This interferes with the view that there are two ways of watching such programmes. You can, so the argument goes, either suspend disbelief entirely and get thoroughly caught up in the machinations of J.R. or Alexis, or enjoy the whole thing as kitsch: sit back and laugh at the melodramatic twists and turns, the absurdly unnatural beauty of the heroes, and the ridiculous demonic quality of the villains. But most of us appear to watch with an attitude pitched somewhere between these two: an involvement in the plot which may indeed be strong enough to arouse anger or bring tears to the eyes, but also with a nice amused background sense of how far away it all is from our own home and family.

> TRB: Is there any resemblance between your family, your own family, and the Ewings or the Carringtons [the family in *Dynasty*]?
> MARY (39): We all sit down to dinner together. That's the only resemblance really.
> JACKIE (41): It's windy out in my garden, same as at the Ewings.

This attitude to viewing is quite firmly linked to American soaps. Only here did we find the regular use of words like 'escape' and talk about how pleasant it was to 'get lost' in the fictional events of the programme.

> ANNE (45): They give you a little bit of what we all would like.
> MOLLY (41): Yes, definitely. [*Most agree.*] I think it's seeing how another half lives.
> ANNE: Yes, what we would all like to have sometimes.
> MAUREEN (39): It's make-believe and fantasy. And a lot of plotting and intrigue.

The word 'escape' has been far too casually used in the past to characterise the audience's involvement with television. Sometimes it has served as an account of the total television experience. Even those subtler souls who might allow that the word hardly applies to the Weather Forecast, *The Antiques Road Show* and *Gardeners' World* have gone on to apply it indiscriminately to the viewing of all soaps and drama series. But we soon found clear signs that viewers wanted to make a distinction between the way they watched different programmes, even within this genre.

> LENA (29): Oh, when they float down for their breakfast off a silver tray, it's already cooked for them.
> ANNA (34): Oh, I love the Ewings. The way they walk about.
> JEAN (38): They're *so unreal*.
> ANNA: Oh, I have to watch it.
> JEAN: I think it's an escape, because it's so unreal.
> TRB: If that's an escape, then what are *Coronation Street* and *Crossroads*?
> LENA: It's you and me – us.
> JEAN: It's like watching yourself.

It seems important to believe that *Coronation Street* and, to a lesser extent, *Crossroads* are, for all their occasional lapses from reality, essentially more 'real' than the American products. One of our groups battled with the distinction for some time. At first members championed the greater reality of the *Street* by pointing out how audiences had gone up when Deirdre and Mike Baldwin were having 'a relationship'. In Martin's (37) words: 'That reflects what people are interested in. A real situation. Unless the situation is real, people lose interest.'

> JIM (29): But they don't. They don't. I mean *Dallas* has got a very high rating now. And that's not really real, is it?
> GEORGE (31): Well, it's certainly not real to us.
> GEOFF (37): It's real to somebody, though. There *are* those types of working people. In Dallas.

So what does that have to say about their respective realities? After all, if you don't know what America is like, might it not be the case that *Dallas* and *Dynasty* bear the same sort of relationship to American life as *Coronation Street* to ours?

> TRB: The world of *Dallas* and *Dynasty* – is that more or less like real life than *Coronation Street*?
> MOST OF GROUP: We don't know.

But one member of this group had checked it for herself.

> LOUISE (42): It's less real. *Dallas*. To be honest with you, I went to America and I was expecting to see all these beautiful women walking round with really outrageous clothes wherever I went. But they weren't. They were all fat. No different to us. And the clothes in the shops were horrible. It was no better than England.

At the level of plot, though, it was difficult to make too much of a distinction. Nobody wanted to say that people in the *Street* had more to put up with than the denizens of Southfork or Denver. In Anne's words, 'They all have problems every day.' But she went on to insist that there was still a difference. And it lay in the emotional reaction of the characters. In *Dallas* and *Dynasty* and *Falcon Crest* and *Knot's Landing* (other glamorous American soap operas), they might get very angry indeed, become positively suicidal, downright jealous, furiously competitive, but just one emotion was missing – an emotion which was at the heart of the *Street*:

> ANNE (45): What you don't see is the *sadness*. You know, when you've got a problem and how down you get and you just let yourself go. And you're sad. They're never sad. They're all still looking good.

A Touch More Realistic

Nowadays there are more dimensions to this debate than the *Coronation Street/Crossroads–Dallas/Dynasty* axis. There are also two other much discussed British serials which both make claims to be more realistic than the average soap opera: *Brookside* and *EastEnders*.

Brookside started with a blaze of publicity in which 'realism' was given full play. There was a realistic set with thirteen permanent houses and several flats on a genuine estate five miles from the centre of Liverpool; the cast of actors included several who were taken straight from the street (that is, real people) and, what's more, in some cases they could boast they were just as feminist or as radical in real life as they were in the storyline. Our 'soap reporter' from Fleet Street, Keith Little, provided the details:

Look at Ricky Tomlinson [Bobby Grant: trade union official, proud father]. The clothes he wears on and off the set are owned by *Brookside*. He wears them at home. At the weekends. In the evenings. He was one of the 'Shrewsbury 2' [militant trade unionists] and was unemployed for something like eight years. He reckons he'll need another year of *Brookside* at about £600 a week to pay off all his debts. And then Amanda Burton [Heather Haversham: career girl accountant, divorced, unlucky in love] is very anti-sexist. Or take Shelagh O'Hara [Karen Grant: rebellious, university hopeful]. Her father was a doctor. Very political again. Brought up in a very political working-class family. Goes on demos and marches. So much that an MP complained about her the other day.

But whatever the radical credentials of the actors, the solidity of the set, the intentions of the producer, is *Brookside* actually more believable? Even though it now enjoys an audience of 6 million, one of its main defenders still felt the need to introduce it.

DAVID (41): I don't know if anyone else watches it, but what I find with *Brookside* is that it's somewhere between the level of wealth that you get in the American soaps and the breadline level in *Coronation Street*. And admittedly a lot more things happen to the characters than would happen to any individual in real life – that's the way it's got to be in 'soap' – the things that do happen are all reasonably credible. There's been divorce, a woman with a grown-up family having a baby, a bloke who's a trade-union official, and living across the way another fellow who's really anti-trade union. Of all the soaps it's the easiest one to watch, the easiest one perhaps to identify with.

Unfortunately, we did not have enough regular viewers of *Brookside* to pursue the case that its growing popularity was related to its greater 'realism', but Keith Little was cynical. In his opinion, its main difference from the other soaps lay in its calculated appeal to the upwardly mobile:

After all, no one in it is actually working class, otherwise they wouldn't be living in that Close. And it's certainly become a lot more middle class. They are now actively trying to compete with other soaps. The press officer phones me up three or four times a week telling me: 'We're doing this or we're doing that. Would you like to do a competition?' If you look at it, it's also becoming more homely: 'homely' in the sense that like other soaps they're staying more in the home. And the language is more restrained. In the early days, Damon [painter-decorator on YTS, Jack the Lad] said everything but 'fuck', and 'pissing' was a popular word. They've calmed all that down.

Some viewers are clearly anxious for *Brookside* to move away from 'dull' realism:

Dear Mr Redmond

I am an avid fan of Brookside and **can** say
in all honesty that I have **never** missed a single episode
and even usually watch each episodes twice. -I therfore
hope that you do not think me too presumptious in suggesting my idea for a storyline that you and your merry
band of highly talented scriptwriters could incorporate
into your tremendous script. It occurred to me that while
the fire-conscious nose of George Jackson is locked up
there could be a fire. It would be a shame to **allow** this
to happen to poor Marie as she has had enough lately but
why not let it happen to either the Grants or to the
Collins family. You could make it a little more dramatic
by making it happen to them in the middle of the night .
I realise that contracts with the thespians concerned
would **not** allow you to write anyaone out of the show so
the fire does not have to be of a fatal nature.

I would also be happy to see more scenes with
the sexy men of Brookside scantily clad. These men
include Terry Pat Damon Stuart and Gordon.

i feel I also have some other suggestions for storyl
lines. Why not make Heather become pregnant and have to
forsake her career . PerhapsKaren could develop some
mysterios illness and Lucy Collins could return from
abroad married. Michelle could be involved in a serious
accident and Damon could become involved in drugs. Annabel
could undrego a hysterectamy and Paul could have an
affair. Bobby could become involved in a scandal of a
sexual nature and finally,Gordon could become violent and
have to undergo psychiatric help.
IF YOU COULD USE ANY OF THESE SCRYLINES I WOULD BE DELIGHTED.

KEEP UP THE GOOD WORK

Jennifer Morgan

Jennifer Morgan

There are undoubtedly those who are not attracted by claims of greater
'realism': they tune in to soaps on the grounds that they *are* soaps. Some purists,
for example, would insist that even *Dallas* and *Dynasty* might not be admitted to
the pantheon. Soap fan and *Daily Telegraph* critic, Gillian Reynolds, lists the
essential qualifications:

> The real thing rolls on, week after week, year after year. *Dallas* and
> company come in batches. This means the pace is very different. True soap
> opera moves very slowly but with a lot of situations happening to a lot of
> people. It is more fragmented and a great deal of background material is

built up in a way Mr Buckman [Peter Buckman, author of *All for Love: A Study in Soap Opera*], 1984) exactly describes as 'pointilliste'.

But others who are less receptive to the appeal of pure fiction may need to be persuaded that any new soap is much more realistic or true to life than others. So it was with *Coronation Street* in the early days: 'Here was a brainchild which moved nearer, much nearer to real life and real people' (H. V. Kershaw, the original script editor). And so it was with *Brookside*, and *EastEnders*. Julia Smith, the producer of this latter programme, publicly declared that she wanted a format that would reflect 'everyday life', a programme that would be as 'topical' and documentary as possible. She had, she said, recently talked to Phil Redmond about *Brookside* and he said, 'it takes you six months to find out what you've got wrong and six months to put it right'. Mark (28), drawing upon television history, doubted if such a leisurely timetable would be available:

> The little I've seen of *EastEnders*, it's clearly going for the tough social issue approach; prostitution, drugs, glue-sniffing, the street-level approach. And that is why I don't think *EastEnders* will be a success. Because *Angels* [hospital drama series focusing on nurses] which was done by the same team was a soap; nurses running around a hospital, people dying, getting disease. And *Angels* disappeared. Too many social issues. That's why I don't think *EastEnders* will last.

But Simon Hoggart in *New Society* (28 February 1985) more astutely envisaged that the first flush of 'realist' excitement would soon wear off and the essential conventions of British soap opera establish themselves:

> The characters we're supposed to like are, for the most part, simply dull. At the end of the first two episodes I found I had no interest in what the future held for any of them. This places *EastEnders* firmly in the tradition of British soap operas, and I have little doubt that it will in time be a huge success.

New Soaps for Old

The 'tradition of British soap operas', and with it the distinctive sense that we get from watching such programmes, may both be imperilled by current developments in the soap boom. For a start the success of the American up-market series has prompted a search for a British soap formula which might rise above the 'breadline' *Street* and the 'hopefully upwardly mobile' *Brookside*. At the moment Granada are busily working on a project code-named *Knutsford Dallas*. According to Keith Little,

> It's about a wealthy family based around the Knutsford area with all the kind of *Dallas* things thrown in. This will have the luxuriant image. A family of six. All drive the same colour car. So Dad has a white Rolls. Mum

has a white XJS, eldest daughter has a white Spitfire. There's another one –
they're revamping *Compact* [early BBC soap opera based on magazine
publishing]. This is going to be very big. You remember *Compact*? Ronald
Allen? He's going to be in the new one. They're calling it *Impact*. The
magazine has gone continental and extremely glossy. It will be the world's
first Euro-soap. They're doing a deal with the Italians and the French,
because the French have just got into soap. They've got one called *Château
Vallon*, their own *Dynasty*. This *Impact* will be dubbed into each language
but recorded and made in English. That'll come in early 1986. Extremely
expensive. And there's also interest from the States. It will be the first global
soap.

And to supplement up-market British soaps and glossy Euro- or global soaps
there are more flashy imports on their way. 'There's a Texan one called *Yellow
Rose* with David Soul. They've had teething problems with that. Central have
the option. *Paper Dolls*, starring Morgan Brittany, slumped in the States. *Glitter*
with Morgan Fairchild is already doing well. *Glitter* also got a bad press over
there but it's been redone.'

Anyone perturbed by the sight of this off-shore soap slick drifting ever nearer
can perhaps draw some reassurance from the very high audiences still watching
those traditional and new British soap operas which offer something more than
an escape from reality. This is not to deny the appeal of 'glossier' American
products. As the writer and critic Richard Hoggart has observed, the world buys
American television programmes not just because they are cheap, but because
they 'accurately gauge what will amuse most people in the world today'. There is
no such thing as the development of a cultural immunity to these products: 'I
have little doubt that, even after sixty years of earnest and culturally pure
communications within the USSR, American soap operas would have massive
majorities among Soviet viewers within a week if restrictions were lifted.'
(Richard Hoggart, *An English Temper*, 1982.)

Children and Realism

Questions about the relative 'realism' of television drama series or soaps become
more urgent when the programmes concerned are watched by those who, it is
thought, may not only take them as depictions of the real world, but will actually
seek to copy them. Although we occasionally hear about impressionable adults
in this context, the usual cause for concern is children.

In the past, the Saturday morning cinema and the comic allowed some sort of
popular, serialised, but still quite secret childhood culture: adults might know
enough about it to complain but were rarely active consumers. Matters are
different nowadays with such cult children's television programmes as *Grange
Hill*.

There's absolutely no doubt about the popularity of producer Phil Redmond's series among the young:

> One location set . . . was recently disrupted by 2000 school children desperate for a lunchtime glimpse of Tucker Jenkins, the programme's third-form Jack the Lad. Autograph hunters even included the policeman, young enough to have watched many of the early episodes, who was sent to clear the crowds.
> (Colin Shearman, *Guardian*, 5 January 1983.)

Nor is there any question about Redmond's own concern to maintain the exclusive quality of the series.

> [He] keeps a close eye on the *Grange Hill* industry – diaries, annuals, pencils – which has grown up around the programme. It was at his insistence that the three novels [based on the series] were originals. 'If you keep faith with the kids,' he says, 'and give them value for money, they'll stick with you.'
> (Ibid.)

But none of this alters the audience composition figures which show that although 25 per cent of the viewers are between ten and fifteen, 10 per cent between four and nine, and 12 per cent between sixteen and twenty-four, there is still a solid 18 per cent of viewers over fifty-five. (Not that we know if this is a mixed audience of fifty-fives to seventy-fives or an exclusive group of octogenarians: for some strange reason – probably not totally unconnected with the wish to keep advertisers unaware that millions who watch the average TV programme are far too old to want to go out and buy tight jeans or fast cars – the standard audience composition figures shovel approximately 15 million people into a single '55+' category.)

All in all, each episode of *Grange Hill* is watched by just over two million people who're still at school and by three and a half million who've already left. (Amazingly, in television terms, this is successful targeting. The producers of *Dangermouse* [a popular cartoon character], for example, must occasionally pause for thought when they have to take into account the fact that although their programme is watched by a million four- to nine-year-olds, it is also the choice of 1·5 million people over fifty-five.)

Some of the adults who take their place alongside their children in the living room to watch not *Flash Gordon* or *The Perils of Pauline* but *Grange Hill* get very disturbed about it all being much too close to home.

> I have been very concerned about some of the attitudes portrayed in *Grange Hill* . . . as I have boys aged 9 and 10 who will probably go to comprehensive school soon.
> The episode which prompted me to write this letter was the one in which one of the teachers was bullying one of the boys by forcing him to do extra PE until he was almost exhausted. This teacher was finally punished by the

head of department by a blow in the face within hearing of his class.

I feel this is a very bad example and not even realistic. Surely a head of department would take the PE teacher aside in the staffroom and reason with him.
(Mrs M. J. Holden, *Radio Times*, 21 February 1981.)

It is usually in circumstances where personal interests are directly threatened – in this case presumably the peace of mind of Mrs Holden's sons – that arguments about the reality of television *plots* are raised. Nobody worries about the story in *Dallas* and *Dynasty* because it is partly within the sheer unreality of its twists and turns that the enjoyment resides.

Others who dislike what they see in *Grange Hill* may not, however, wish to challenge its 'realism'. As though recognising that this is not a charge that would normally be brought to bear on a dramatic offering, they allow the plot to stand and instead raise arguments about its *typicality*. Whereas clearly *Dallas* and *Dynasty* hardly stand comparison with any other world (unless it be such other fictional domains as *Falcon Crest* and *Knot's Landing*), *Grange Hill* might be seen as representing all comprehensive schools.

Are those nasty, grumpy, spiteful and unhappy children of *Grange Hill* school really typical problems of our State education? If so, I have every sympathy with parents who put themselves on the breadline in order to afford to send their children to private schools (where kindness and decent behaviour are taught).
(E. Price, *Radio Times*, 24 March 1984.)

But even if *Grange Hill* isn't 'typical of our state education' there's still another problem to be faced. How might we persuade children that although *Grange Hill* is realistic in the sense that it certainly reports what really goes on at some schools, it is unrealistic in the sense that it suggests that all the elements are housed under one roof?

Children accept schools portrayed on television as typical, whereas of course, they are not. For the purposes of providing incident and entertainment the series [*Grange Hill*], at the very least, compresses incidents into the one school which might possibly have occurred separately in many different schools. *How do I convince my children of this?*
(D. J. Gilmore, *Radio Times*, 21 February 1981.)

When we could stop the children in our groups from simply saying that 'Grine Jill' was 'great', it wasn't at all clear that they needed convincing of the unreality of the popular school. In fact some of the things that they saw happening there could only be explained by the fictional setting.

JESSICA (10): They're cheeky. All cheeky.
TRB: So the children are much more cheeky in *Grange Hill*?

School's bullies copied Grange Hill mob

A TEENAGE gang of school bullies, who modelled themselves on TV's Grange Hill kids, may be expelled.

The boys, aged between 14 and 16, stopped other children in the street and demanded money, a Devon police spokesman said yesterday.

The ringleaders at first asked to borrow 5p or 10p while the other members of the gang held their victims and searched their pockets.

Youngsters who would not pay up were beaten up or bundled into cupboards.

Gripper

The probe began after a worried parent complained to the headmaster of the 2,300-pupil comprehensive school at Exmouth School in Devon.

He told headmaster Philip Thorne that he had heard of allegations of thefts of small amounts of money from pupils.

The ruthless gang leader is believed to have modelled himself on a Grange Hill character called Gripper, a notorious bully in the series.

Six pupils have been interviewed

(*Sun*, 24 February 1983)

ALEX (9): Yes. [*All agree.*]
TRB: Why do you think they are so cheeky?
JESSICA: And sometimes they swear.
VICKY (9): Well, it's a programme, isn't it?
JESSICA: It's television.
TRB: So they are allowed to be cheeky?
JESSICA: Yes, they are.

Even if this seems to show a nice line between what's allowed on television and in real life, it might also mean that the children who watch wish that life was more like *Grange Hill*.

TRB: Why do you watch it then, if the kids are cheeky and they get expelled?
MANDY (10): I like *Grange Hill* better than I like the way we act.
TRB: You mean you prefer *Grange Hill* to the real thing?
MANDY: Yes.
TRB: Do you wish you were there sometimes?
ALL TOGETHER: Yes.

It's quite different, though, to wish that you went to *Grange Hill* and to believe that there's a real possibility that you could. Like most of the adults who send wreaths and flowers to characters in *Coronation Street*, these young children were able simultaneously to believe in *Grange Hill* and its characters and to know that it belonged to a different reality from that of their own school.

> TRB: Is Grange Hill a real school?
>
> MANDY: Yes, because it can't be in a studio because otherwise they would have to have loads and loads of rooms.
>
> JAYNE (10): I think it is a real school.
>
> GAIL (9): It's just been redecorated.
>
> TRB: So, it's a school they just use for *Grange Hill*?
>
> GAIL: Yes.
>
> TRB: Where do you think it is?
>
> REBECCA (9): Is it on a hill?
>
> SUSAN (9): Somewhere around Grange, wherever Grange is.
>
> TRB: It's near Grange, is it?
>
> MARY (10): Yes. [*Most agree.*]
>
> ALEX (9): Near London.
>
> SUSAN: Or in the north somewhere.
>
> MANDY: It might be in America for all we know.
>
> MARY: Not really . . .
>
> MANDY: It might be.
>
> SALLY (10): But they don't have American accents.
>
> MANDY: Yes, I know.
>
> GAIL: I think it is in England.
>
> JAYNE: Somewhere in Britain.
>
> TRB: Where would you like it to be?
>
> MARY: Right next to our school. [*All agree.*]

When we asked if the series contained real children, there were further difficulties. First of all, the children said that they were probably older than you thought. 'Some of them are eighteen.' But when pressed as to how they could be eighteen and yet look thirteen, Alex had a straightforward answer which avoided any suggestion that her favourites might be some sort of freaks:

> They use make-up – that's what makes them look smaller.

So, then, could you tell that these people were older than they pretended to be? Yes, they agreed, you could.

> TRB: But how can you tell?
>
> JAYNE: I don't know.
>
> TRB: How can you tell how old they are?

Finally Gail produced the answer which satisfied the rest.

> You can tell because you know which form they're in.

Of course.

Live and Half Live

No one should be surprised by the difficulties that we sometimes have in deciding between the different levels of reality which are to be found in an average evening's viewing. At the cinema or theatre it is relatively simple. Godard and Pirandello may play their tricks but the cinematic and theatrical frames bind the material securely. We have no doubt on our way home that what we saw was a play or a film. The play was evidently live – the film was not.

But such matters and many others are up for debate when it comes to television. The word 'live' slips and slides between several meanings. In relation to rock music, as in 'Bruce Springsteen live at Olympia', it now means nothing more than that Springsteen had an audience at the time – theoretically, *any* time in the past at which the programme was initially recorded.

In such usage, the promoters are exploiting the peculiar fact of television's double audience – the audience who was there at the original event and for whom Springsteen was clearly live, and the television audience. The presence of a studio audience in any prerecorded show similarly ensures that the presenter and that audience may be in happy cahoots about the liveness and unexpected-ness of everything that happens, while the producer relaxes in the knowledge that it is always possible to 'roll back' for a quick retake if the unexpectedness turns out to be a little too unexpected. Or again, as in *Top of the Pops* (a long-running BBC popular music show), we may be confidently assured by the *Radio Times* and the presenter that the programme is 'live' in the sense of happening now, only to discover that the live musicians are in fact miming to 'dead' – recorded – music. And, what's more, don't seem to know quite when the music's stopped.

> JIMMY (13): They've got no leads out of their guitars.
> TOM (14): You can sometimes see the lead singer, when the music stops, still going like this [*strumming guitar*].
> GREG (14): When the band's been on for a certain amount of time, the camera goes back to the DJ and everyone starts clapping. And the band are still playing away. But they aren't making any noise.

In addition, the liveness of the programme will be frequently belied by the introduction of a number of prerecorded videos. And as a final flourish, there may be the occasional musician (Billy Bragg was the most recent example) who will break the rules about miming to recorded music, and actually sing and play live – perhaps one should say *live* live – during transmission.

Elsewhere during the evening will be performers or presenters who refer to the occasion as 'live', which may usually be taken to mean (although no guidance is available on the matter from any source) that the programme concerned was recorded only shortly before transmission. Viewers in America are at least assisted by the phrase 'live on tape', but in Britain, where 70 per cent of the TV output is recorded, the issue is fudged. Not that this throws everyone off the scent. The groups are discussing Michael Aspel's *Saturday Night Live* (a chat show):

> JENNY (41): That's not quite live on the day.
> SUE (39): I think, although Aspel comes on in the evening and says *Saturday Night Live*, it's not really live.
> ANNE (27): But it is live, the clock says the time.
> ROS (41): It's got to be live.
> ANNE: Yes, it is live, the clock's there.
> JENNY: No, I think that's fast.
> ANNE: Fixed?
> ROS: I wouldn't have thought so.

Even when the cameras swing outside the studio and claim to be recording events as they are happening, more problems arise about reality. Certain sporting occasions – motocross or motor scrambling or wrestling, for example – seem to be waiting for the cameras to arrive rather than running to their own timetable. And there is a general appreciation of the fact that courses might be redesigned, new events developed and enthusiasm generated for the benefit of the domestic viewer rather than that of the lone punter standing in the mud on the hillside watching the bikes go by. In America the cultural critic and historian, Christopher Lasch, has noted not just the clock but the calendar adjusting itself to television's requirements.

> When the television networks discovered surfing, they insisted that events be held to a prearranged schedule, without regard to weather conditions . . . Television has rearranged the athletic calendar and thus deprived sports of their familiar connection with the seasons, diminishing their power of allusiveness and recall.
> (*The Culture of Narcissism*, 1978.)

We wondered if this well-documented interference with sporting reality held true in more sacred areas; in religious broadcasting, for example:

> MARY (59): You can't rehearse a Mass. You've got to actually have a Mass. It's not different on television. They might get the vicar to say how long he would actually take over a service, so they could cut some verses out of the hymn if it was too long. But that's all.

Questions about the fragility of religious reality in the face of television interference surfaced in the IBA's research report on audience reaction to the *Communion* programme – a studio-based service of communion transmitted in most regions as the first programme of the day on Sunday. After some theological reservations about 'telecommunion' (apparently, within the Church of England the concept contravened eleven conditions of canon law) a simple ceremony was devised in which each celebrant was supported in the studio by a handful of people drawn from his home congregation, and the service took place across a plain table with 'a cross behind suspended before a blue background'.

Despite such elaborate preparations, only half of those who watched were prepared to say that it was the 'same as real communion' and many of these believed that the communion was 'live on air' although in fact it was prerecorded. On being told this news, a quarter of the sample immediately said they found this 'dissatisfying'. Neither did the series prompt the sort of active participation which might have been expected. Although a quarter of the sample claimed to have thought of placing their own bread and wine in front of the television whilst watching the programme, only four said they had actually done this.

The researchers reasonably derived some overall comfort from the general approval given to the programme, but it was still clear that many viewers found the lack of 'liveness' a real impediment to regarding the occasion as 'real'; what's more, they felt that this was in some way not properly 'religious'.

At the other extreme are the problems which arise when some representations of reality are made too real. On BBC's *Crimewatch*, highly skilled directors using first-class actors film quite elaborate reconstructions of unsolved crimes. During the transmission of the programme viewers are encouraged to ring in and pass on any useful information which might have been prompted by the film to one of a large group of policemen who are seated by telephones behind a glass screen. (Apart from a number of scurrilous calls during the miners' strike naming 'Scargill' as the guilty man, this method has had considerable success in catching criminals.)

However, the very authenticity of the programme can not only be distressing to some viewers but also confuse levels of reality. Following one recent reconstruction of a horrific rape and murder in which the suspect was shown with bloodstained hands buying a drink in the local pub, a caller rang in to insist that she knew who the man was, and that the crime was solved.

The policeman who took the call carefully explained that recognition was not the point of the exercise, that the man was only an actor who was being used to jog people's memories about the occasion. This hardly satisfied the caller, who proceeded to explain that she actually knew the man's name.

'It's Frank,' she declared. 'I recorded the scene on my video and have just played it back and held it still at the moment when he buys a drink. When you do that you can just see a card in his wallet with his name on it. It's Frank. That's his name.'

She was right. What she had seen was the actor's Equity membership card.

As a complement to this viewer's confusion between reconstruction and reality, it was interesting to find another viewer in one of our groups who claimed that *Crimewatch* itself juggled reality in order to improve the dramatic effects of its reconstruction.

DEREK (49): There's one that sticks in my mind. Had me on the edge of my seat. A family was held at ransom, and this guy shot their dog. They reconstructed it as nearly as they could: tied this young lad up, threatened the father, started to rob them; I was terrified. It happened. It could happen to me. That really could be me there. You're saying to yourself: 'Bloody hell, that was true.'

TRB: Did any of the rest of you see that programme?

ALAN (42): I happen to know a little bit about the story. The real dog that was killed was actually a vicious guard dog. In the story it came out as a Labrador pet. I'm not saying they should have shot it, but it was there for a job. That's how television, even a true programme like that, does change something to make it sound better . . . if 'better' is the right word.

JOHN (42): It helps to get the emotions going.

ALAN: Yes. I mean a soft old Labrador pet coming in, this big guy shoots it, and you think, Oh dear, oh dear, a poor old family pet. The impact would be less if the programme said, 'A guard dog got killed by the raiders.'

Here, if Alan was to be believed, was a case of a little fiction being introduced to beef up reality. Television and radio drama can occasionally be found reversing the process, placing real events or real people in among the make-believe.

PAT (47): In *Dynasty* the other day, they went to a dinner party and who should walk along but ex-President Ford. 'Oh, good afternoon, Mr President. How are you?' And there he is in the programme.

Ex-President Ford lines up alongside compatriot Nancy Reagan who has also made a soap appearance. Back in Britain, Graeme Souness, the ex-Liverpool footballer, met his greatest fan Yosser Hughes in the drama series *Boys from the Blackstuff*; Kenny Dalglish, also of Liverpool FC, took his turn in another drama, *Scully*; Princess Margaret busied herself opening a fête for *The Archers* (the rural radio soap opera); Larry Grayson, the camp comedian, acted as chauffeur for Meg Mortimer's marriage in *Crossroads*, driving his own Rolls-Royce. (Unfortunately in the last case the producer felt the need to cut the few extra ad-libbed lines in which he complained to Meg Mortimer, actress Noele Gordon, about how noisy he found his motel room. 'Someone next door appears to be keeping ferrets,' he remarked.) *Crossroads* has also featured writer Arthur Marshall, one of its greatest fans, in a small walk-on part, and George Michael of Wham! is rumoured to be negotiating a similar role in *Brookside*.

Maybe these 'role' appearances do something to compensate for the shortage of references to real people in popular drama. Bobby Grant refers to 'Thatcher' in *Brookside* and the *Street* had a Duran Duran fan for a while, but otherwise the outside world of the Bishop of Durham, Mick Jagger, Ian Botham, Enoch Powell, Steve Cram and Neil Kinnock (apart from his quick flash in Tracey Ullman's video) goes largely unrepresented.

Neither is the matching of the external calendar particularly meticulous.

Christmas is observed – especially in *Crossroads* when Meg still reigned – but references to Easter or Guy Fawkes Day or other anniversaries are sparse. On the radio, *The Archers* perhaps deserves a special mention for its self-conscious role as adviser on country life and manners:

HELEN (37): They often bring the country code into it. They remind you about shutting gates, and picnicking, and dropping litter.
ANNE (51): And cows being killed with polythene bags. Tom Forrest will tell you real things. Why they are putting the daffodil bulbs in this week. And you think, that's right, I've got to go and put the daffodil bulbs in. Each week they put a thought in your mind. And they give real advice to farmers.

Although in some cases a little tinkering with reality is needed to bring it off:

I think the period when I did most nail-biting was when we decided to have an outbreak of SVD at Brookfield. SVD, or swine vesicular disease, to give it its proper name, cropped up for the first time suddenly and devastatingly in December 1972. It rampaged through the country causing the compulsory slaughter of hundreds of thousands of pigs. It was an obvious subject for inclusion in *The Archers* but the trouble was that no one knew how long it would last. Every time the Ministry of Agriculture vets announced that they thought it was under control, it broke out again. And I kept wishing that we had, after all, decided to give Phil's farm a dose of the disease.

Eventually we came to a point in November 1973 when we decided to take the plunge. The Ministry vets wanted us to deal with SVD because it could be used to put across a lot of points they needed to get over to farmers, farm workers, hauliers, dealers and others. It obviously had great dramatic potential, with Phil Archer's pigs being wiped out. The question was, would a disease which we were discussing at script conferences in November still be around by March when the resulting scripts were broadcast? No one knew, not even the Ministry. Suppose it were all over in January or February and we were stuck with an outbreak in Ambridge in March – not an odd scene which could be scrapped without difficulty nearer the time but a story running through the scripts for several weeks? I outlined my predicament to the Ministry vets and managed to extract a promise from them that, whatever happened, they would not announce the eradication of SVD until after the Hollowtree outbreak. On that basis I went ahead. I must have been the only person in the country praying for the odd outbreak in January and February 1974. We got the necessary trickle of cases and then the Ambridge flare-up. I need not have worried. Unhappily the disease is still with us in 1980.
(Anthony Parkin, Agricultural Story Editor, in Smethurst, ed., *The Archers*, 1981.)

Matters were a little more under control when, in another *Archers* coup, Clarrie's baby was timed to coincide with the birth of Prince William, so that he might be named after his royal progenitor.

But like its television counterparts, *The Archers* does not score highly when it comes to the inclusion of references to real people and events. The Falklands and CND have at least been mentioned, and Eddie Grundy makes the occasional reference to Dolly Parton, while Lucy Perks busily hunts for tickets for the Wham! concert in Birmingham, but politicians' names – even the Minister of Agriculture – are never heard. Perhaps the problem is that *The Archers* simply do not know such names: no one in the series appears either to watch television or listen to the radio.

A Little too Real for Home

Even the most liberated among us have probably had the experience of sitting in a cinema or theatre with a loved one and feeling that peculiar embarrassment which arises when the characters on stage or screen behave in a rather more explicit way than we ourselves have yet managed in normal life. But at least at such times we can stare intently forward and hope that the slight flush in our cheeks is not visible in the dark.

There are fewer options when we are members of a television audience. Conspiracies of silence are difficult to maintain when some of the possible conspirators are under twelve – 'Mummy, Mummy, what's that man doing?' – and there's no disguising embarrassment in a well-lit room.

It's at times like this that some will comment, as they did in the IBA's research project on 'bad language on television', on 'decadence' being 'poured into the home'. They will complain that swearing has been 'thrust' or 'inflicted' on the family, or that it is allowed to 'creep' into programmes. Some will refer directly to the bad effect this has on children:

> I think TV is responsible in the main for the many four-letter words being used by seven-year-old kids. Also the word bastard is repeated so often . . . during one episode of *Penmarric* [a period drama series based in Cornwall] it must have been used twelve times. My three-year-old son said it twice the next day. Okay, he should have been in bed by then – but he wasn't. I actually shiver if I hear kids saying [four-letter words], and just lately I've been shivering quite a lot.
> (*Offence and Defence in the Home*, IBA, 1980.)

A sizeable group will emphasise that their objection is not to the material as such but to the problems of coping with it when others are present (particularly when 'it is suddenly spoken or shown on television'). Here are two viewers' reactions to scenes in *Brideshead Revisited* (based on the Evelyn Waugh novel):

> As a heterosexual I found the display of affection between men (in my own living room) distasteful and I fortunately missed those episodes (or blinked at the right time).

The love scene on the liner I felt to be too explicit. Also highly embarrassing when viewing with one's family.
(*Brideshead Revisited*, IBA, 1982.)

Some commentators regard such complaints as evidence that television conventionally shields the viewers from any direct involvement with anything disturbing or abnormal.

Broadcast TV is . . . disturbing for its viewers when it represents something that is repressed in most domestic situations. The largest scandals about TV broadcasts have occurred in Britain when a few TV programmes have dared to represent activities which are censured or go unrepresented in many families.
(John Ellis, *Visible Fictions*, 1982.)

But this is too sweeping. There are undoubtedly those who would like to prevent members of their family from hearing and knowing about certain subjects, but there is also a genuine concern for the susceptibilities of others. Few of us would simply march our children or aged parents off to the cinema or the theatre without considering the possible bemusement or embarrassment which might be caused by what they were to see. To sit in a living room in similar company and find, often quite suddenly, that this embarrassment has just occurred provides grounds for concern which do not have to be rooted in anything so formidable as 'repression'.

It's also difficult to know precisely how many people are offended by the intrusion of these aspects of reality. 'Scandals about TV broadcasts' are often more representative of the activities of small pressure groups than genuine signs of domestic alarm. And asking people for their views on the subject ignores the importance of the context. Language which might be taboo in *Question Time* can be shrugged off in *The Young Ones*. But at least such surveys do show how the presence of others increases concern.

Blasphemous language in TV plays and comedies

Not offended	46%
Yes – if others present	25%
Yes – even if by self	26%

Sex or bodily function

Not offended	52%
Yes – if others present	29%
Yes – even if by self	15%

Swear words

Not offended	41%
Yes – if others present	34%
Yes – even if by self	20%

(*Offence and Defence in the Home*, IBA, 1980.)

Neither are those most offended a tribe apart. The IBA research suggests they are not religious fanatics or television haters – but rather those who welcome some privacy in their lives (e.g. when getting dressed or having a bath). They are likely to be older people and working class.

Members of this group can at least feel reasonably assured that there will be one area of television which excludes some if not all domestically embarrassing aspects of reality.

> PAULA (25): And they don't swear at each other in soap operas. You don't get bad language.
> WENDY (26): It wouldn't suit the programme somehow.
> TRB: Bad language doesn't suit *Dallas* and *Dynasty*?
> ALL: No.
> SALLY (29): No, I couldn't see Jeff say f . . . off.
> WENDY: But in America they're not allowed to say such words, are they?
> JUNE (28): It just wouldn't go with the programme.
> WENDY: It's odd really. They're allowed to stab and shoot and rape but they're never allowed to swear.

An early radio set for hikers – the first Walkman?

2

Tears and Fears

JOYCE (42): My husband was sitting on the settee watching *Coronation Street*. Tears streaming down his face.

The Night Bert Tilsley Died

Although we think of emotions – of sadness, love, fear, anger and happiness – as somehow natural and beyond our control, we are remarkably good at managing them. We save our tears for the moment when the coffin is lowered at the funeral, wait until the laughter at the theatre has got under way before joining in, and during a lengthy game of poker, keep our emotions firmly to ourself. But even if we know how to behave emotionally in public, we are less well informed about what goes on in private homes. When we are visiting relations or new friends, and the television is switched on, we may have to spend several uncomfortable minutes latching on to the emotional tone. Does one shout with enthusiasm during *Match of the Day*? Angrily protest about the remarks of politicians on *Question Time*? Allow a small tear to well up at the plight of a victim on *TV Eye*?

Unfortunately questions about ordinary emotional reactions to television have been largely obscured by the debate about whether or not it might induce an extreme emotional response with consequences for others – violence. We have little evidence to offer on this subject. Nobody in the discussion groups admitted to such feelings after viewing, so we turned to the 3000 people in our national sample and invited reactions to two statements.

- 1. I sometimes wish that violence in programmes like *The Sweeney* [a British cops-and-robbers series] was more realistic.
- 2. Sometimes I can feel quite violent after watching crime programmes.

We could hardly expect that the second question would produce much agreement: it's probably difficult enough to admit to oneself that one is overtaken by such an antisocial emotion, let alone to an eager visitor with a clipboard. And we were right. Only 2 per cent strongly agreed with the statement. Question 1 was a little more subtle: *The Sweeney* is generally characterised as the most explicitly violent of the British cops-and-robbers genre on the screen and therefore those who wanted more realistic violence within it would seem at least to have an appetite for the stuff. (Actor John Thaw has said: 'I know we've been criticized for our strong scenes. But we don't have gratuitous violence. The fact is we're doing a series about policemen, and the squad aren't called the Heavy Mob for nothing. They have to counter violence with violence.') But again, our national sample seemed relatively mild-mannered about their television diet: only 4 per cent wanted anything more explicit than they were already getting.

It's also salutary to consider the actual nature of the audience for *The Sweeney*. There's no evidence whatsoever of members of the most violent age group in our society – sixteen to twenty-four – rushing home for their weekly fix. Quite the contrary. Television viewing in general is lowest amongst this age group, and *The Sweeney* and other cops-and-robbers programmes do nothing to change this viewing profile. In fact only 7 per cent of those watching fall into this critical age group and they are outnumbered seven to one by those over fifty-five. If 'violent' programmes were quite as criminogenic as is sometimes claimed, it is difficult to see why there has not been the slightest change in the behaviour of this group during the twenty years or so in which television 'violence' has been available to more than 90 per cent of the population.

Tears of Farewell

Many accounts of how television induces violent feelings in the viewer are remarkably unconcerned with context. A young gullible person witnesses a violent scene and is then stimulated to reproduce it. The emotional reactions to television which were described by viewers in the groups were very different. In fact nothing could be further from the stereotyped image of the solitary impressionable individual suddenly aroused by a scene on television than the complicated blend of real events, family life and fictional involvement which produced tears or laughter or fear in our viewers.

> JOYCE (42): And it was only a few days before Bert Tilsley [Ivy's husband from *Coronation Street*] died that our dog had got knocked over. My husband was sitting on the settee watching *Coronation Street*. Tears streaming down his face. I said, 'What's the matter with you?' He said, 'I'm thinking of the dog with Bert Tilsley dying.' Fancy comparing the two. You've never seen anything like it. Tears rolling down his face.

Even though experts have assured us that men do not like soaps – even despise them – it was interesting to see that an all-male group on such programmes quickly produced some allies for Joyce's husband. The men moved quickly from a slightly macho togetherness over Deirdre's foolishness in returning to such a wimp as Ken (from *Coronation Street*) towards individual admissions of particular events in the *Street* which reduced them – or raised them – to tears.

ALAN (37): Well, Ken and Deirdre, when they were having that bust-up, that was so emotional. It was very good TV. It choked you up a bit.
JOHN (44): It was saddest, though, when she went back to him.
ALAN: Yes.
JOHN: Yes, I reckon she should have left him.
DENNIS (49): I sometimes get sad about Hilda. She gets put upon. Sometimes Hilda gets put upon.
DENNIS: I must be perfectly honest, I watched it when Stan died, I watched it and I cried. I sat down and watched it when Stan died, because it was so real and I could relate to it. I just sat there and cried.

When it comes to television sadness, it seems that some viewers not only lack inhibitions but have the capacity to lower them in others: especially when the public funeral which is being observed is for *Dynasty*'s Fallon.

TRB: And you cried, did you?
AUDREY (32): Oh, it broke my heart. It was so sad. Blake stood at the grave and said: 'I've loved you from the day you were born and I'll go on loving you even though you're dead.' And he was so upset. He was so upset.

(At which the transcriber of the tape – otherwise anonymous – felt compelled to add in brackets: 'It's making me feel like crying and I'm only typing it.')

Television is truly a family medium: a medium which presents hundreds of television families – Garnetts, Ogdens, Barlows, Ewings, Carringtons, Trotters – to millions of real families. Yet not much attention has been paid to the degree and kind of identification between the two familial scenes; the extent to which television scenes recall biographical incidents, elicit unspoken fears, desires and memories, and obliquely allow more public expression of family emotion than might otherwise have been possible.

Often a family sit in a room looking at a family sitting in another room. And even if the actual family which looks is quite unlike the one which is observed (only about 5 per cent of the population live in the classic TV family of working father, housewife mother and dependent school-age children), the setting is nevertheless familial. At times the close-up face of the television character on the screen is of approximately the same size as that of someone sitting across the room from us. Their voice is at roughly the same level. On the set immediately above the fictional talking heads will often stand photographs of our own children or relatives.

Not surprisingly it is the British soaps which are most likely to evoke particularly strong family identification. At the heart of it seems to lie the fact of 'carrying on', of 'coping'. What most moves viewers to tears is the sight of a stoical character, one who has endured all the sufferings or hardship which can be unleashed upon them by a diligent scriptwriter, finally giving in.

JOY (27): It was so very sad when you saw it, the funeral, and then her, Hilda [from *Coronation Street*], who'd been so strong through all of it. And then when her son went, and she unwrapped the parcel, didn't she, with his clothes? She broke down. At the sight of the clothes. In the end it was too much for her.

Good and Bad Riddance

It is not customary in most media to *rage* against the dying of fictional characters. A few tears and some regrets are usually enough before one turns the page or begins to see the cinema screen once again with unblurred eyes. But television viewers – and especially soap viewers – can be simultaneously sad about the death of a fictional character and angry with the scriptwriter or producer who decreed that it should happen.

Dorothy Hobson was able to devote several chapters of her book on *Crossroads* to the emotional reactions of viewers to the decision to write Meg Mortimer (actress Noele Gordon) out of the script.

> I think the way they have treated Noele Gordon is shocking . . . I have watched her on television for many years and also *Lunch Box* [midday magazine programme] and *Stars on Sunday* [religious, songs and celebrities]. I know I am old 88 years but I am a good judge of people. All I can say keep going Meg we will miss you! I live alone and over 70 and look forward to seeing *Crossroads*. I feel she is a friend come into my home. I do hope that you can do something to save her.

In a chapter entitled 'Whose Programme is it Anyway' Hobson forcibly argues:

> Television is very important to the elderly and housebound and while the rest of society fails to alleviate the situation for many elderly people who live alone, the entertainment and sense of contact which programmes like *Crossroads* provide for its viewers are surely among the most valuable aspects of the medium . . . the reassurances which they derive from fictional programmes should not be underestimated.
> (Dorothy Hobson, *Crossroads*, 1982.)

Even viewers who were much younger at the time of her departure told us of their sadness at the event, a sadness they were well able to combine with astringent comments on other aspects of the programme.

> TRB: How did you feel when Meg Mortimer left?
> AMY (47): I didn't like it. It was sad. I cried.
> JOAN (51): It seemed as though a big chunk had been taken out of the programme.

AMY: Yes, she *was Crossroads* really.

JOAN: I always hoped they'd bring her back.

SUSAN (42): I thought they would but they were very adamant about her not coming back.

TRB: Where did she go?

JOAN: Ended up going abroad.

AMY: Australia. She's remarried.

JOAN: Made a new life for herself.

TRB: So some of you actually cried when she left?

SUSAN: Oh yes, I usually have a cry.

JOAN: I like a cry.

TRB: Are you going to cry when David Hunter [the more recent central character] goes?

JOAN: No.

TRB: What are you going to do when he goes?

SUSAN: Have a party.

Susan will have had her party by now. David Hunter's addiction to roulette and the breakdown which accompanied this pathological trait have now ensured his departure from the series. It's been a relatively smooth passage by current standards, almost comparable to that bestowed upon such a beloved character as Doris Archer who was discovered dead in her armchair at home, a demise which allowed the actress concerned, Gwen Berryman, to sit in her nursing home sipping a cup of tea and listening to the broadcast of her own funeral: not a fictional radio ending granted to Grace Archer, who was burnt alive on the opening night of ITV, or Polly Perks, killed in a collision between her car and a milk tanker.

Altogether it is not too fanciful of Alice Walker of the *Daily Mail* to claim, 'They ought to pin Murder Incorporated on the door of those scriptwriters. They've got a licence to kill. Bert Tilsley [blown to pieces in a gas explosion] will be the twentieth character in the *Street* to meet a violent end. They've had *Street* personalities shot down by gunmen, pushed under buses, electrocuted and burnt.' (*Daily Mail*, June 1983.)

Not all these deaths or disappearances provoked tears or outrage. In several cases the scriptwriters moved hand in hand with their viewers' or listeners' emotional prejudices. The death or mutilation of the characters seemed to everyone appropriate revenge for all the months and years of infuriating behaviour. Lacking a clear example from current soaps, we invited viewers to select a 'living' soap character they would like to remove from the screen and then devise a 'perfect death' for them. We offered a wide choice of 'deaths' to allow the expression of different degrees of vindictiveness. The most popular choice of victim was undoubtedly *Dallas*'s Lucy ('A neckless blonde sex grenade only half as high as everybody else,' Clive James, *The Crystal Bucket*, 1981; also known as 'the Poison Dwarf'). Here are the deaths we suggested:

- Road accident
- Fire
- Drowning
- Mugging
- Suicide
- Poisoning
- Strangling
- Stabbed in the back
- Shooting
- Illness

Here are the assassins being briefed:

> TRB: All right, let's take Lucy. I want you to devise the perfect death for Lucy.
> KIM (29): Oh, I'd like a suicide.
> DEE (28): Or a poisoning.
> KIM: No, I'd like a suicide.
> WENDY (33): I think I'd like her to be strangled by that bloke she's going out with.
> DEE: I was thinking the same as that.
> WENDY: Because she's going out with that bloke who's got nothing, isn't she, and I think he's the type who'd lose his temper and strangle her.
> KIM: I'd like a suicide, not a murder.
> DEE: I think so as well.
> BETTY (27): I'd like to see her slash her wrists.
> YVONNE (28): That's too horrible.
> BETTY: Because she is depressive, isn't she? It would make sense.
> KIM: Or she could take too many pills.
> BETTY: They could save her if she took pills. But if she slashed her wrists they'd be more likely to arrive too late. And she'd be dead.
> YVONNE: But they can't have her slashing her wrists. They're not allowed to show blood in an American programme.
> KIM: Aren't they?
> YVONNE: You never see a bit of blood in American programmes.
> DEE: In *Hill Street Blues* [an American cult cops-and-robbers series] they once killed one of the gang and he had blood coming from his mouth.
> TRB: Have you made up your minds?
> DEE: No, we're still killing her.
> KIM: If she commits suicide, then they're going to have a post mortem, and they'd have to drag all the nitty gritty out, which would be quite nice.

The final preference, in this and the other two groups who discussed the same question, was suicide. Far from this being a kindly option, it might be seen as a demonstration of viewers' ability to distinguish between fictional and factual retribution. In the context of *Dallas* or *Dynasty* a mere suicide is dramatically ignominious: truly interesting characters have truly interesting deaths: in *Dallas* Renaldo (an Italian kidnapper) gets shot, Jock dies in a plane crash; in *Dynasty* Fallon (a reformed nymphomaniac) is also lost in a plane crash (although reconstituted into another actress by plastic surgery), and Mark (a macho tennis player) may have been murdered by Alexis.

A Share of Happiness

Critics on the look-out for the most calculated television tear-jerker are inclined to nominate *This is Your Life*. There is something about the 'show-biz' choice of guests, and the almost perfunctory way in which they are reunited with their former acquaintances and friends, which seems unlikely to carry quite the emotional impact of a carefully constructed soap reunion. Neither does presenter Eamonn Andrews's use of the second person – 'You leave the army, travel to Barnstaple and meet a young librarian' – seem likely to aid identification. The apparent superficiality of the proceedings led TV critic Lucy Hughes-Hallett to comment in the *Standard* (5 April 1984):

> The programme is a bit like the beginning of a formal wedding reception, with the guest star playing bride, groom and both sets of parents-in-law. He kisses everyone, whether he knows them or not, murmurs something about it being so kind of them to come, while they, speechless with embarrassment, clasp his hand or guffaw raucously for no particular reason. Everyone is in their best clothes and over each head floats an invisible bubble reading: 'My, how fat he's become!' Or 'Oh, did I ever really fancy her?'

But viewers, particularly older viewers, derive great emotional comfort from the form of the programme, from the fact that it brings together people who were formerly apart and, what is more, that all those who have been separated appear to be delighted that a plane or boat or train has been made available by Eamonn to effect the reunion. The fantasy must be particularly appealing to the lonely. If only such facilities could be made available to one's own relations.

When older viewers talk about their emotional reactions to television, about what they like to feel when they are watching, the word 'happy' predominates.

> EILEEN (51): I like the programmes that are happy. I don't like miserable things because I get very down in my own life, you know, and I think, Oh, it's not worth watching if it's going to make me worse.

And the 'happiest' programmes for many seem to be the quiz and game shows – such programmes as *Name That Tune*, *Give Us a Clue*, *The Price is Right* and *Blockbusters*. These are all great favourites among those over fifty-five – particularly working-class women. (They are hardly ever watched by men in social grades A and B.) And their popularity is growing. While twenty years ago there were five game shows a week totalling two and a half hours (*Take Your Pick*, *University Challenge*, *Beat the Clock* (with £400 in prizes), *Criss Cross Quiz* and *Double Your Money*), now, in an average week, there are at least twenty to choose from – at least half of which attract more than 10 million viewers each.

Among those who like such shows there is remarkably little sign of the 'competitiveness' or 'greed' which according to so many critics constitutes their fascination. The size of the prizes was never mentioned as a reason for watching, which tallies with the statistical finding that there is no relation between the popularity of game shows and the size of the prizes they offer. This is just as well for their producers, given the IBA guidelines:

> At present, the maximum value of any single prize awarded in a programme to contestants appearing before the cameras may not normally exceed £1750. Exceptionally the IBA may agree to a larger sum, up to £3500 being awarded once, say, every four weeks, provided that the average value of the maximum prize over that four-week period does not exceed £1750.

Far from revelling in the competitiveness of it all, the general opinion seemed to be that shows were best when there were not obvious losers:

> TRB: Do you ever enjoy seeing people lose? Or do you prefer to see them win?
>
> KATHY (51): Win. Always. I like to see people winning.
>
> MARIE (56): Yes, I only like it when they win something. I hate it when they don't get anything at the end of it.
>
> MAUREEN (58): That's why I think that the big prizes, the caravans or whatever, are too much. Everyone who goes on should at least get something.
>
> MARIE: Yes, when people win a big thing, which is worth, say, two thousand pounds, that's too much.
>
> KATHY: Yes, because with all that money you could have three or four winners. [*Others agree.*]

This view is also in line with the results obtained by the 1984 BBC research into 'What Makes a Good Television Quiz Programme?' More surprising is the small proportion of respondents who feel that quiz programmes should make you care who wins (since this is closely allied with competitiveness).

Such findings hardly suggest that as a society we are moving very rapidly towards the fulfilment of the prediction made in 1961 by a Nuffield Foundation team investigating 'Television and the Child': 'The nightly gloating over rich rewards for puny efforts must in the long term encourage the development of false sets of values.'

No doubt there is a degree of cynicism among game-show impresarios, promoters and perhaps even presenters about the merit of their product. But there still remains this solid sense of 'happiness' which some viewers persistently derive from them. The only explanation is that they do present the quite unusual television picture of large numbers of people apparently enjoying themselves. The especial popularity of *The Price is Right* is surely directly related to this. There is nothing about the size of the prizes or the skill of the game or the charm of the presenter to distinguish it from many other programmes. What is different is the atmosphere. Lots and lots of very happy – and sometimes quite ecstatic – people. Just the type of communal enjoyment we might revel in elsewhere. As Bill Stewart, the show's producer, points out, we are quite used to seeing the British enjoying themselves at pop concerts, football matches and the last night of the Proms, so isn't it pure prejudice to expect only solemn behaviour in a television studio?

It is a feature of television, and one which is obscured by those who attempt to apply a single critical 'art' or 'information' measuring rod to its entire output, that at times it functions as a mood machine. Even upper-class men who keep well away from the mass hysteria of *The Price is Right* may switch on a late-night cops-and-robbers series more for the general feeling of action and suspense and tension which it displays than for the actual niceties of storyline or characterisation.

A related sense of togetherness and reunion is prompted by another favourite programme of the over-fifty-five age group: *Songs of Praise* (religious singsong). Although the format could hardly be more different from *This is Your Life*, viewers spoke in similar terms about the pleasure they derived from the way it brought people together; the way it somehow made them feel 'happy'. One man quoted in the BBC report *Songs of Praise* (December 1984) said, 'The thing is there are people there from all denominations. If it's a Roman Catholic church they're in that day it's not just Roman Catholics but all denominations.'

Older viewers spoke of the feelings of stability and serenity which the programme induced, the sense of comfort and security, the feeling that Sunday was now complete. 'You think that the world isn't all bad,' said Doris (67), 'and what's more if you know the hymns and there's a good congregation and an organ, you can sing along with them. You feel together with them.'

Look Behind You!

It is often suggested that the almost pathological nature of some viewers' emotional involvement with fictional TV and radio characters can be best gauged by their predilection for sending bouquets and wreaths and other messages of hate and love to the fictional characters of radio and television. But subsequent interviews with those who have acted in this way rarely reveal any fundamental inability to distinguish fact and fiction. Yes, say the viewers, we do know that these characters don't really exist but that does not alter the fact that 'they are behaving badly or being treated outrageously'.

Dear Sir

I am writing to you about the Disgusting treatment of Mavis in Coronation Street. May I say that the way Sally went behind her back was the most Deceitful thing that I have ever Seen. It has made poor Mavis a nervous wreck. That second reporter was even worse. I've a good mind to write to the press council to see if something cannot be done about the way he gets his stories and that Derek Wilton just who does he think he his. It wasn't enough jilting her at the alter he now has to rub it in by humiliating her in the paper. I honestly feel as though I could really punch him on the nose.

I am sure a lot of people would be grateful if you could use your influence and have this harassment stopped **IMMEDIATELY**

I would like you to send my support to Mavis tell her that she'll get over it and not to worry too much. I would look forward to a reply to answer a few of the ~~POINTS~~ I have mentioned in this letter

yours Faithfully.

R. Heron

52

Mr Heron of Ripon is not just concerned about the 'disgusting treatment' of Mavis but also about Sally's deceit. It is indeed this inability to let characters know what is being done behind their backs – to convey to them the viewers' special knowledge of the situation – which is a frequent cause of extreme irritation. The desire to let *Coronation Street*'s Ken Barlow know that his wife Deirdre was having or about to have an affair with Mike Baldwin, or the wish that in *Dynasty* Alexis's children – Fallon, Adam and especially Steven – could once and for all grasp the nature of their mother's delinquency, can become overwhelming.

> MAUREEN (39): I would like her own children to see her for what she really is, especially Steven.
> EDNA (42): Yes.
> MAUREEN: I would like him to see through her and know what she's done. And then he could say, 'Well, she is still my mother, and I'm still going to love her, but now I know what she is like and in future I'm not going to trust her.' Because she does terrible things, and they find out, and in the next breath she says, 'Oh, but it wasn't me, why do you always think it's me?' And then they say, 'Well, perhaps it wasn't her this time.' I would like them to see through her. Just once.

Often it's not so much the torments visited upon characters which provoke such outrage, but the pusillanimity of the characters in the face of such provocation. Doris (42) was particularly incensed by the long-suffering way in which Barbara Hunter (of *Crossroads*) put up with her husband David's infidelity:

> DORIS: She should have a go. Not put up with it. What's she keeping quiet for?
> ANNE (45): I wouldn't keep quiet. I'd smash him. [*Laughs.*]
> DORIS: I think any normal wife would have a go. Very unreal . . .
> ANNE: Very unreal. She didn't say a thing, not a thing. I mean I'd have him by the jugular if he'd gone off like that.

Homely Fears

How frightened are we by what we see on television? We checked the incidence of this emotion by asking our national sample:

- Nowadays, are you ever frightened by any programmes you see on television?

More than a quarter agreed that they were. If we allow for people's unreadiness to admit to what sounds like a slightly neurotic (or cowardly) reaction to television programmes, this suggests that a sizeable minority of the population are capable of being frightened by that box in the corner of the room. When we leave the formal questionnaires and ask people to talk in depth about their fears, we run straight into a paradox. On the one hand the home is seen as a thoroughly pleasant and appropriate place in which to indulge a taste for suspense or even horror:

> JANET (31): Oh, I love horror films on TV.
> TRB: Do you?
> JANET: I love being frightened. Feeling frightened.

Even if *some* thoughts of the outside world do intrude, these can often be successfully put aside:

> DEE (27): I like to stay up and watch 'the horrors', especially if I'm baby-sitting. I love to watch those. I sit there and think, Oh, I've got to go home after this, oh dear, but I still watch them.

Fearful episodes on television have to fight for their effect against a plethora of mundane familiar objects, teapots, chairs and tables, and often also against the laughter or derision of at least some of those present. At the cinema, by contrast, it may be precisely the failure to know quite where you are, the shock of encountering alien others, which is directly bound up with the fearful experience. Here is one example taken from a book on cinema audiences which first appeared in 1948:

> I liked *Trader Horn* the first time I saw it, it made a shocking hole in my manners. The black men were swinging across the river on branches, whilst crocodiles snapped at their legs. As one of these men was taking off, I suddenly swung myself out of my seat into the lap of the person, an entire stranger, next to me. I held my feet as high as I could in the air, so as not to be bitten. Ye Gods, what a commotion, it was many moons before I had sufficient courage to go back to the Empire, Leicester Square.
> (From J. P. Mayer, *British Cinemas and their Audiences*, 1948.)

Although in one sense it takes no more effort to walk out of a cinema when you're frightened than it does to switch off or walk out of the room at home, in practice the differences are great, as Susan insisted:

> SUSAN (41): At the cinema you're on *foreign territory*, you've got people around you you don't know; you've paid money out to see the film; you feel that you want to get your money's worth, so you don't really want to walk out in the middle. And if you did you'd feel as though you'd failed the test. And you're much more likely to forget where you are and get yourself involved. Whereas at home, the phone might go . . .

Another group was of the same opinion:

> TRB: So what is it about watching a film in your own home that makes it less frightening than watching it in the cinema?
> JOANNA (36): The size of the screen.

SUE (39): And you can always get up and make a cup of tea, can't you?
PAULINE (32): Yes, at the cinema you're stuck there.

But there is another perspective, one which may help to explain the existence of that 15 per cent who experience some fearful sleeplessness at night, one which not only allows for the presence of all the familiar objects and loved ones, but actually sees them as somehow related to our anxiety. This is to suggest a specific television fear which is far removed from crocodiles and the Empire, Leicester Square: the fear that the very sense of cosiness which surrounds the television viewing could quite suddenly be shattered by intruders.

MICHAEL (49): The only thing that I object to in these programmes is that sometimes they show you people getting into houses and things like that.
GEORGE (38): People knowing how to get in through windows.
MICHAEL: And through doors. With Barclaycards.
GEORGE: That's what's frightening.

Even if other parts of a mystery story are dismissed, the domestic violation still strikes home:

DOREEN (29): You see films – I mean, the whole plot might be unreal but that part of the programme obviously can be done. Getting into a house. It gives people ideas.

These fears were amplified in *Crimewatch*, which claims to depict real events:

MARIE (41): That was terrible, wasn't it?
DENISE (38): It was.
MARIE: I think it's because you know it could happen to you.
MARIE: There was a chap lying down on a settee.
JUNE (39): Oh yes, and they came in through the windows.
MARIE: You think, that could be anybody's house – it could be mine.

Crimewatch was regularly referred to as a frightening programme – even if the crime had no specific domestic reference.

Dear Nick Ross,
   At the end of *Crimewatch* last night you said, 'Don't have nightmares', and implied that these crimes are rare.
   I had watched with horror the awful facts as they unfolded, and I couldn't sleep. I wonder if the fact that three women mentioned on that programme suffered violent deaths has made a significant impact on the minds of our MPs, judges etc. Plus the poor little boy savagely murdered and the young girl who has not been found.
   I hope you had some satisfactory answers last night, but I am sorry, I won't be watching again. Too terrifying.
   Yours sincerely,
   JOAN BRYANT (Mrs)

This may, in part, be due to the skilful filming of the unsolved crimes, but also perhaps to the differences which exist between this programme and other established fictional crime series. *Crimewatch*, for example, does not provide a heroic detective, a tough reporter or a trained scientist with whom the viewer may identify. Neither does it provide the other consolations of the crime genre, a clear motive for the central crime or a nice dénouement in which mysteries are solved and wrongs righted. Instead the picture sometimes conveyed is of a relatively arbitrary act committed by unidentified villains who are still on the run and quite free of the attentions of Inspector Kate Longton (of *Juliet Bravo*), Dempsey, Makepeace, Kojak, Reagan (of *The Sweeney*) or even Dixon of Dock Green. No wonder that the fear is even thought to extend to members of the cast:

> JUNE (39): I don't know if I actually saw this programme or read about it, but they showed a scene where two women were jumped upon.
> ANN (43): Yes, as they were walking back late at night.
> JUNE: Yes. And apparently the women, the actresses in the scene, said they were absolutely petrified. They had to retake the thing so many times. They could feel the fear as they were doing it, although they're actresses. I think that was pretty hair-raising, to think they were frightened as well.

Not that there is any indication of a large number of viewers deciding to give *Crimewatch* a miss because of the fear that it induces: the latest BARB figures show that it is still among the most popular of all BBC television programmes.

Only two recent programmes were spoken of as being too fearful to watch – BBC2's *Threads* and the American TV film *The Day After* – both concerned with the consequences of nuclear war. The research conducted by the BBC into reactions of those who did see *Threads* suggests that the nonviewers' concerns were fully justified by the content of the programme. While 36 per cent of those who saw it agreed that it was depressing, 31 per cent found it convincing and 33 per cent, a third of the viewers, strongly agreed that it was 'frightening'.

Unfortunately we cannot easily put a figure on those who were too frightened to watch. A range of more acceptable reasons came easily to hand:

Not in/busy	40%
Not interested	24%
Didn't know it was on	13%
Watched other side	15%
No reason given	9%

In the group discussions on the subject, more personal, dogmatic and xenophobic reasons for not switching on were produced.

> DENISE (38): *Threads* was frightening. I was frightened by that.
> MARIE (41): I don't watch anything like that at all. I don't want to see them.

DENISE: You didn't see it?

MARIE: No, I just don't watch those programmes. If it's going to happen it's going to happen, that's how I look at it.

DENISE: Did you watch the American one about the end of the . . .

MARIE: No. I don't believe in Americans.

3

Experts and Their Reputations

JIM (41): The trouble with [James] Burke is that you have to look over his shoulder to see what is going on.

Animal Experts

When we asked our national sample of 3000 viewers if TV had made them 'much more interested' in politics, 70 per cent of those who had feelings on the matter said it had not. Animals fared much better. Nearly 80 per cent of those expressing views felt that television had definitely increased their interest in this area. The other 20 per cent (whom one imagines all squeezed together at the end of a long settee otherwise occupied by cheering ranks of amateur zoologists) declared that they were now *less* interested than before.

Not that any old animals will do. Viewers, in the same way they prefer some humans to others on the screen, have animal favourites. It was precisely such preferences which were investigated by a research project enquiring into the most suitable ingredients for a television quiz game on the subject of wildlife. On this occasion top ratings were given to short films featuring 'A Honey Bird', and 'A Jay with Ants', but those starring 'Green Frogs' and 'Pelicans' were rated as less entrancing.

Similar opinions were evident in our own groups on wildlife programmes, where a heated debate developed over the size of the animals that were ideal subjects for such programmes as *Survival* and *Wildlife on One*. One group member, John, maintained that television was particularly suited to the study of insects. Insects were, he argued, simply more interesting than larger animals. It was 'very very exciting' to see the complexity of their organisation. But Wendy, who was equally addicted to such programmes, was unimpressed.

WENDY (31): All right, it's interesting on a very high plane but I still don't think you can say it is as exciting as the lion, or cheetah, going in for the kill. It's not that kind of excitement.

JOHN (41): But once you've seen a lion kill, you've seen it, haven't you? It's straightforward.

WENDY: But once you've seen ants running around, that's it as well . . . I mean ants don't do a lot more, do they? They run round in different ways.

BOB (33): They spend all their time building. They're doing something. And it's quite interesting how they help one another . . .

It was clear from later discussion that viewers were often as fascinated by how the pictures were obtained as by the animals themselves. 'You wonder how the hell they get so close.' 'The camera seems to be so clever you almost forget there is someone controlling it.' It made it all so different from life.

JOHN: If you're walking along in the country and see a rabbit run across a field and go down a burrow, that's the last you see of it. It's so fast. But on television the cameras follow it down.

But how much was this an illusion? Was the rabbit glimpsed by the camera at some distance the one that we then saw running underground?

MIKE (42): With rabbits I suppose you could put them back down again if they came out.

LARRY (37): It'd be quite easy to do that if they wanted to.

GARETH (32): They might even be tame rabbits, mightn't they? And there might only be one entrance and one exit so you'd know where it was going to be.

Once doubts were raised in the group, others rushed in with their own theories about how even the most apparently 'wild' incidents could be simulated.

DAVID (41): This is interesting. Because sometimes they quite clearly say, although we don't know whether they're lying or it's true, 'we hung around for three weeks'. Sometimes they say they've been waiting for a lion to kill. And you think to yourself, Well, I wonder if they've covered themselves in case nothing turns up. Put a deer in a van, pushed it out and said 'run' and then quickly filmed the lion following. I sometimes wonder about that type of thing. But I have just about enough faith in human nature to believe it's true if they actually say so.

What seemed to make the matter of such significance in both groups was that certain individuals who admired animal programmes, in particular the David Attenborough programmes, liked to regard them as more 'natural' than the rest of television. Whereas soap operas and game shows and quizzes were perfectly dispensable, and current affairs could be learnt about from elsewhere, such programmes were unique in that they offered (in many cases for the first time) a chance to see the living world – live. Any notion that effects might be fabricated interfered with this viewpoint. John rounded on the 'simulation' faction.

JOHN: I saw David Attenborough, he was down in Indonesia somewhere, making a programme about a gorilla, and he went right into the middle of the gorillas. I don't know what sort of gorillas they were but he went into the middle. Now, I can't imagine for a minute someone was prompting those gorillas. They weren't being set up. No one was giving them a piece of sugar and saying, 'Quick, get ready, he's coming. Here he comes.' [*Laughs.*] '*Attenborough's coming.* You've got to do the right thing.'

Of all the Attenborough programmes it was *Life on Earth* which was most loved. ('It was obvious from the first episode that thousands of new zoologists would all be conceived at once, like a population bulge,' wrote Clive James perceptively in *The Crystal Bucket*, 1981.) And consequently the notion that there might be anything less than the real thing in this series was especially disturbing, a reflection on the expert who presented it:

MIKE: You know, I think some were fabricated in *The Living Planet*, or *Life on Earth*, the David Attenborough programmes. Some of the underwater shots were actually filmed in a tank at the studio. I know that.
JEFF: But you found that out afterwards. When you're watching it it still does seem natural, a reflection of what really happens.
JOHN: Yes.
DON: Anyway you're not going to train insects.
GARETH: I was sure he just went out there, set the cameras up by a watering hole and just let them roll. If nothing happened that day, they waited until it did.
JOHN: No, no. That's not right. The water shot in a river is done in a tank, isn't it?

Andrew Longley, the author of a new book, *The Making of 'The Living Planet'*, 1985, is certainly right in his calculation of some viewers' reactions to the news of how various pieces of film in the series were obtained:

You may be surprised – even outraged – to learn that the happy-looking armadillo on your screen was, in fact, fresh out of a zoo. Surely all these animals are supposed to be in the wild? The fact is that, sometimes, the only economic way of getting pictures of some species is to film them in captivity. The giant anteater seen earlier in the same programme was also from a zoo, as were some of the snakes, rodents and fish in subsequent programmes.

But this reassurance may not be enough to allow everyone to accept the subsequent example with equanimity.

Strangest of all was the affair of the flying snake. This extraordinary reptile seems to swim through the air by spreading its ribs, but it proved impossible to obtain a clear shot of one performing in the jungle. So a specimen was taken up 300 feet in a balloon above an airfield in Brunei, and simply dropped overboard. The resulting film is unforgettable, and the snake suffered no ill effects at all. (From *Radio Times*, 7 June 1985.)

Views of animals derived entirely from television may not always further our understanding of the natural world. The teacher who assisted our research into four- and five-year-olds' opinions on television described to us a lesson held in March 1985 during which she talked to the class about hibernation, about the various animals and insects who were now awakening from their winter slumber to greet the spring. In this context she referred to bees and asked the class if any of them had seen any this year. There was silence, until a four-year-old volunteered that he has indeed seen 'bees' recently on the television. 'Good,' said the teacher. 'Very good. Will you tell all of us what they were doing?'

'They were coming down this road, miss, and they were huge, and all these soldiers were firing at them.'

Simply Obsessed

As we have said, it was almost impossible to separate viewers' respect for animal programmes from their admiration for David Attenborough. He was the only television person to emerge from all our discussions without a single critical comment against his name. If there was one aspect of his appeal which stood out it was the feeling that we – the viewers – had been privileged witnesses to the development of his interest: we had been drawn into this world by his genuine curiosity and then watched as he went about satisfying it.

JIM (41): What makes it for me is that Attenborough is simply obsessed with animals. At the beginning it was a part-time interest. But now it's completely taken him over. He goes everywhere for years and years. His whole heart and soul are in it. He is genuinely still surprised.

This sense of being in the presence of an obsessive, someone who was even a little crazy in their pursuit of a single objective, and who actively went out with all the zeal of an early Christian to convert others to their cause, was something which many viewers looked for in the television expert. It also made Patrick Moore an admirable television figure.

PAUL (37): I get the impression he spent half his life looking through a telescope.
ALAN (42): Yes, even from a boy.
PAUL: Yes, that's the impression I get.
ALAN: He came to it because of a genuine interest. He knew enough about the subject to actually flog it to television. It's not exciting like wild beasts all wandering around the field.
TRB: But does he make it exciting?
BOB (51): Oh yes. [*All agree.*]

Moore and Attenborough are sometimes carelessly referred to as television personalities, which might suggest that their fame is largely a result of simply being well known, of their ability to differentiate themselves in small ways from other personalities, of their lack of any 'specific attributes'. But in fact they are rarely spoken of by viewers (at least by the viewers in our groups) without reference to their achievement.

In terms of scale, Attenborough's 'achievement' would certainly seem heroic. For the thirteen-part series, *Life on Earth*, he and his team travelled 1,500,000 miles in more than thirty countries, and shot more than 1,250,000 feet of film. A single three-second scene of the birth of an amphibian took 300 hours of observation before the filming was completed. (In terms of television 'miles', it is possibly something of a comparable achievement for Patrick Moore to have travelled successfully across our screen with *The Sky at Night* for nearly thirty years!)

Other television 'scientists' and 'intellectuals' may aspire to the heroic expert status accorded to Moore and Attenborough but seem less qualified to achieve it. Although they may have the necessary obsessiveness, the abiding curiosity, the desire to convert others, there is sometimes a feeling that these attributes have not developed slowly in front of our eyes (as with Moore and Attenborough) but were put together in a television workshop.

DENNIS (27): I like David Bellamy very much but you do get distracted and keep half thinking that he's hogging the limelight, that he must know he's being funny, that he's putting it on slightly.

What's more, alongside the undoubted admiration expressed for Bellamy were some concerns about whether he was 'going off' and might 'not be as good as at the beginning'. These temporal terms were never applied to Moore or Attenborough – an indication perhaps that Bellamy still risks that dissipation of appeal which is the characteristic of the pure 'TV personality'.

The management of identity is a peculiarly tricky problem for television experts. They depend upon some 'personality' to get the message across, but this must not be exploited. It seems to be a matter of 'credit' ratings. For whereas Patrick Moore is able to appear on *Blankety Blank* (a television quiz in which celebrities guess simple words) and *Face the Music* (a musical quiz show) without any apparent loss of status, several viewers felt strongly that another 'expert' had imperilled his identity by appearing in an inappropriate setting.

JIM: It was after he [Magnus Pyke] appeared on the *Morecambe and Wise* show that his attitude changed.
DOUG (48): Yes, you could see him wanting to be a comedian. He wanted to be a personality.

Perhaps a clue to the distinctions between Moore, Pyke and Bellamy also lies in the capacity of viewers like Doug to spot the motives of the performers. By now we are all experts in reading the merest facial flicker of a few dozen soap-opera stars; it's hardly likely that this judgement is left behind when other less fictional characters appear before us. If this rigorous examination suggests that such experts do indeed 'want to' be comedians or performers, this immediately belies their claims to an obsessive concern with their own subject.

Most television 'scientists' or 'experts' depend initially upon their outside reputation. Only a few are home-grown. In recent years the doyen of these has undoubtedly been James Burke, a graduate in English literature from Oxford who after a period of teaching English in Italy obtained his first job in television as a reporter for *World in Action* (fast-talking investigative current affairs). In his series *Connections* and *The Real Thing* he set himself up as a plain no-nonsense fellow who was able to make sense of science and metaphysics. More recently, in *The Day the Universe Changed*, he turned his attention to the origins of Western knowledge. Viewers were not greatly impressed:

ALAN: Supercilious.
DEREK (49): He's too much in front of the camera all the time, huge centre screen: 'Look how wonderful I am.'
JIM: The trouble with Burke is that you have to look over his shoulder to see what else is on. [*Laughter.*]

Some others were distracted by his aeronautic displays.

ALAN: I'm not sure I like the way he moves about . . . his programmes were on a large set and he kept leaping from one set to the other, didn't he? He'd introduce one aspect of a subject and then he'd fly across to another place. He'd never settle down.
PAUL: I could never understand what he was on about at all.

When it came to the more popular programmes on television, it was rare to find complete convergence between the views of television critics in the quality press and those held by typical members of the audience. There was, however, general agreement over James Burke's limitations – particularly when he was, say, compared to other 'experts'. 'Give Patrick Moore a studio and he transports you to the stars with his enthusiasm and knowledge,' Nicholas Shakespeare wrote in *The Times*, 24 April 1985. 'Give James Burke the world and he hops about like a flea on heat, making precious little sense at all.'

And while the 'personal' authority of the presenter (Bellamy, Attenborough and Moore) is regarded as a distinct virtue in other series, when used as a description for Burke's programmes it carries, if the *Guardian*'s TV critic Nancy Banks-Smith is to be believed, a rather different meaning.

'Let me,' said James Burke, 'tell you a joke. Someone went up to the great philosopher Wittgenstein and said, "What a lot of morons people back in the Middle Ages must have been to have thought what they were seeing was the sun going round the earth!" To which Wittgenstein replied, "Yeah, but

I wonder what it would have looked like if the sun had been going round the earth.'' The point being of course,' Burke added helpfully, 'it would have looked exactly the same.'

Yeah (as the great philosopher Wittgenstein used to say), that's a real rib-tickler but I prefer the one about the great philosopher Kierkegaard. He was standing one day in a flowerbed lost in thought when he was spotted by the park keeper, who called out angrily, 'What are you doing there?' 'What are any of us doing here?' replied the sage sonorously.

It was a question which recurred to me with increasing force during *The Day the Universe Changed* (BBC 1), subtitled A Personal View by James Burke. The phrase 'a personal view' is an encoded message meaning 'Look, it's nothing to do with me. Take it up with that chap waving his arms about.' (*Guardian*, 20 March 1985.)

The Bubble Reputation

Such attacks upon James Burke's reputation as an expert raise interesting questions about television reputation itself. The medium has a peculiar capacity for mixing together different kinds of reputation. On a single programme, there may appear people with credit ratings derived from quite separate areas of the medium. It seems to be this original rating which determines whether or not their appearance will add to their reputation, detract from it, or leave it untouched. What they actually say or do is of rather less significance. Consider, for example, the profits and losses which might be incurred by some well-known figures if they accepted an invitation to appear on the panel for *Blankety Blank*. We gave viewers four names to assess.

Glenda Jackson. It was unanimously agreed that such an appearance would lower her reputation. For although she appeared on the *Morecambe and Wise* show, the fact of her appearance in such a setting was itself the point of the appearance. As a panellist on *Blankety Blank* she could only be another participant.

Michael Aspel. There was less certainty here, but a majority thought his reputation would be diminished, because as a presenter himself, Aspel would by such an appearance give up the usual authority he enjoys on television. He would be on a panel rather than 'behind a desk'.

David Bellamy. This fitted in with predictions. Bellamy would lose by such an appearance. For although Patrick Moore may come on such shows regularly without loss of reputation, appearance for Bellamy at this stage of his television career might raise further doubts about the truly obsessive nature of his botanical interests.

Ian McCaskill (weather forecaster). Everyone thought he would gain by it. The timing would seem just about right. Weather forecasting has, under the influence of breakfast television, become increasingly an 'entertainment' slot – and McCaskill is a leading performer in the genre.

This is far from being purely an imaginative game. Considerably more sophisticated versions of such 'reputation accounting' go on every day of the week in the offices of agents and impresarios.

While on the subject of experts we introduced another, more refined test of public 'reputation'. We drew up a list of 'experts' and others and asked:

● If you saw this person taking part in a television commercial, would your estimation of them *decrease* or remain *unchanged*?

The theory is that if a person's reputation is decreased by such an appearance, then we may say that they have a reputation which also counts in the real world. However, if a person's reputation is unchanged by such an appearance it may be assumed that their reputation is confined to television.

● What would happen to their reputation if they appeared in a television commercial?

	Reputation would slip	Reputation unchanged	Unable to agree
Esther Rantzen	√		
Jimmy Hill	√		
Ian McCaskill		√	
Angela Rippon		√	
Melvyn Bragg	√		
Robert Robinson	√		
Russell Harty			√
*Hilda Ogden (Jean Alexander)			√
*Jean Alexander (Hilda Ogden)	√		
Magnus Pyke		√	
James Burke		√	
David Bellamy			√
Patrick Moore	√		

* In the first example Jean Alexander would appear in the commercial character of Hilda Ogden, in the second as the actress who plays the part.

The group found little difficulty in agreeing that the reputations of such presenters and experts and hosts as Esther Rantzen, Jimmy Hill, Melvyn Bragg, Robert Robinson and Patrick Moore would be marred by such an appearance. Similarly there was agreement that Ian McCaskill, Angela Rippon and Magnus Pyke would be unaffected.

There was uncertainty over Russell Harty (perhaps promoted by knowledge of Wogan's activity in this field), David Bellamy (as predicted by our earlier comments) and Hilda Ogden (possibly a surprise in view of soap star Larry Hagman's recent exploitation of his fictional J.R. persona from *Dallas* in advertisements for tyres).

We should also mention one disagreement which is not recorded in the list of responses. Paul (47) insisted that James Burke's reputation would not remain the same after his appearance in a commercial. It would be enhanced!

4

A Touch of the Blarney: Television's Hosts

● Who is or was your favourite chat-show host?

1. Terry Wogan
2. Michael Aspel
3. Russell Harty
4. Michael Parkinson

---

5. Des O'Connor
6. Lennie Bennett
7. Larry Grayson
8. Simon Dee
9. Eamonn Andrews
10. Clive James
11. Frank Delaney
12. Derek Nimmo
13. Maria Aitken
14. Gloria Hunniford
15. Janet Street-Porter

'Please Say Something'

There was not much doubt in the viewers' minds about the competitors in this league, or their order. And when it came to the top four, agreement was absolute. It is a feature of this segment of television life – the arena of 'pure' personality – that matters can be different by next month, and are almost certain to be so by next year. Popular newspapers continually report subtle shifts in popularity ratings: in June 1985 they commented on Wogan's possible decline and began to pronounce the last rites over Parkinson. Keith Little remarked: 'Parkinson, you see, is already Second Division. And Wogan's not pulling in the audience. You can't say that sort of audience isn't around at that time. The *Coronation Street* audience is there – which is 17 million – and Wogan's pulling – what? – *eight*.'

In the background stand examples of those whose 'personality' has apparently not been enough to sustain their career: the famous case of Simon Dee (host of *Dee Time*, April 1967 to December 1969) and the dramatic decision of the BBC in 1982 to axe the *Sin on Saturday* programme which was intended to launch Bernard Falk upon a chat-show career. ('He sounded confident that he was going to be the next Michael Parkinson when he was telling me about *Sin on Saturday*.' Margaret Forwood, *Sun*, 26 August 1982.)

Although all four top personalities in our list have a long career of work in the media, a curriculum vitae stretching back for ten or fifteen years, they have now firmly severed their links with this past in order to take their chances with the affections of huge national television audiences. (It is left to a small elite to mourn the passing of Wogan the radio performer and Parkinson the journalist.)

It is partly the recognition that they have taken this risk, that they are not claiming any special expertise as critic, journalist, commentator or performer, but are putting their own individuality on the line, which forms one aspect of the 'personality deal'. Only those who make themselves so vulnerable to public taste seem to be granted, however temporarily, the kind of massive popular support, empathy and identification which allow us to talk of a 'personality cult'.

The fact that involvement may momentarily swing away from them during the show – say towards the ventriloquist Rod Hull's Emu as it proceeds to savage Parkinson – or Grace Jones (the black singer and actress) as she hits Russell Harty across the head ('a confrontation of deep personal embarrassment' – Russell Harty) does not interfere with the overwhelmingly sympathetic view which people hold of their favourite hosts.

Even when we specifically asked viewers if they would welcome a few more things going wrong on these shows – if they would welcome some return to say, the relative chaos which used to characterise Eamonn Andrews's original live chat show, they stuck firmly to their identification with the presenter. It would, they said, hardly be pleasant for him.

TRB: If one of the guests on a chat show turned out to be a little drunk, how would you feel then?

BERYL (32): No, I wouldn't like it.

PAT (33): I wouldn't like it.

FAY (40): Was it Robert Mitchum? They couldn't get an answer out of him.

PAT: No, he was absolutely sloshed, wasn't he?

FAY: He went 'yep, yep', and . . . Aspel said to him, 'Is that all you're going to say all night?', and he went 'yep'. [*Laughs.*]

TRB: Well, suppose the guest suddenly swears?

SUE (31): Wogan would probably say, 'Enough of that bad language.'

FAY: He'd say, 'This is a family show.'

TRB: Do you ever hope that something like that might happen?

PAULA (28): No. [*Others agree.*]

TRB: Something a little embarrassing?

BERYL: No.

FAY: No, he's too nice for that.

Neither was such loving concern confined to Wogan. Viewers were equally solicitous about the relatively out-of-favour Parkinson.

> TRB: What about some of the others, like Parkinson? How do you feel if there's an awkward silence? If the guest stops talking?
> FAY: You tend to feel sorry for him. You think, Oh, please say something to him. *Please.*
> TRB: So you feel more for the host than you do for the guest?
> FAY: Yes. Much more. [*Others agree.*]

And if your audience is really with you, it stays that way even through minor disasters.

> JACKIE (41): D'you remember when Terry Wogan was walking onto the stage . . .
> SUE: The night he fell over?
> JACKIE: Yes. Elton John and Wogan fell over the step and he landed flat on his back. It was hilarious. But he carried it off beautifully.

Unlike television 'experts', personalities like Wogan and Aspel are to be judged not in terms of specific skills but rather by the criteria that we might apply to our own lives and those of our close friends. They are successful to the extent that their self-presentation, however glamorous or show-bizzy, must still allow us to see through to some recognisable inner person – someone who looks and sounds much like us. Such a person – someone, in Boorstin's words, who is known principally for 'his well-knownness' – is, ironically, a perfect subject for us to identify with: 'His qualities – or rather his lack of qualities – illustrate our peculiar problems. He is neither good nor bad, great nor petty. He is the human pseudo-event. He has been fabricated on purpose to satisfy our exaggerated expectations of human greatness.' (Daniel Boorstin, *The Image*, 1961.)

However 'fabricated' such personalities might be, their persistence rests upon a strong belief that there is little to choose between their private and public lives. Although actors and comedians and commentators might be damaged by revelations about the contempt in which they held their public, they would not be destroyed: a 'pure' personality, by contrast, would be breaking the only significant term of their contract.

When viewers were talking about such people they regularly spoke of their private and public lives as interchangeable. An observation that 'Wogan is this' or 'Parkinson does that' was thought likely to be true both on and off the screen. (Any discrepancies between the two worlds could be easily handled by such statements as 'Well, you can tell he's like that from looking at him' or 'I'd have guessed that about him' – the covering phrases of the loving parent who 'knows' their offspring, whatever they might occasionally get up to.)

However, that didn't mean that no distinctions were made *between* the chat-show hosts themselves in this respect. Viewers found no difficulty in ranking the top four when we asked:

- Which personalities are most like themselves in real life?

1. Terry Wogan
2. Michael Aspel
3. Russell Harty
4. Michael Parkinson

This order of 'integrity' exactly reproduces the order of popularity of the four individuals. The more you are thought to be 'like yourself' on the screen the more you will be liked (or, to put it another way – the more you are 'liked' the more you will be seen as 'like yourself'). This didn't mean that Wogan 'could do no wrong' – that he would come out top of any poll merely because of his overall popularity. When we turned to more specific attributes, he scored less well: you don't have to be 'good' to be a top personality.

- Who is the most 'modest' at home?

1. Michael Aspel
2. Michael Parkinson
3. Terry Wogan
4. Russell Harty

- Who is most pleased to meet new people at home?

1. Russell Harty
2. Terry Wogan
3. Michael Aspel
4. Michael Parkinson

However, Wogan came back well on a further integrity measure:

- Who is most 'truthful' at home?

1. Terry Wogan
2. Michael Aspel
3. Michael Parkinson
4. Russell Harty

– and in a final flourish (which may have owed more to Irish stereotyping than careful assessment):

- Who drinks the most at home?

1. Terry Wogan
2. Michael Aspel
3. Russell Harty
4. Michael Parkinson

Trivia of Personality

These, of course, are only fictional differences between such personalities –
more interesting for what they say about our imagination than the reality of our
heroes' lives. If we turn to something more concrete, to the actual differences
between the personalities as they appear before us on the screen, Boorstin
suggests that in this area of the merely famous, we can expect to find people
'differentiated' only by 'trivia of personality'.

Certainly viewers had very strong opinions about the relative merits of all four
celebrities. An identification with any one personality seemed to ensure either a
hostile or an ambivalent attitude to others. 'Wogan' people are unlikely to find
many good words to say about 'Harty' or 'Aspel' or 'Parkinson' people. If we
concentrate on the present Number One – Terry Wogan – what can be said
about his differences from the others which amounts to more than 'trivia'?

Certainly, some opinions about him do not rise much above an almost
maternal concern about his clothes and eating habits.

> ROSALYN (31): In my opinion Wogan is perhaps just a little bit overweight
> for his chair.
> WENDY (33): Yes, I feel that.
> ROSALYN: I'm always half expecting the chair to collapse underneath him.
> He always looks bigger than other people who're on with him.
> BETTY (27): But that's perhaps because he wears suits that are too small for
> him.
> WENDY: He should adjust his clothes, I think. Get something which fits.
> Because it must be uncomfortable when he has to keep on going like that.
> [She puts a thumb inside her belt and mimes Wogan easing the pressure on his
> stomach. All laugh.]
> BETTY: It makes you feel uncomfortable to watch.

But some, in a manner which was less easy to reconcile with Boorstin's notion of
the trivial difference, focused much more closely on Wogan's particular interviewing skills:

> ALAN (42): What's unusual about Wogan is that everyone likes him. It's as
> simple as that. People he interviews are glad to meet him.
> DENNIS (27): They're smiling at all the funny things he's said before they see
> him.
> PAUL (31): They know that they're not going to be 'sent up', or only in the
> way that he always does.
> ALAN: And he leaves *himself* wide open. The guests know that they can have
> a dig at him.

There were other references to Wogan's 'clubby' approach to guests, his
easy-going assumption that most people who came wandering onto the set were,
like him, slightly bemused by this crazy world of show business; that, like his,

their lives were just a bit precarious; but that nevertheless, for the moment, they would sit astride their temporary fame and chatter amiably.

This aspect of Wogan's interviewing style was well enough known to be criticised by some viewers, particularly by those who had been briefed by the newspapers about unsavoury aspects of the stars' lives. In these cases, it became difficult for them to watch a conversation which made no reference to such matters. Instead of a friendly chat it appeared that Wogan was somehow colluding with the guest.

> NATALIE (37): Sometimes you only get to know what the stars want you to know. Like Victoria Principal. [Pam Ewing in *Dallas*. Sex-film past. In real life married to a plastic surgeon.] Before she was twenty-one she was the most revealing woman going. She was in sexy films. But when she came on for her interview with Wogan it was all about the years *after* she was twenty-one.
>
> NORAH (57): I think the problem is that the interviewer himself would like to ask some juicy questions, but he can't.
>
> JOAN (51): Nosy questions.
>
> NORAH: Yes, nosy questions, but he can't. Someone like Wogan has got a very hard job, because he's always got to do what other people want.
>
> HEATHER (49): Maybe Terry wanted to say other things to Victoria Principal that day and people were holding up boards saying, 'Stop it, stop it.'

Others agreed that chat-show hosts did not have much control over the programme. Despite the relaxed picture on the screens, frenetic activity was just off camera.

> TRB: Who do you think makes decisions about how long guests are going to stay on?
>
> DEREK (43): The producer.
>
> DAVE (41): You've got someone in the wings saying, 'Quick. Hurry up. Get off.'

John saw the whole business as rather more relaxed, but his identification was still firmly with the host.

> JOHN (39): It must have something to do with how well the interview is going. If the director, or whoever is behind the camera or in the wings, can see that Terry's not going to be able to get an awful lot out of this person, they just wind it up and allow a little bit more time for the next person and hope that goes well. Or maybe there's somebody famous, really famous, at the end, who will have plenty to say – and they just give them the extra minutes.
>
> MIKE (47): I thought that with Fallon from *Dynasty* he was struggling. He kept asking her questions, but she kept giving him the same answers, as though she wasn't listening.

And if 'Fallon' was to blame for the monotony of her answers, Bo Derek seemed incapable of taking a joke.

MOLLY (41): I don't think Wogan liked Bo Derek very much. I think he found her boring. You could tell from the way he spoke.
JEAN (42): He was making fun of her.
MOLLY: Yes, gently taking the mickey.

At least 'Fallon' and Bo Derek did not challenge the assumptions at the heart of the Wogan show – that one's show-biz personality must be worn lightly, and not spoken about in too obviously careerist terms. For one group this was not true of another Wogan guest:

JO (29): You know who I dislike – Selina Scott. She thinks she's so important.
PHILLIPA (27): I think I like her.
JO: I did. But not now. Not after she was interviewed on Terry Wogan. She was such a shirty cow. She makes out she's sexy. She's going to do this and that and then she'll do this.
BERYL (32): She sat there the whole time like this, didn't she? [*She leans back and shows legs.*]
JO: I hated that.
BERYL: And she gets more than the Prime Minister gets.
SUE (31): She gets *eighty thousand pounds*.
BERYL: A year?
SUE: Eighty thousand pounds a year.
JO: But she's only on for an hour in the morning.

Eye-Lining

Even being as generous as we can to Wogan and his defenders, his interviewing skills hardly seem distinctive enough to explain his popularity. What else might constitute the marginal difference between him and other hosts? One character-istic, cited far more by critics than by ordinary viewers, is the degree of collusion that he is said to be able to establish between himself and the audience: the sense that he is somehow sharing a joke with them about some aspect of the game or chat show in which he finds himself enmeshed. Although this eye-line to the audience might seem very strange on sports programmes, current affairs and documentaries, it is as much a convention of talk shows as was the soliloquy in Elizabethan drama.

Because the talk shows are about visual witness not the battering of ideas and opinions, [Johnny] Carson [the American chat-show host] can afford to ignore or disdain his guests, his face glazing over with boredom or his eyes

widening in disbelief as he darts the visual equivalent of an aside into the camera which is reserved throughout *The Tonight Show* for close-ups of his reactions. The guests are engaged so that Carson can react to them, beckoning us to join him in the wry act of looking.
(Peter Conrad, *Television: the medium and its manners*, 1982.)

And in this country, Wogan, sitting at his simulated marble coffee table, shares his use of 'visual asides' with such a heterogeneous bunch as Russell Harty, Jimmy Tarbuck (comedian and quiz host), Bruce Forsyth (comedian and game-show host) and Larry Grayson.

Once this channel of communication is opened, different messages may be sent along it. Conrad suggests that Carson is primarily conveying a wry boredom or disbelief about the proceedings: wide-eyed comedians such as Forsyth and Grayson mostly use it to mime such phrases as 'Did you hear that?', 'Oh – *really*' or 'Get him'. Harty's look disingenuously announces that he seems to be getting into deeper emotional water than he had ever intended: 'What *did* I say?'

Wogan's asides are subtly different to all these, in that they do not so much exclude or 'place' his guests by commenting on their tediousness (Carson), their absurdities or pretensions (Forsyth and Grayson), or their propensity to make damaging revelations (Harty), but rather unite viewers and guests into a genial commentary upon the whole business of the chat show itself. 'His persona is based on amiability, interest, self-effacement and the sense that he is a bemused, yet conspiratorial pawn in the great showbiz game.' (Dave Hill, *City Limits*, 10 October 1985.) This is far less subversive than his treatment of the disc-jockey role on Radio Two, or his approach to the game show in *Blankety Blank*, but it is still distinctive, however much critics see it as a retreat from a much richer former persona.

> It does seem sad that Wogan himself has become a Johnny Carson clone, eschewing confrontation of any kind in order to appeal to the widest possible audience. The Wogan of the morning radio show was free to meander alone (apart from the sparring matches with Jimmy Young) through the letters and records in his own idiosyncratic way. On television he has to keep a studio audience laughing, as well as entertaining a large number of guests. Making jokes at his own expense is not much of a substitute for the individuality he used to possess. (Peter Buckman, *Listener*, 25 April 1985.)

Not that Wogan's special form of collusiveness can count for much if it goes unobserved. We asked viewers if they always felt they knew who chat-show hosts were talking to. Where were their eyes – on the guest, the studio audience or the people at home?

MICHAEL (49): On the guest. [*Others agree.*]
TRB: Always? All the time?
REG (43): No, not all the time.
MICHAEL: Sometimes on the audience or the camera. Looking at us.

REG: When he gets a certain answer, he laughs, and then he turns round and faces the camera, and then we're supposed to laugh. He's asking us to laugh at it as well.

TRB: So when he looks at you he's asking you to laugh?

REG: I think so. I don't know. I tend to laugh.

MICHAEL: You feel you want to appreciate him and what he's doing.

No one, however, regarded Wogan's visual asides as a practised technique, or considered the technical facilities which might be needed for him to bring them off. They were part of his personality. The way he was. The reason other chat-show hosts did not employ a similar style of communication was also thoroughly personal – part of themselves, not calculated.

JOHN: Parkinson avoids looking at you.

MICHAEL: But that's because he's shyer on the whole. He's a much shyer person. So he tends to look away more.

TRB: What about other chat-show hosts? Do they give any signs to the audience at home?

FRED (41): Michael Aspel does. Sometimes.

REG: That's his twitch. [*Laughter*.]

TRB: What does Aspel do which seems to be for the people who're watching?

FRED: I can't quite describe it. He occasionally gives an embarrassed sort of raise of the eyebrows – if it's cheeky.

TRB: And then you know he's looking at you?

FRED: I'm not sure. Maybe he's looking at the producer behind the camera but it appears he's looking at the audience at home.

(Strangely, we could find no one who felt sure that their favourite personalities were looking directly at them. They felt they might be, hoped they were, even laughed at the idea that such a thing might be happening. But then the sense of being 'looked at' by those on television is complicated. Although everyone who directly faces the camera appears to be looking at the audience, people rarely feel 'looked at' by those who most adopt this technique – the news readers.)

Barnsley Chop

If Wogan's distinctiveness was difficult to characterise, it was even harder to elicit views on Michael Aspel's personality or special technique. He was 'nice' and 'pleasant' and 'not too pushy'. Above all there was something endearing about his complexion. When Anne (25) referred to his 'big blue eyes or whatever colour they are' and 'his nice soft face – gentle face', there was general agreement that this was the key to his success. He always looked smoother than anyone else, as though photographed through a special lens. (If any current celebrity deserves Kitty Muggeridge's classic account of Frost's television career, 'He rose without trace', it would appear to be Aspel.)

Michael Parkinson, on the other hand, aroused many specific comments. In several groups he was roundly criticised. Although he was hosting a game show (*Family Secrets*) rather than an orthodox chat show, there seemed little enthusiasm for the proposal that he might return to his former setting:

JANET (33): Oh no, I think he's just a big bore.

MARY (35): Yes, he is boring now.

JANET: I mean it's like me sitting here going [*her voice slows down and becomes expressionless*] 'NOW – WHAT – DO – YOU – THINK?' *Scratch. Scratch.* He's just past it. He should be put out to graze.

JUDY (29): But I do think it's a shame.

MARY: I get blood pressure because he just can't ask them anything interesting.

TRB: Has he always been like that?

JANET: Oh yes, I think so.

MARY: But he smiles a lot. He smiles continually.

Parkinson undoubtedly still has many fans – the moderator who took two of the groups concerned with chat shows was among them – but it certainly seemed as though his favoured techniques were now regarded as out of date.

JIM (41): He has a clipboard. I always see him as with a clipboard, and he goes on to the next question whatever happens. And sometimes he's got the second question in before the guy has answered the first.

PAUL (37): Yes, but I think when he was on originally, he came at the right time. There wasn't anybody else as good as him then.

DEREK (49): But since then it's all developed into a bit of a fine art and people have developed new styles, and he's been left behind.

The contrast between then and now was not confined to the presence of the clipboard.

LIZ (37): It comes down to ad-libbing. You can carry off a bad interview just by jokes.

JAN (37): Aspel covers anything. Watch the *Six o'Clock Show* [early evening variety and chat show]. So many things go wrong. He just sort of carries it off. Smooths it over.

LIZ: That's experience, isn't it?

JAN: Parkinson's given his script. All puns and everything. Drives me up the wall. It's all scripted. I feel it's not like that with the others. Not with Harty. He's just himself.

Behind some of the animosity towards Parkinson, it was possible to detect a hint of moral retribution. He was after all one of the original television personalities, with a programme (or 'show' as he liked to call it) which began on 19 June 1971 and ended on 3 April 1982 after he'd interviewed 1050 guests. During that time he had been on the line like any other 'personality', but now there was the suspicion that he was merely giving performances.

JOAN (42): He always looks as if he can't wait to get home . . .

The paradox in all this is that the 'new styles' spoken of by Derek have moved even further away from the inquisitorial form of interviewing, which Parkinson at one time was regularly blamed for not adopting. Critic after critic accused him of being too soft, too starry-eyed, too obsequious, too inclined to let the guests off lightly. The comparisons in those days were with tougher interviewers:

GEORGE (36): Well, the best example I can think of is Frost. That amazing David Frost programme, where he interviewed that guy, that Indian guy – there was never such a hated man in all my lifetime – Savundra – that's it. That was a piece of master television, a piece of master interviewing.

Parkinson now seems to some to be too investigative, too journalistic, too full of set questions for the modern chat-show ethos, which, despite Wogan's occasional incisiveness, is largely conceived of as a relaxed two-hander in which both guest and host have an opportunity to display their general charm and 'niceness'.

In such 'no-win' circumstances he might be forced to look for consolation to at least some of the 'obituaries' upon his personality which followed the last edition of *Parkinson* in 1982.

On a deeper level, Parkinson has not neglected to allow his own firm but gentle convictions to reveal themselves when necessary. His loathing of apartheid, for instance, and his total lack of colour prejudice has been voiced on more than one occasion, notably in the course of a conversation with an unusually excited Muhammad Ali.

It is this combination of deceptive professional ease and rooted personal commitment that has given Mike Parkinson the kind of authority that has outdistanced so many rivals. I don't suggest he's everybody's cup of tea, but he has lasted the course and will be missed.
(Herbert Kretzmer, *Daily Mail*, 6 June 1982.)

If Parkinson is yesterday's chat-show host as far as viewers are concerned, who among the present top three hosts is most likely to join him in the near future? We asked our groups the somewhat brutal question:

• For how many more years do you think the following will be successful as chat-show hosts and top television personalities?

Wogan's huge following was enough to secure him an average future of fifteen years, with six votes of twenty years and over. Aspel, true to his ranking in the top chat-show-host league was considered to have another nine years of fame to look forward to, while Harty was allocated a modest four and Parkinson a mere two.

To see if this 'life span' would give the stars an adequate chance to salt away some savings for their later, less famous years we also asked:

● How much do you think chat-show hosts are paid per programme?

		(average estimate)
1.	Wogan	£2600
2.	Parkinson	£2300
3.	Aspel	£1000
4.	Harty	£700

(Parkinson's high placing possibly suggests that behind some of the viewers' doubts about his present television status may have lain a feeling that he was overpaid compared to the more popular Aspel and Harty.)

Viewers on Harty

If we are to judge 'personalities' by their public pronouncements then there is probably no one more prepared to accept the idea of his imminent demise than Russell Harty. In 1982 he chose to begin a short essay on his life and times by quoting the following paragraph from the fourth volume of Anthony Powell's memoirs:

> The television personality is positively encouraged by the conditions of existence to be answerable to no one but self, under no sort of restraint other than remaining a recognised 'personality'. The impression often given is that prolonged expenditure of the personality (as the Victorians used to suppose of masturbation) is cruelly hard on mind and body.
> (Anthony Powell, *The Strangers are All Gone*, 1982.)

Some people certainly detected an element of self-consciousness in Harty which was less evident in Parkinson, Aspel or Wogan. He was regarded as the least truthful chat-show host in real life, as well as the least modest. But some enjoyed the more 'acted' or affected manner which he brought to the part and could see how it worked with some of the less 'show-biz' guests he favoured on his programmes.

> MARY (52): I think he likes to show off himself. He enjoys doing that. And as a result other people start to show off as well. They all go a bit mad.

But his formal turns of phrase – 'You have, have you not?' – were less appreciated.

> VAL (51): He's always saying 'one this' and 'one that' – 'one would say' or 'one would say this'.
> DOT (37): And 'one would not'. He does talk to the person he's interviewing but I think it's all done with a big air of 'look at me, I'm somebody'.

Others found it difficult to see past his slightly camp manner towards the more cutting edge of his interviewing style.

> DOT: Harty is the one I hate. He's somehow all flabby. And I'll swear he's a bit funny.

However, when we asked 'Which of the following chat-show hosts avoids asking their guests difficult questions?', Harty actually tied for first place with Wogan – which in the context of the present belief in Wogan's infallibility gives him some sort of moral victory.

Unfortunately, in one group, more detailed discussion of Harty's precise 'personality', the critical differences which marked him off from other chat-show hosts, was pre-empted by some 'hard' news from the real world.

> DOT: He's a snob in real life. I know that for a fact. I mean I saw him in a restaurant and, my god, I don't know who he thought he was. So stuck up. I thought, well, I can afford the same restaurant as you.
> TRB: Where were you?
> DOT: In a restaurant up in Notting Hill.
> LORNA (40): A Wimpy, actually. [*Laughs.*]

It was a form of encounter already well described by the highly self-conscious Harty in *The Third Age of Broadcasting* (edited by Brian Wenham, 1982): 'Construction workers hang over building sites and make remarks about your manhood. Small crowds discuss your identity within your hearing: "Can't remember his name but he's the one your mother doesn't like." Girls at the checkout counter at Marks and Spencer pick out your purchases and mouth at each other "Fancy *him* buying food".'

Chitter, Chatter

Chat-show hosts, as we have argued, are examples of the 'pure personality' – those whose lack of specific attributes, whose capacity for appearing to be exactly what they are, make them ideally suited for identification. What we appear to want most of all in this format is not the provocative investigative interview (there is a place for this elsewhere) but rather the sense of easy sequential talk – an elevated version of chatter between friends in which what is said may even be less important than the pleasure which can come from the mere fact of talking.

There may be some truth in Peter Conrad's claim that 'Talk on television isn't meant to be listened to', not just because, as he suggests, 'the words gain for us the time to look at the talker', but because there is also pleasure to be had from watching people chatter. (Lounge bars on Saturday evenings are full of such happy auditors.)

What's more, because chattering is something that every one of us can manage with some degree of success, there is a particular pleasure in having someone we feel to be just like us – the pure personality – doing the job on our behalf.

All this may tell us one more thing about Wogan's especial success in this domain. On several occasions we were told that 'he had kissed the blarney stone', that he had the gift of the gab – a fascination with simply talking. Indeed, what made his Radio Two programme so successful was primarily his ability to take hold of the usual inconsequential chatter which disc jockeys sandwich between records, and make a virtue of its pointlessness. In this sense, far from lacking any specific attributes which might explain his success, he may have one which matters a great deal – a clear notion of exactly what lies behind the appeal of that odd segment of television output, the chat show.

Not that everyone in our teenage group seemed to have time for such subtleties.

GARY (14): He's boring, he's crap really . . .
TRB: Why do you say boring?
GARY: Because he's always on.
SEAN (15): He might not be boring to older people, but to kids, that's not the sort of thing you want.
PETER (14): I can't understand what he's saying.
GARY: Yes, that's because he's Irish, isn't it?

The Game Show Presenters (and Participants)

Nothing on television so exercises the critics as the game shows. One of the more recent offerings – *The Price is Right* – opened to the usual rave notices:

'Unspeakable vulgarity, ghastly materialism and unedifying greed' (*Daily Mail*).

'A load of rubbish' (*Daily Mirror*).

'The noisiest, most money grabbing show so far' (*Guardian*).

'The most nauseating game show for this past couple of decades' (*Daily Telegraph*).

'The most naked celebration of consumerism since *Double Your Money* . . . the whole tatty show is aimed at advertising greed' (*Standard*).

And as is usually the case, the show shot straight into the top ten programmes in the UK, regularly attracting 13 million viewers: one out of every four men, women and children in the country. Meanwhile another 25,000 people are busily writing in each week applying for a place in the audience, and thereby a chance to take part in the actual programme.

Criticism usually swings between two poles: the show is either said to cater to the greed or consumerism of the participants (*The Price is Right, Sale of the*

Century, *Family Fortunes*) or to exploit their emotional frailty (*Game for a Laugh*, *The Ultra Quiz*). There is nothing very new about such concerns. Back in 1955 *Double Your Money* with Hughie Green was condemned as 'vulgar and materialistic', while in the same year A T V's *People are Funny* (hosted by Derek Roy) was actually taken off the air.

We first of all asked fans of *The Price is Right* (a show cruelly but accurately referred to by David Frost as '*The Antiques Road Show* on speed') about the part played by the participants – people like Mike:

> 'Mike,' says Crowther, calling down the next contestant, 'this mini-snooker table is made from polished wood and comes with a set of balls. Isn't it exciting?' Mike agrees. 'Have you got a table like this at home, Mike?' Mike says he has. 'Well, Mike,' says Crowther, 'now you have got another one, haven't you?' Again, Mike finds it hard not to agree with Crowther. (Hugo Williams, *New Statesman*, 4 January 1985.)

> TRB: Do you think the people who take part ever fake their excitement?
> LORNA (40): Oh yes. They join in. They get carried away. Get excited over a decanter and six glasses.
> BERYL (51): Things that they wouldn't normally be bothered about.
> MAVIS (47): They all have to scream. They all have to do it on *The Price is Right*. They have to come down the stairs and shake their fists with delight. *Hooray. Hooray. Hooray.*
> PATRICIA (49): And you even get some who are screaming and crying at the same time.
> BERYL: Did you see when that coloured chap was on? He really went mad. He was jumping in the air and dancing. He was very good at it.

What seemed to be important about the participants – what made them 'very good at it' – was their ability to let themselves go, to go 'mad'. Yes, they were faking it, but that didn't seem too important. No one could *really* be that excited about a decanter and a few glasses, but somehow it didn't matter much whether the emotion was genuine. Perhaps, as in the wrestling match described by Roland Barthes, 'What the public wants is the image of passion not passion itself.' And to pursue the analogy, greed here was no more the dominant motive for the participants than a desire for violence might be dominant among a wrestling crowd. Something which looks like violence, something which looks like greed, provides an occasion for the organised release of feelings – in the case of *The Price is Right*, collective euphoria.

Although the hosts certainly have a central role in game shows, there's less opportunity for 'personality' play than in chat shows. They are often too busy getting people enthusiastic about the value of the prizes:

> LESLIE CROWTHER: Hello there. Welcome once again to *The Price is Right*. Ladies and gentlemen, in our Treasure House of Prizes tonight, eighteen

major prizes can be won and two magnificent showcases. [*Twelve seconds' applause*.]

Or winding up the participants:

L.C.: Mark, *three* of those *four* items can be yours – provided – provided – you avoid the Danger Price.

Or dealing with the sheer mechanics of the game:

L.C.: Vivienne, what is your bid?
VIVIENNE: Hundred and twenty-nine. [*Some shouts from audience*.]
L.C.: One hundred and twenty-nine, says Vivienne. [*All shouting*.] Maureen, what do you think?
MAUREEN: Seventy-eight. [*Extended shouting*.]
L.C.: Seventy-eight, says Maureen. Leslie, your opinion?
LESLIE: Seventy-nine . . . [*Shouting to overcome shouting*] Seventy-nine.
L.C.: Seventy-nine, says Leslie . . . Mark?
MARK: Ninety-seven.
L. C.: Ninety-seven . . . [*dong*] . . . well, that's a very good start except you've all bid over. Now the lowest bid was seventy-eight from Maureen so you've all got to bid lower than that, and we will start again. Vivienne, give me your new bid.

In fact the only part of the programme in which Crowther was not fully absorbed with the progress of the game occupied approximately five seconds – a tiny bit of banter with one of the participants:

VIVIENNE: Forty-six . . . [*Shouting*] Forty-six.
L.C.: Forty-six?
VIVIENNE: Forty-six.
L.C.: Forty-six?
VIVIENNE: Forty-six.
L.C.: Well, fine, bit of a difference. Maureen, how about you?

Opportunities for 'personality play' in *The Price is Right* are, however, much more scarce than in such other contemporary game shows as *Play Your Cards Right*, where a great deal of 'space' is provided for Bruce Forsyth to bounce verbally off the contestants and even to parody other game shows and his own role in the present one. But even this relies less on 'personality' than *Blankety Blank* with Wogan (and, to a lesser extent, Les Dawson) where the whole edifice rests on the joke of nobody taking the silly game very seriously or thinking much of the prizes (and where the presenter is palpably overqualified for the task in hand). Crowther's relatively anonymous role more readily parallels that of such other hosts as Gordon Burns in *The Krypton Factor* (it is a popular joke in game-show circles that after hosting this programme for over eight years Burns has still to be recognised by anyone in the street), Jim Bowen in *Bullseye* and Tom O'Connor in *Name That Tune*.

We did, however, find that game-show enthusiasts were able to make some distinctions – particularly when they'd had a chance to compare two people fronting the same programme.

> BERYL: And I must say that I think Max Bygraves in *Family Fortunes* is rubbish. He's not as good as Bob Monkhouse at the job. He can't seem to find his way round, can he? He trips over everything.
> MAVIS: Yes, he's a bit fumbly. He doesn't seem to recognise people until he's right up to them. And sometimes he goes to the wrong team and forgets where he's put his notes.

The *Sun* inimitably invited its readers to give their opinion – although the letters and verse printed (7 February 1985) hardly made clear the criteria by which any judgement might be made. First Bob's qualities:

> And with Bob in the chair it was a lively show.
> Now poor old Max, he tries his best.
> But somehow he has trouble getting the words off his chest.
> With his hands in the air, he yells 'Big Money'
> On your bike, Max, you're certainly not funny.
> Bring back Bob with his zing and his zest
> And the show will be back to one of the best.
> ANDREA, GLORIA, CHRIS, VAL and YVONNE, Gravesend, Kent.

> I appeared on the show two years ago with Bob Monkhouse and I can say in all honesty what a nice, genuine man Bob is.
> At the rehearsal, he spoke to all of us.
> We were fortunate to be the first family to win more than a thousand pounds and Bob couldn't have been more pleased for us.
> Max Bygraves has turned a good show into a laughable flop.
> MRS S. HULL, Ashby, S. Humberside.

And then Max's:

> Max is very good for *Family Fortunes*. I agree with what he says about Bob Monkhouse, he is oily.
> And when I see him put his arm round the shoulders of the contestants, with that silly grin on his face, it makes me shudder.
> Carry on with your Big Money, Max. I think you're great.
> IRIS PRATT, Royston, Herts.

> Everyone in my family watches the show and we all agree that it has been better since Max Bygraves has been in charge.
> It seems more relaxed, and Max looks as if he enjoys doing the show rather than seeing it as just another job.
> D. PARSELL, Hemel Hempstead, Herts.

> I much prefer Max. His warmth and Cockney charm can put anyone at ease. He fits in so well with the show.

Bob was okay but he seemed to want the limelight, whereas Max involves everybody.
R. RAYFIELD, Oxford.

Max may not be so good with the ad lib but at least he isn't sarcastic like Bob Monkhouse.
Carry on Max – let's have *Family Fortunes* ending with a Singalong.
MRS P. MAHER, Ashford, Middx.

Finally, in these tabloid hustings, one spoilt paper:

Who is best – Bob or Max? It's like asking which you'd prefer – a headache or a stomach ache. Give me Bruce Forsyth any day.
MRS VALERIE HAINES, Ewell, Surrey.

We tried to bring a little more precision to the area by asking viewers to evaluate the following game-show hosts:

Leslie Crowther	*The Price is Right* (16 million viewers)	ex *Crackerjack*
Bob Monkhouse	*Bob's Full House* (10 million viewers)	ex *Golden Shot* and *Family Fortunes*
Jeremy Beadle	*Game for a Laugh* (12.5 million viewers)	
Nicholas Parsons	*Sale of the Century* (7 million viewers)	ex Arthur Haynes stooge
Max Bygraves	*Family Fortunes* (12 million viewers)	ex *SingalongaMax*
Bruce Forsyth	*Play Your Cards Right* (14 million viewers)	ex *Generation Game*

First, we asked which of the above 'felt as enthusiastic about their work as they sounded'. Bruce Forsyth was a clear winner – no doubt an indication of the opportunities provided within *Play Your Cards Right* for him to express some opinions which sound as though they might be his own rather than the scriptwriters'. At the bottom of the list came Max Bygraves in *Family Fortunes*, whose showing on other criteria certainly suggested that as far as our game-show viewers were concerned he was far from being the host with the most.

When, for example, we asked, 'Which of the chat-show hosts really likes doing the job?', Max again slipped into bottom place with Bruce Forsyth leading the field.

But at least he scored better on the 'Who really likes the participants?' question, in which the wooden spoon went to Nicholas Parsons of *Sale of the*

Century. In fact Parsons emerged with a rather strange profile, for although apparently feeling superior to the participants, he also easily led the field on 'Who really thinks the prizes are valuable?' (This perhaps suggests that he'd like all the prizes for himself and so resents giving them away to nasty contestants.)

To try to find some further distinctions between the six hosts, we then asked, 'Who is really proud of what they're doing?' This did indeed differentiate the six, with Bob Monkhouse, who scored well on all other measures, coming first, while Jeremy Beadle (senior host on *Game for a Laugh*, who may well be known to viewers for his appearances in rather more serious television programmes) came a resounding last.

As a final calculation we combined all the scores obtained on the different questions (Who likes the participants/the job? Who gets excited/is proud? Who thinks the prizes are valuable?) in order to produce a 'host of hosts'. The clear winner was Bruce Forsyth, with Leslie Crowther some distance behind, but just beating Bob Monkhouse into second place.

Full Table	*Host of Hosts*
1	Bruce Forsyth
2	Leslie Crowther
3	Bob Monkhouse
4	Nicholas Parsons
5	Jeremy Beadle
6	Max Bygraves

Bruce Forsyth is not only top game-show host but also the most prolific producer of game-show catch phrases with 'Didn't he do well?', 'Good game, good game' and 'Nice to see you – to see you, nice'. But he has nothing at the moment which quite matches the sheer populism of the invitation issued weekly by Leslie Crowther at the beginning of his programme and offered at the end as a lure for the one to come.

> L.C.: You have won a health unit, a TV and video recorder, a beauty case, a pair of decanters, a four-poster bed, two side cabinets, two table lamps, and *one* holiday for *two* – in Spain.
> *Yes. That's great.* Ladies and gentlemen, I know you're going to join us next week when once again I'll be able to say to you, *come on down*.

5

Here are the News Readers

CHRISTINE (31): It's almost as though she [Jan Leeming] is going to a dinner party afterwards, isn't it? And wants to be dressed beforehand. Just popped in to read the news.

In 1954, the BBC stated its policy for television news: 'The object is to state the news of the day accurately, fairly, soberly and *impersonally*.' We are not directly concerned here with questions of accuracy, fairness or sobriety (these can hardly be assessed by viewers who do not have access to reliable other sources), but there can be no doubt that the news is now thought to be about as 'impersonal' as the Wogan show. The news readers or newscasters are, in the words of one writer, 'stars – whose glamour, attractiveness and self-assurance invest them with the same magical aura that surrounds others in show business who are universally known to be universally known'. (Leo Bogart, quoted in Percy Tannenbaum, ed., *The Entertainment Functions of Television*, 1980.) And this despite the fact that they are typically confined within a slick production straitjacket which provides them with even less opportunity for 'personality play' than that allowed to the presenters of fast-moving and technical game shows.

Here is the script for a typical BBC *Six o'Clock News* for one day in 1985, with interruptions from some of our viewers:

At 30 seconds before 6 pm 'cue dots' appear in the top left-hand corner of television screens all over the country. At 10 seconds to 6 they disappear. In BBC Television Centre the instruction is given, 'Run V.T.', and the P.A. [production assistant] counts down on a stopwatch, 10−9−8−7−6−5.

At 5 seconds before 6 the announcer says on air, 'This is BBC 1.'

1. V.T. (Videotape)/   OPENING TITLES (a computer-generated graphic of the world turning itself into a Venetian blind – the message is: NOW you can see through to the world outside).
IN:(MUSIC)

2. O.O.V. (Out of Vision)/ Announcer (Sonorous. Slight Echo Effect): 'The Six O'Clock News from the BBC with Sue Lawley and Nicholas Whitchell.'

3. W.S. (Studio Wide Shot)/ Sue and Nicholas sitting at a long desk. She is angled looking at him. He is scribbling some last-minute notes.

(It takes longer and longer to get to the news these days. Indeed, there are so many visual and auditory effects, so many curtains going up, that you're a little surprised to find that behind the last one lies not the Dalai Lama on a throne of gold but Sue Lawley and Nicholas sitting upright at a good old desk.)

TRB: Why do you think they have two news readers nowadays?

MICHAEL (39): So that there's some variety.

JANE (29): Yes. You get a single news reader just sitting there all the time and you tend to get bored with looking at him or her as the case may be. You need a different face. If you've got two of them the camera can switch from one to the other. You can imagine what goes on between them. See how he gets the bad bit, she gets the good bit, or she gets the bad bit and he gets the good bit.

JAN (41): Sometimes on *News at Ten* they show a little thing going on between them, some little comment in between the bits of news. A look or a smile. It goes down well. I think it's great the way they look at each other as they finish off the stories.

4. M.C.U. (Medium Close Up)/ Sue Lawley – the desk is now out of vision. Sue: 'Good evening. The headlines.'

6-02.

What interested – even fascinated – viewers about the news and the news readers was the tension between the formality and the informality of the occasion. (You can almost grade programmes on television according to the formality of their tone, all the way from the 'spontaneous', 'unrehearsed', 'plenty of mistakes' look of *The Tube* [Tyne-Tees' libertarian answer to *Top of the Pops*] through to the stark impersonal out-of-vision voices of BBC TV's continuity announcers.)

The news, with variations depending on channel and time of day, always establishes a certain formality by its reliance on stiff postures, fairly formal clothes, grammatically complete sentences, a general lack of emotion, and the use of either long shots (as of Sue and Nicholas at the desk) or a respectful Medium Close Up (for most of the programme).

But over the years there has been a carefully controlled increase in informality. Some viewers saw good reasons for at least one of the changes:

TRB: Why do you think they got rid of the desk?
JAN: Too far away. You have to have the camera too far away to get the desk and the news reader in. But now you can get very close into the news reader.
JOAN (51): It's stuffy anyway. You associate a desk with your boss. It's a sort of stuffy atmosphere. It reminds me of Gilbert Harding [the original *What's My Line* 'personality'] and all that sort of thing.
SALLY (42): And when you see the desk and it's very hot you can imagine them sitting there with their feet in a bowl of cold water.

5. M.C.U. (Medium Close Up)/	Sue Lawley: 'Nearly 200 people have been killed in the latest attack by Tamil terrorists in Sri Lanka.' (One and a half seconds' pause to indicate a change of mood.) '*And* – a "hair-raising" attempt to set a new world record.'
6. S.F. (Slide File Picture)/	Woman with very long hair dangling from a crane.

6-04.

We aren't all that good at remembering what we've seen on the news. If we are asked the next day, we can on average recall about two items in eight. And neither is our comprehension much better. Indeed it's only just possible to claim that we understand any more about news items as a result of having seen them on television. The pictures certainly don't seem to help a lot. Those who sit with their backs to the sets do just as well. A lot depends on how much background knowledge we already have, how much the item affects us or can be seen in personal terms – and also upon exactly where it occurs in the bulletin. But this all makes sense if much of the time we only watch the news to see if there is anything there which might affect our own lives. If there is not, then nowadays we can still be given a small reward for watching in the first place, a bit of showbusiness which briefly sends up the formality of the previous proceedings:

JILL (31): I like it when they do a joke at the end.
JOANNA (32): Yes. [*Most agree and laugh.*]
JILL: I always wonder what they say to each other when the . . .
JOANNA: I'd love to know. [*Laughs.*]
JILL: Yes. They always say something. The picture zooms back and shows the two of them sitting there, and I wonder whether they're saying, you

know, 'Where are you going for lunch tomorrow?' Or just moving their mouths.

So popular have these little 'rewards' or 'strings' become that ITN has thought it worthwhile to bring them together in a book with a foreword by one of the newscasters (a title preferred at Independent Television ever since Aidan Crawley insisted that news people should be journalists and not merely 'readers').

'And Finally . . .' – two words in the last minute of *News at Ten* which promise at the very least the raising of an eyebrow or two, at best that a good laugh is on the way . . . part of a long-running understanding between us and you at home that even on those days when the news seems a little gloomy, we'll try our best to send you to bed with a smile . . . like a passing encounter with an old friend – before Alastair, Sandy, Pam or I say goodnight, the closing music crowds in, and, judging from your letters, everyone wonders what on earth the two newscasters are saying to each other in that closing 'two-shot' that has become a *News at Ten* trademark. Forgive me if I don't give the game away on that.
(Martyn Lewis, from Preface to '*And Finally*', 1984.)

7. M.C.U. (Medium Close Up)/	Sue Lawley. 'Last night in Londonderry a teenage boy was taken to hospital with serious head injuries after rioting, in which police patrols came under attack. This report from Neil Bennet.'
8. O.B. (Outside Broadcast)/ Run V.T.	Neil Bennet standing outside a polling station. 'In what police described as an orchestrated attempt to disrupt the poll, the RUC were attacked by petrol bombers as they collected ballot boxes. A car belonging to a candidate from the SDLP was set on fire. He blames supporters of Sinn Fein.'

6-06.

Television news has been described as 'excitement governed by order'. Items quickly follow each other, generating confusion about the exact number in a single broadcast.

TRB: How many separate news items do you get in a half-hour bulletin?
BOB (51): Thirty to forty different items, I should think.
TOM (36): I'd say about twenty. You never seem to stop on anything for more than a minute.
DEREK (49): Twenty-four.

GLENDA (38): Fifteen.

JOHN (42): Twenty.

TRB: So anything between fifteen and forty?

JOHN: It's so quick. They try to make it as quick as they can.

(The average six o'clock bulletin contains fourteen separate items.)

In addition, there are frequent moves from the studio to outside reports. Even when the cameras are not there for the action itself, going over to a spot near where it occurred and then introducing some fast cutting between different scenes (in the short Bennet film there were five different scenes shown on camera) creates a sense that something has happened.

TRB: Can you tell a difference between real backgrounds – when the correspondent is actually there – and when it's a film of the place?

ALICE (35): Oh yes. But I can't tell you how.

ELIZABETH (35): With a film, you can have a fair old wind blowing yet the bloke's hair isn't a bit out of place. It's quite uncanny. It doesn't fool anybody.

TRB: Do you think all those special correspondents – in Northern Ireland, Beirut, wherever – do anything else apart from their little bit on the news?

DAWN (27): I'm sure they must do something else.

ELIZABETH: Because they don't call them every day. Sometimes you don't sort of hear from them for weeks if places are quiet.

CHRISTINE (31): But you get some reporters, television reporters like Brian Barron, who are always going from country to country, and I suppose that is their job. Just sending back reports. But I think the other special correspondents must be doing other things, until they're needed.

ELIZABETH: They're for ever assessing the situation.

9. M.C.U. (Medium Close Up)/	Sue Lawley: 'As nurses' leaders appeal for a better wage – one nurse tells us she is *over*worked, *under*paid and the system is *over*stretched – *and* a "hair's breadth" from death. The woman who wants to break a world record.'
10. S.F. (Slide File) /	Repeat of picture of woman with long hair dangling from a crane.

6-10.

Over and over again the personality of the news reader emerged as the most interesting feature of the bulletin. How much individuality was appropriate to the job, though?

News At Ten is 15 years old on 3 July. To celebrate the occasion, Nigel Bunyan asked each of the past and present newscasters for their anecdotes about a now established institution

FIFTEEN YEARS ON...

ALASTAIR BURNET
1967-

"There was a great deal of opposition to News At Ten in the early days. When things were particularly bad I remember Geoffrey and me having a meeting at which we discussed changing the signature tune. To do that would have been to admit defeat, so we fortunately decided against it. As it is, it has stood the test of time."

SANDY GALL
1967-

"I had awful problems once when I was switched from one story to another. I was supposed to be covering a story in Germany when a call came through to divert to Uganda. It was winter, we were all in anoraks and snow boots, and we couldn't get any new clothes until we arrived. It seemed a very long journey from the airport!"

LEONARD PARKIN
1967-76

"The night Bosanquet had to interview Lee Kuan Yew, the Prime Minister of Singapore, he forgot to move out of his seat and into the interview area. As a result, he had to conduct the interview at the top of his voice from one side of the room to another. Lee Kuan Yew didn't seem to notice anything was wrong . . . at least, he didn't let on!"

ANDREW GARDNER
1967-77

"The summer we started was ferociously hot. With the studio lights on it became unbearable. We couldn't work in our shirtsleeves — that wasn't done, old chap! — and it would hardly have been decent to take our trousers off.
"In the end, we rigged up electric fans and placed ice buckets beneath the desk."

REGINALD BOSANQUET
1976-79

"I was on the brink of resigning after about the first week. I'd been sent to Rhodesia to interview Ian Smith and returned to find Alastair's desk where mine had been. My own was nowhere to be seen. Some bureaucrat had reasoned that Alastair and Andrew, as presenters, should be in the same office. Fortunately the editor was horrified and it was sorted out amicably."

ANNA FORD
1978-81

"Working with Reggie was very special. We used to write each other notes and limericks between items. People were always asking us what we said to each other at the end of the news. Usually it was things like 'your turn to buy a drink', but I also used to call Reggie 'Old Bean' or 'Old Has-Been'. Occasionally lip-readers would write in and ask: 'Don't you realise we can tell what you're saying!' "

MARTYN LEWIS
1977-

"The closest I've come to not getting something on the air was during a shipyard dispute. I remember running down the corridor with a film editor, Jim Hosack. He was holding the film story on a spool in one hand, and I was holding the sound. As we sprinted down the corridor we could actually hear Reggie introducing the item. Luckily we made it in time — but only just."

SELINA SCOTT
1981-

"A few days before the Royal Wedding I'd gone down to interview the Guards at the Hyde Park stables. I was trying to do a piece to camera with a massive horse — 16 hands high and fresh — blowing down the back of my neck and nibbling my ears.
"I was supposed to be smiling throughout the whole thing, but was actually terrified!"

(*Sunday Express Magazine*, 4 July 1982)

JOAN (45): Sue Lawley's always turned out very nicely. She always looks well groomed, and I think *that's* why I like her.

KAREN (32): And Jan Leeming, she wears terrific tops.

CHRISTINE: But I think it detracts from what she's saying.

ALICE: Oh, no, I don't. I like to see what she's got on.

TRB: Do *you* think it detracts from what she's saying?

DEB (32): I think so, yes. I sit there thinking, Look at all those frills. That really isn't appropriate. Not frills. I'm not saying she should be soberly dressed, but I think her clothes are too fussy for reading pieces of news.

CHRISTINE: It's almost as though she's going to a dinner party afterwards, isn't it? And wants to be dressed beforehand. Just popped in to read the news.

11. M.C.U.   Nicholas Whitchell:
    <u>(Medium Close Up)</u>/ 'The headlines tonight. The pit deputies' union –
                            NACODS – is starting an immediate ban on
                            overtime. It's a protest at the way the Coal Board
                            is closing pits. Today the Board announced the
                            closure of two mines in Yorkshire. There's been
                            more interracial violence in Sri Lanka . . .'

                                                    6-16.

MARIE (29): I like Sandy Gall. The one with the big bags under his eyes. He's
a sort of down the rugby club and let's have a few pints.

SAMANTHA (36): He always looks to me as though he's just this minute got
back from somewhere. He does a lot of special assignments.
JULIA (27): It's their ties I notice most of all.
SUE (31): Oh yes. Their ties and shirts don't match at all.
MAGGIE (33): Yes. That Leonard Parkin, the stripes he wears. He's a real old
fuddy-duddy. You imagine him still getting things out of the back of his
wardrobe that went out years ago. [*All laugh*.]
MARY (35): Sandy Gall is just as bad. He wears the most atrocious ties.
MAGGIE: There's one on the BBC that I like now. He *always* wears a white
shirt, *always*. Grey hair? I can't think. He's always in a dark suit . . .
SAMANTHA: John Humphries, is it?
BARBARA (39): That's it, he's always got a white shirt, *always*.
SUE: The other one I like is forty-two but all the girls like him. He's very
nice-looking. Can't think of his name.
MAGGIE: Oh, I know who you mean, Richard Whitmore?
SUE: *That's it*. Yeah, oh, I think he's lovely. He was on breakfast TV the
other day, reading the news, very casual, wearing a nice jumper.

How much should news readers respond to this type of reaction – how much
should they cultivate the 'personality' which they have acquired from newsreading? We asked what viewers thought, for example, about the careers of Anna
Ford and Angela Rippon.

PAT (47): They were in competition with each other, weren't they? All the
time they were on it was a battle between them.
TRB: Do you think they wanted to do other things?
JANET (32): Yes, Angela Rippon, I think she did. But I think Anna Ford was
virtually pushed into it, wasn't she?
JUDITH (40): Angela Rippon was a star anyway, starred in a lot of things.
PAT: Came over as a snooty type.
MAUREEN (39): I think the thing that put me off was the fact that those two
in particular, Angela Rippon and Anna Ford, that wasn't all they did. The

men news readers – that's all they did. That's their job, but Angela Rippon does horse riding, nature programmes.

ANNE (45): She was in the *Morecambe and Wise Show*.

JUDITH: You don't think of them as serious after that, do you?

ANNE: You associate people with what they do.

JUDITH: Once you've seen her legs up in the air, all over the place, you can't take what she says as serious.

MAUREEN: Yes, but she pushed *herself* forward. Anna Ford was pushed into it.

MOLLY (41): You always saw them in the papers more than you did Reginald Bosanquet or the other news readers like Trevor McDonald. It was usually them. Funnily enough it's mostly women who go on other things. But I wouldn't like to have seen Reginald Bosanquet dancing anyway, would you?

12. M.C.U.	Sue Lawley:
(Medium Close Up)/	'At the Old Bailey three men have been convicted of stealing cheques from the Duke of Devonshire. They include the son of his butler. They will be sentenced on Monday.'

6-20.

Private Eye's references to Anna Ford as the 'well-known auto-cue reader' play upon the belief that news readers enjoy considerably more respect than is warranted by their acquisition of the modest skills required for newsreading. But this doesn't seem to be a widely shared view. We asked the 3000 people in our national sample if this was one of the jobs which they thought they'd be able to manage on television: 84 per cent thought that it would be beyond their talents.

TRB: Do you think they rehearse the news before they read it?

EDNA (42): They must study it.

MOLLY: They're usually word perfect, aren't they?

PAT: They must do because some of those words, the names of foreign diplomats, are totally unpronounceable. They must go somewhere and learn to pronounce them first.

MOLLY: You can see they're reading because they sort of turn their head rather than their eyes. They keep moving their head slightly.

ANNE: If something comes through like a news flash they get it in their ears. You can see them listening while they're talking.

MOLLY: Do you remember how the phone used to ring in the old days?

| 13. | M.C.U. (Medium Close Up) / | Sue Lawley: 'And that was the 6 o'clock news *on the day that*:

The Coal Board announced plans to close two more Yorkshire pits and the pits deputies started an overtime ban.

And the *day* that Mrs Thatcher said –' |
|---|---|---|
| 14. | S.F. (Slide File) / | Mrs Thatcher's face.
SUPER (superimposed words on screen)
'I shall not stop carrying on . . .' |
| 15. | V.O. (Voice Over) / | Sue Lawley: 'I shall not stop carrying on . . .' |
| 16. | M.C.U. (Medium Close Up) / | Sue Lawley: 'I shall carry on.'
Sue Lawley smiles as though to say, 'That's Mrs Thatcher for you.' |

6-29.

Although bias in television reporting has been a constant matter of debate in the last five years – in particular since the work by sociologists in Glasgow on the treatment of industrial news – not much of this work has focused on the viewers' own opinions (often, presumably, because the 'bias' is supposed to create its impact in ways which are not immediately obvious to those who are subject to it). When we raised the matter in our groups it quickly became personalised. Some news readers were regarded as consistently more biased than others – judgements possibly relating more to demeanour, accent and style of dress than to the actual content of the news they were reading – but, nevertheless, an interesting indication of how 'right-wing' or 'left-wing' bias in the news might be confirmed or negated by what was thought of the political views of the person who read it.

We asked first about past and present news readers' involvement with the news that they read. In particular, were viewers able to detect signs of sadness, distress or emotional concern in the reader's attitude or voice when certain items were in the headlines? Despite the anxieties expressed by many about her overflamboyant dress, Jan Leeming easily topped this poll in all six groups. Sandy Gall was agreed to be second, and Trevor McDonald tied with Sue Lawley for third place.

When we asked, 'Which news reader do you think is politically most right-wing?', Anna Ford, surprisingly in view of some of her public pronouncements, shared first place with Alastair Burnett, followed by Richard Baker and Angela Rippon, while Sandy Gall topped the 'left-wing' list, with Trevor McDonald and Moira Stewart a close second and third.

There seemed to be some connection between 'left-wingness' and 'integrity' in that two out of the three 'left-wing' readers, Trevor McDonald (first) and Moira Stewart (third), were also in the top three when we asked for those news readers who, at home, were most like the personalities they displayed on screen. Robert Dougall, although he had not been on the screen for some years, was well enough remembered to take second place.

Finally we asked viewers to say which of past and present news readers seemed to them to be 'most anxious to put over their own personalities'. Anna Ford topped this poll, with Angela Rippon second, and Jan Leeming third. Sue Lawley and Nicholas Whitchell were both unplaced.

Although viewers certainly discussed the news readers' personalities before they discussed the actual treatment of the news, they did so in order to make distinctions. They had very clear ideas about how 'personality' should be kept under control in news bulletins. As Fay (40) put it:

> You've really got to take second place to what you're doing. You've got to get across what you're saying, rather than *you*, so they've got to sort of subdue their personalities slightly, which I think Jan Leeming doesn't.

And Jan Leeming, as we've noted, was less censured in this respect than Anna Ford and Angela Rippon. Indeed, Anna Ford and Angela Rippon may in some ways be said to have created a bottom line for the exploitation of the news reader's personality. Whatever their own feelings on the subject, there can be no doubt that their 'personalities' were inflated beyond the level which is reached by most current readers – something no doubt which was related to the newspapers' success in stimulating (or simulating) the competition between them. The fact that even now they still top viewers' lists of those news readers 'most anxious to put over their own personalities' suggests that they may have been exceptions. Normally, the personality of a news reader is not expected to be quite substantial or evident enough to be carried across to such other non-news programmes as *The Morecambe and Wise Show*. It should not take over from the job. In this respect viewers might well be said to recognise that the news is finally more important than the reader – even if what they prefer to talk about is the latter.

	CLOSE	
17. Q. (Cue)/	MUSIC.	
18. Q. (Cue)/	LIGHTING (Set darkens) Sue and Nicholas silhouetted at desk.	

CLOSING
TAPE

The computer-generated graphic
of the blue Venetian blind
closes up on the world.   6-30.

'The dream set of the future: a vision of radio in the year 1960, when the world will be commanded by wireless, television, etc.'

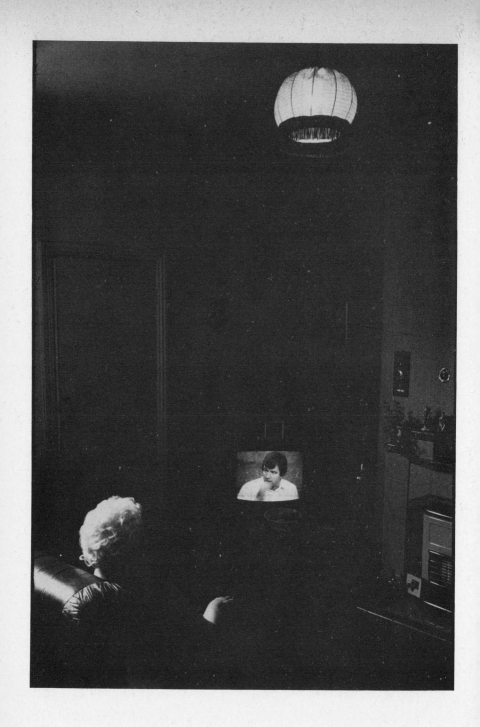

6

The Ogdens and the Windsors: Memory and Imagination

MARY (48): *And the cat.* You see that cat on the roof. That cat has always been there.

A Living Tradition

As is clear from hundreds of examples in this book, many of us know a great deal about the characters, plots and personalities of television. Not only are we able to talk about the programmes we see on the screen, but some of us also have a mass of information derived from daily and weekend papers about the relative popularity of this or that series, the personality of the actors who play the principal characters and the future storyline of the major series.

Those who only switch on the occasional minority programme no more sample this culture of popular television than those who confined their early cinema-going to German expressionism could be said to have been members of what Michael Wood, the film critic, called the 'universal movie audience'. The comparison between the former audience for film and today's television viewers can be pushed further. Wood, in his book on American films of the 1940s and 1950s (*America in the Movies*, 1975), talks about tens of millions who saw movies as members of a coherent world – 'a country of familiar faces . . . a system of assumptions and beliefs and preoccupations, a fund of often interchangeable plots, characters, patches of dialogue and sets'. Movies referred to other movies, actors made references to other portrayals. In this way the Hollywood films of that period made up 'a living tradition of the kind that literary critics always used to be mourning for'.

But however rich this tradition may have been – and however far removed from today's experience of the cinema – it looks thin alongside the television culture. Apart from our children's teenage discussion groups, all the viewers we spoke to had lived through most British television history. In the twenty-odd years since 1966 (when 90 per cent of the population were known to have access to a set) they have been developing their familiarity with its characters and conventions. Neither will it do to claim that the ephemeral nature of television means that the word 'tradition' is misplaced. Even if people do forget some of the things they have seen in the past, as American academic Daniel Thorburn sharply reminds us,

> television's capacity to make its history and evolution continuously available (even to younger members in its universal audience) is surely without precedent, for the system of re-runs has now reached a point of transforming television into a continuous living museum which displays for daily or weekly consumption texts from every stage of the medium's past.
> (Horace Newcomb, ed., *Television*, 1982.)

In Britain, the present 'system of re-runs' would allow a truly dedicated viewer to watch no fewer than 4500 repeats a year (as well as 2600 old films).

We asked viewers to ignore these re-runs and try to remember some of the earlier episodes of their favourite programmes. Could they, for example, remember some characters from *Coronation Street* who were no longer in the series?

JOYCE (49): Martha.
BILL (51): Martha . . . Minnie Caldwell.
JILL (37): Ena Sharples.
JOYCE: Elsie . . . Gerry . . . eh, what happened to Gerry?
MAUREEN (42): Gerry . . how did he go . . . M-m-m-m-m-Mavis [*a reference to Gerry Booth's stutter*]. He used to work with Len Fairclough.

Those viewers who have known characters for five, ten or twenty years have at least as great a sense of the continuity of their characteristics as the scriptwriters themselves – perhaps at times they observe a development in the characters which may be as much part of their own imagination as of the writers' craft. Nora felt, for example, that she could use history to throw some special light on the Ogdens – Hilda and the recently deceased Stan:

NORA (57): I think in the early days when they were on, they were the same sort of people as the Duckworths [from *Coronation Street*], weren't they?
JAN (39): No, not really the same.
MOLLY (56): Hilda was not as hoity-toity.
NORA: Well, if you ever see the old ones, ten or fifteen years ago when they first turned up, I think they *were* the same sort of people.
SANDRA (38): You reckon they've mellowed with age, that sort of thing?
NORA: Yes, I do.
SUE (39): They have mellowed a lot.
SANDRA: Stan was always like that, wasn't he, but in the end he got your sympathy because they aged together.

Not that you needed to have a constant reminder in, say, the present-day appearance of Hilda Ogden, of all that had gone before. Viewers were perfectly capable of recalling characters who made relatively brief appearances – particularly if a certain presumptuousness on their part was quickly followed by the scriptwriter's retribution.

One group of regular soap watchers vividly remembered a character from *Dallas* who had not appeared for some time, Katherine of the long black hair.

ANN (31): She was a cow.
TRB: Who's Katherine?
ANN: She was Pamela Ewing's sister.
TRB: Was she like Alexis from *Dynasty*?
MAXINE (32): She was after Bobby.
SUE (27): She manipulated people.
MAXINE: She went for him tooth and nail.
ANN: She tried to shoot him. She thought if she couldn't have him no one ought to have him, so she tried to kill him. [Three weeks after this interview, she reappeared – and did just this.]

As with conversations about current happenings, those which recall past events and characters can uninhibitedly mix biographical details of the performers' personal traumas with those experiences which befell their fictional selves. The talk within one discussion group was far too fast for anyone to have time to make the distinction – even if it was ever felt to be necessary:

EDNA (42): Who was the Irish girl [in *Coronation Street*] whose mother used to work in the bar sometimes, and her father got crushed to death?
MO (37): Oh yes, by that lorry or something coming through the window?
EDNA (42): She was an Irish girl, and she turned to drink, didn't she . . .
ANNE (45): That's right, yes.
JACKIE (43): I just can't think of her name.
JO (47): Black hair. She was in the corner shop, wasn't she?
JACKIE: That's right, and the father got crushed.
JULIE (38): Lucille Hewitt.
EDNA: That's it, Lucille Hewitt. She drank a lot . . .
JO: I didn't like her, anyway.
IRENE (37): It was her father, wasn't it, that got killed by the lorry, when it fell on him. And Len [Fairclough] tried to get him out.
JULIE: That's right, yes, he died.
IRENE: I thought that was very dramatic.

But were the actual characters in *Coronation Street* as nostalgic as these viewers evidently were about past members of the *Street*? Had they simply forgotten about those who had disappeared?

Four faces you won't forget

STEPHEN HANCOCK, 59, joined the Street in 1971 to play Ernie Bishop.

In 1978 Ernie was shot dead in a wages grab after Hancock was refused changes in his contract. Now he mixes acting with writing music.

Hancock, who lives in Stratford-on-Avon with his wife, Jocelyne, says: "I never watch Coronation Street, but it's not because I'm bitter about Ernie being killed off."

PHILIP LOWRIE, 47, joined The Street in 1961 to play Elsie Tanner's tearaway son, Dennis.

When he left, in 1968, his salary dropped from £250 a week to £20 in rep, and he had to sell his country mansion.

But Lowrie, who now lives in a small house in Fulham, London, says: "I've never regretted leaving. There was no further challenge—they never let Dennis grow up."

JENNIFER MOSS, 40, was only 15 when she joined Coronation Street as problem child Lucille Hewitt.

By the time she left in 1973, Jennifer was a problem herself — she was an alcoholic.

Since then she has rebuilt her life, and now she and her fourth husband, Paul Howard, 23, live in a one-room flat in Liverpool where they make and sell jig-saw puzzles.

REGINALD MARSH, 58, found the odds were against him when he played bookie Dave Smith in The Street.

The trouble was that flash Dave did not appear regularly enough for Marsh to pay his grocery bills. So in 1972, after eight years, he left.

Marsh, who lives with his wife in a country house in Hampshire, has kept busy with TV work, including Terry And June.

(*Sun*, 14 May 1985.)

SALLY (41): They mention them sometimes. Not for long though.

JOANNE (37): The only one who is still mentioned from the past is Ena Sharples.

SALLY: She's not forgotten. She was mentioned in the programme for quite a while. They never wrote her out.

RITA (51): I mean she WAS *Coronation Street*, wasn't she?

What then was their earliest memory, something which reached back towards that opening scene transmitted on Friday, 9 December 1960 – remembered here by script editor H. V. Kershaw:

At seven o'clock precisely Eric Spear's music drifted from a host of television receivers, the title of the programme appeared on the screen for the first time, the director cut to the shop interior and Elsie Lappin, the departing shopkeeper, addressed Florrie Lindley, the new arrival, with the words, 'Now next thing you've got to do is get the sign-writer in. That thing above the door will have to be changed.'

(Kershaw, *The Street Where I Live*, 1981.)

TRB: Your earliest, earliest memory?

LIZ (51): *Da da da da da da* . . . [*All start singing* Coronation Street *theme*.]

TRB: The first scene. The first character.

LIZ: The roof.

MARY (48): And the cat. You see that cat on the roof. That cat has always been there. They've never changed the cat. That's stayed the same.

JAN (47): And the rooftops of the houses.

MARY: Yes, the rooftops.

Often people talked as though they had always known the characters from their favourite programmes – almost as though they wanted to stretch the fictional biographies so that they fully overlapped their own. Or perhaps it seemed that characters like Alexis and J.R. and Hilda Ogden had lived so long simply because so much had happened to them. It takes a lot of normal life to fit in all the problems and traumas which can occur to soap-opera characters in a single year! Certainly there was a tendency to overestimate when we asked all our groups:

• How long has the following programme been on television?

YEARS:	Max	Min	Average	Actual
Dallas	12	5	8	6.6
Dynasty	5	3	3.5	3
EastEnders	1	0.25	0.5	0.25
Brookside	4	2	2.75	2.4
Emmerdale Farm	20	6	10	12.6
The Practice	1	0.25	0.25	0.25
Crossroads	25	15	22	20.6
Coronation Street	26	20	25	25

(Poll completed June 1985.)

Evenin' All

Although there was much talk of Ena Sharples and some of *Bonanza*, *Emergency Ward Ten* and *Muffin the Mule*, one figure more than any other stood like a lighthouse amid the mists of time. A lighthouse with a helmet: PC George Dixon of Dock Green.

MARY (47): The oldest one, the very oldest one, and the one that sticks in my mind, *Dixon of Dock Green* with Dixon saying, 'Goodnight all.'

MAVIS (52): 'Evening all.'

MARY (47): That's right.

Several people were determined to talk about the very last image of the programme. It seemed essential to get it absolutely right.

JOHN (42): He'd stand there and say 'Evenin' all' and then the camera would go up from his head.

MICHAEL (47): Yes, it would go up and there's the POLICE sign. And that was ages ago. It just shows you how well that has stuck in my mind.

Perhaps the shot was accurately remembered by many viewers because it so neatly encompassed the priorities of the programme. George was first of all a kindly human being chatting to us at home about what we had just seen – the final 'Evenin' all', was always preceded by a set piece straight to camera – and then, *secondly*, a member of the POLICE.

The timing of the programme was probably also important. In the early years of mass television, it was much more customary for the set to be switched on for general viewing at certain times rather than left flickering constantly in the corner.

> JOHN (37): Yes, we used to religiously watch *Dixon of Dock Green*.
> REGGIE (42): Every Saturday evening, wasn't it?
> JOHN: Either after or before *Dr Who*.

Inevitably the family nature of these occasions was also closely tied in to the memories: not just the memory of sitting with the rest of the family watching, but also the feeling that Dixon himself was part of one's own family – despite the promotion that he received towards the end of his career.

> CHRIS (36): He was a sergeant, but he was a fatherly figure, wasn't he? He never got beaten up or anything, never came anywhere near the violence, did he?
> DAVE (31): He could have never been on *Hill Street Blues*.
> MICH (33): No. [*All laugh.*]
> JEFF (34): He wouldn't know what a drug addict was.

For others he was old enough to fulfil another family role.

> BOB (51): He was one of those old policemen, wasn't he, when they used to have bobbies on the beat walking round. He was real. Like your granddad.

But what the viewers found so interesting about Dixon and the family was that, unlike most contemporary policemen, he actually had a family of his own.

> MARGARET (47): He was just a nice family man, everybody's friend, and he lived with his daughter and her husband and it was a lot about their life and their family troubles. There was always a moral – a lesson to be drawn. He'd point it out.

It was strange how far back into television memory viewers wanted to push George Dixon. He was on 'fifteen years ago' or 'twenty years ago' or 'ages ago'. Although the first episode of *Dixon of Dock Green* was indeed transmitted on 9 July 1955 – certainly 'ages ago' in television terms – the last live, as distinct from repeat, transmission went out as late as 1976. What seemed to be happening was that Dixon's traditional approach to policing was not remembered as a particular fictional style, but as a mirror of the reality at the time when he made the programmes. Historical time had again to be adjusted to television time.

TRB: What sort of man do you think he was, Dixon?

MICHAEL: Well, he was a local bobby. In those days you had a local bobby. Someone who was respected. [*All agree.*] You could ask him the time, he would show you the way.

GEORGE (42): He would give you a clip round the earhole.

MICHAEL: Yeah, a telling off.

DAVID (39): Caught on rubbish tips, *wallop*. 'What are you doing over there?' 'Nothing, mister.' 'Don't do it again.' [*All laugh.*] Now you're likely to get a social worker.

It was difficult to believe from these loving accounts of George Dixon's life and times that he was around in 1976, or that a very different version of contemporary policing was simultaneously available to viewers during most of his period of office: *Z Cars* was first transmitted on 2 January 1962 and ran successfully until 1978. There were many other less avuncular images of the police available during the same period:

Popular crime and cops-and-robbers series

1950s	1960s
Murder Bag	*The Untouchables*
Shadow Squad	*77 Sunset Strip*
Fabian of the Yard	*Perry Mason*
Dragnet	*Ironside*
The Naked City	*Department S*
Highway Patrol	*The Saint*
Mark Saber	*Special Branch*
Dial 999	*Gideons Way*
Interpol Calling	*Riviera Police*
Sea Hunt	*No Hiding Place*

The reasons for George Dixon's special place in the memory of viewers are not yet exhausted: one last factor separates him from other TV policemen and soap-opera characters and chat-show personalities. There was thought to be a very special affinity between the man himself – actor Jack Warner – and the character he played. Elsewhere we talk about the ambiguities of this relationship in other characters, about people's ability to conflate biographical and fictional lives – but Dixon/Warner is unique in the general assumption of identity. Warner was Dixon. Dixon was Warner.

> MICHAEL: . . . if you see these actors in very different parts then you realise they're acting. George Dixon, I didn't see him in anything else.
> GEOFF (47): That's right.
> MICHAEL: So you just associate the actor with the character he played.
> DAVID: When he was interviewed, he was exactly the same.
> TRB: Who?
> DAVID: George Dixon.
> MICHAEL: Jack Warner, the actor.
> GEOFF: I've seen him in a couple of films and he was the same sort of fatherly person.
> GEORGE: He was the same.
> GEOFF: But I think years ago actors were like that. They did portray the characters like themselves. They *were* the same.

When we put the matter to a more quantitative test and asked fifty members of our groups individually to nominate the police people who were most like the character they played in real life, George Dixon easily topped the poll, with

Inspector Reagan (from *The Sweeney*) a long way behind in second place, closely followed by a dead heat for third between Inspector Barlow (Stratford Johns in *Z Cars*) and Captain Furillo (*Hill Street Blues*).

All in all, despite a little competition from other avuncularly friendly TV cops (the desk sergeants Joe and George in *Juliet Bravo*, perhaps, and – if private investigators are allowed – Jim Rockford, the amiable detective from *The Rockford Files*), Sergeant Dixon is still probably the only policeman most viewers would be glad to see walking up to their front door.

> GEORGE: I think you'd always imagine him to be riding a bicycle round to your house, rather than screeching round in a Rover 2.5 to other people's. [*Others agree.*]

(Jack Warner died, aged eighty-five, on 24 May 1981. A wreath in the shape of a blue lamp was presented by the Metropolitan Police.)

That Other Family

The loving identification which so many viewers have with past and present television characters closely resembles the 'fictional' relationship which they enjoy with the royal family. Indeed, the only threat to the monarchy in the coming years may be that its familial appeal becomes completely overshadowed by the more credible and intimate family lives offered by television soap operas.

When we tested the parallel between these two worlds by asking viewers if they thought there might be any suitable soap operas for members of the royal family, there was not a moment lost in getting down to actual casting. The Queen Mother was thought to be most suitable for *Crossroads* – not to become intimately involved with the characters but more as a background figure who might add a bit of genteel tone to the rather hurried foreground proceedings. Marie (54) contrived a way in which her visit could be dramatically short-lived.

> I can just see her in that – yes, in *Crossroads*. Yes, I know. As a guest – passing through – on her way up to Scotland.

Princess Anne was regarded as a natural for *Sons and Daughters* – the afternoon Australian soap opera – a somewhat suburban offering which revolves principally around two families, the Palmers and the Hamiltons, and is particularly prized among devotees. Almost every character seems permanently racked with anxiety, typically anxiety about something in the past. It is obviously a good context for Anne to redeem her own slightly unfortunate past of general surliness, wear the concerned face which has now come to be associated with her role as Save the Children sponsor, and generally behave in a thoroughly un-royal suburban manner.

Meanwhile, Princess Margaret, with a certain predictability, was consigned to the top single bedroom of Southfork ranch and the sad, estranged life of Sue

Ellen, a life only enlivened by the occasional appearance of such heroes as the young blond male counsellor, 'Peeder' (Peter, that is).

She was at least saved from competition with Princess Diana who, after some discussion, was agreed to be best qualified for a tearful and elegantly solicitous job in Denver.

HELEN (52): You could see her in *Dynasty* or *Dallas*, couldn't you?
JOAN (51): I think *Dynasty*.
TRB: Playing what kind of person?
JOAN: Blake Carrington's wife. Instead of Krystle.
HELEN: Yes, I was thinking that. [*All agree.*]
JOAN: She even tried to outdo Joan Collins [at a film gala] with that dress.

But would this mean that Charles got left behind? Nobody seemed able to envisage a part for him. Blake? Adam? Steven? Jeff? Dex? Mark (resuscitated)?

ALICE (52): No, he could only play himself. Prince Charles.

This is far from being mere guesswork. Just as television drama can readily appropriate some of the royal family, so can members of that family try to secure themselves a television place. Charles's abilities in this line were recently tested in BBC I's *Jackanory* (children's story programme) on which he read extracts from his own book *The Old Man of Lochnagar*. Individual viewers were not as unkind about his performance as the *Daily Star*, which described it as going down like 'a lead balloon' – and for good measure added in a nine-year-old called Dale, who squirmed, 'I hate this – I like war films', and a fifteen-year-old named Paul who 'stifled a yawn' and muttered, 'Give me *The Sweeney* or *The Professionals* [British undercover police series] any day.'

All in all, though, it seemed best to keep Charles out of our league table for 'Best Royal Television Performer' ratings in which Princess Anne romped home an easy winner.

MARIE (54): I like Anne – she was smashing on Wogan's show. She's so different to what people think of her. You can tell she's nice. She's very humorous and not snobby. She's had too much bad press in the past.

Perhaps Anne was lucky in that a Wogan show appearance provided her with the opportunity for countering public opinion and press. Princess Margaret's media role gave her less opportunity to move into the limelight.

HELEN (52): Princess Margaret has always been in her sister's shadow, hasn't she? She's always taken second place in everything. But I didn't think she was that good in *The Archers* [when she opened an Ambridge fête] really. Mind you, it must be quite hard to suddenly be put into it.

The Queen, of course, has a regular Christmas slot in which to shine as a television performer, and although she was only third in our overall ratings (behind Anne and the Queen Mother), this may well be an improvement on past performance.

ANNE (50): She used to be very stuffy. But recently she's more relaxed.

Mary detected a possible technical reason for this change.

MARY (47): It used to be live as well, didn't it?
CHARLOTTE (50): No, it's done a couple of weeks before, apparently.

But there was a general reluctance to believe that the Queen would submit herself to all the visual rigours of television production.

TRB: Does she rehearse at all?
JANE (58): Not much. She's used to giving speeches so I think just one run-through is enough.
CHARLOTTE: I shouldn't think that she comes in at all until it's absolutely ready and set up right. They'd do a dress rehearsal with a stand-in to get it all focused. Because she usually looks straight at the camera.
TRB: So it's done in a studio?
JANE: Oh no, I don't think so. She has to have all her own things round her, doesn't she?
MARY: It has to be done in her own home.
CHARLOTTE: It's nice to see the photos and that.
JANE: It's human.

Human enough, apparently, for at least some viewers to want more of it.

MARY: Ten more minutes I'd like to see. It's a ritual for me to stop everything and see it.
TRB: Do the rest of you stop everything to see it?
HEATHER (49): Not everyone. The kids don't want to see it. And the men go to sleep.

To complete the television circuit, we asked how much time they thought the royals themselves spent listening to and watching other people. The Queen came highest at thirty hours – well up to the national average – and Margaret a close second with twenty-five. But when it came to radio listening both had to make way for Diana, who was imagined by some to listen to the radio most of the day. What were the actual programmes which so attracted their attention?

A day's listening and viewing at Buckingham Palace must be a complicated affair. It starts simply enough with the Queen and Prince Philip (still in bed perhaps) listening together to *Today* (Radio Four's current affairs programme) but the relative peace is broken at nine o'clock by the sound of Charles and Diana turning up the volume on the transistor to David (ex-'Kid') Jensen's show on Capital Radio. Soon Charles leaves to listen to Jimmy Young (Radio Two's music and chat show) with Dad, while elsewhere the Queen Mother settles down

	FAVOURITE TELEVISION PROGRAMMES		FAVOURITE RADIO PROGRAMMES
Queen	*The Good Life* Felicity Kendal Richard Briers	*Coronation Street*	*Today* John Timpson Sue MacGregor Brian Redhead
Philip	*Wildlife on One* David Attenborough	*Tomorrow's World* Raymond Baxter Maggie Philbin Judith Hann	*Jimmy Young Show*
Charles	*Mike Yarwood* Harold Wilson Brian Clough Denis Thatcher Frankie Howerd	*Morecambe and Wise*	*Jimmy Young Show* [see Philip]
Diana	*Top of the Pops* [see Queen]	*Dallas* and *Dynasty* Bobby Ewing and 'husband' Blake	*Capital Radio* [see Charles]
Queen Mother	*Last of the Summer Wine* Compo Foggy Clegg	*Sons and Daughters* Aussie anxieties with the Hamiltons and the Palmers	*Radio Four* [all of it]
Margaret	*Butterflies* Wendy Craig Mother of two sons Dentist's wife Should she leave husband?		*The Archers* When there's time left o' from opening fêtes
Andrew	*Only Fools and Horses* The Trotters: Del Boy and Rodders	*Knight Rider* Computer-driven car which talks to its driver	*Simon Bates* Radio One's intelligent nice Mr Sincere
Anne	*Panorama* Richard Dimbleby Robin Day David Lomax Fred Emery	*Wogan* Wogan	*Woman's Hour* Sue MacGregor

All television and radio programmes include both past and present personalities

LEAST FAVOURITE TV AND RADIO PROGRAMMES

Any Questions? John Timpson Freddy Grisewood	*Playschool* Magazine programme for the under fives	*Top of the Pops* Mike Read Steve Wright John Peel Janice Long et al.
Today [see Queen]	*Crossroads*	*Dallas*
Capital Radio Alan 'Fluff' Freeman David 'Kid' Jensen Michael Aspel Anna Raeburn and the 'Capital Doctor'	*Coronation Street*	*Match of the Day* Jimmy Hill Bob Wilson
Radio One especially 'friend of the royals' Mike Read	*Songs of Praise* Geoffrey Wheeler Cliff Michelmore	*Question Time* Robin Day, Ludovic Kennedy and 3 men and 1 woman
Gardeners' Question Time Alan Gemmel Fred Loads Bill Sowerbutts	*Starsky and Hutch* David Soul and Paul Michael Glaser jumping over cars; but likes everything	*Tomorrow's World* [see Philip]
Desert Island Discs favourite record when a guest – Swan Lake: LSO/Previn	*Grange Hill* 'Grine Jill' with Tucker, Roland and Suzanne	*Spitting Image*
Capital Radio [see Charles and Diana]	*Sons and Daughters* [see Queen Mother]	*Any Questions?* [see Queen]
	Crossroads [see Philip]	

to *Gardener's Question Time*, and Anne tunes in to Sue MacGregor on *Woman's Hour*.

The Queen Mother is first to the television for *Sons and Daughters* at half-past three, with Andrew dashing in for his favourite *Knight Rider* (a computer-driven car series) just after five. From then the arguments rage. Diana as usual wants *Top of the Pops* but the Queen won't budge, and in another corner the Queen Mother objects most strongly to Philip being slumped again before *Tomorrow's World* (a chatty science programme). In her room Margaret wistfully clicks off *The Archers* and turns to watch *Butterflies* (a situation comedy) on the portable, only distracted from time to time by another shouting match between Philip and Diana over *Dallas*, and the eerie sounds of Charles attempting to emulate Mike Yarwood's impersonations.

Meanwhile in the nursery, Prince Harry is silently preparing for his debut.

JOAN: You see, it's part of their training. I mean that baby is starting already. He turned round once recently and waved just like the older ones . . .

P.S.

Since receiving these opinions on royal choices we have had some confirmation of their perceptiveness from the Prince of Wales (as told to the *Daily Mirror*). Our viewers were, it seems, right in saying that *Dynasty* and *Dallas* were among the Princess's favourite programmes, and right to say that the Prince at that time had not been converted. (He now watches them with Diana.) They also correctly guessed that Charles favoured *Emmerdale Farm* (a British rural soap opera) and was a morning radio listener.

Morning Radio

It was not surprising that so many people envisaged members of the royal family listening to the morning radio. This is the one time of the day when the medium is thought of as 'the most natural choice'. And this is also apparently the time when its heroes are created. When we asked our Radio Four group to select their top 'radio personalities' (excluding any individuals who might also have some 'contaminating' television reputation), they unhesitatingly selected four familiar 'breakfast' presenters:

Brian Redhead   (*Today*)
John Timpson   (*Today*)
Sue MacGregor   (*Today*)
Libby Purves   (*Mid-Week*)

Perhaps because several of the group admitted listening to the *Today* programme in bed, there was also a sense of the actual setting from which Redhead, Timpson and MacGregor operated:

BOB (46): I imagine them with headphones on – they've always got headphones.

MARK (48): And a clean shirt. I always think they've got clean shirts, And a pair of casual trousers.

BOB: Very casually dressed.

MARK: With piles of papers everywhere which they're sorting through.

BOB: Yes – and people coming in and going out. Who they laugh about after they've gone.

ANDREW (39): People they make comments about – you know, 'I see you haven't had a shave this morning'. You always know that someone has come in unshaved or with torn jeans because one of them will comment.

In each case, listeners felt they had a strong idea about what the person was really like when listening to him or her talk. They were like old and close friends.

ANNE (37): Funnily enough I would like to meet Brian Redhead. I've never forgotten two summers ago his boy got killed in a motor accident in France, eighteen years old, and he wasn't on the radio that morning and they gave it out, and that's never gone out of my mind. I always think of that, I always wonder how he could get over it and still be sort of happy.

Neither, of course, was there any great chance of this affectionate identification being spoilt by any incongruous personal characteristics. As nobody knew what their heroes looked like, any physical detail could be sketched in which might supplement the appealing image obtained from the voice.

We decided to see how close the listeners' imagination came to reality by asking them to select the actual photograph of their favourite broadcaster from eighty other pictures (forty male, forty female) of important people whose faces were not so well known as to be readily identifiable.

Although we excluded anyone who thought they might have seen a photograph of any of the four, there was some confidence among the others about the outcome.

TRB: Does anyone know what Sue MacGregor looks like?

ANNE (51): No. But I feel I do.

ANNE (37): I don't *know* – but I think I might *recognise* her.

When the actual exercise began there was some eager hunting around for clues:

TIM (47): I'm not sure about Sue MacGregor. What does she look like?

BOB: Sensible, I should think.

ANNE (37): Short hair. I should think she's got short hair.

MARK: A bit staid. No, that's not the right word.

ANNE (51): She *is* a spinster. I know that. And a bit of a homely sort of spinster.

ANNE (37): I didn't know she was a spinster.

The uncertainty meant that the group agreed to leave Sue MacGregor for a moment and move on to Libby Purves:

TRB: So how do you imagine Libby Purves to look?
MARK: With a name like that she should look nice and scatty.
TONY (39): She's not. She's a keen sailor.

The group fairly quickly divided their choice between the following 'Libby Purves-es': Maggie Drummond, a journalist on *Options* (l), and Angela Heylin, chief executive at Charles Barker (r).

And here is the
real Libby Purves

Andrew led the discussion when it came to John Timpson.

ANDREW: This one here, number thirty-five, is John Timpson.
TRB: You mean you know it is? You've seen him before?
ANDREW: No, but he definitely *should* look like that.

In fact this was enough to ensure that most of the group selected not the real John Timpson but Sir Robin Nicholson (l), with a minority vote going to Robin Hanbury-Tenison (r).

Nobody chose the
real John Timpson

The only unanimous choice (taken from the thirty-eight remaining male portraits in the pile) was of 'Brian Redhead'.

JACK (41): He should look humorous but strict.
ANNE (37): Yes. Strict but kind.

Unfortunately this did not allow Brian himself to be selected. At least his substitute was a fellow journalist, Ian Wooldridge.

The *real* Brian Redhead has a wider smile.

Finally, the group returned to the highly contentious issue of Sue MacGregor.

TONY: You can tell she's a lovely person because she has got a lovely voice.
ANNE (37): I don't go along with that . . . Sue MacGregor might well be a lovely person, I also think she is beautiful on the radio, but she could be a right old cow when she comes off.
TONY: Not with a voice like that.

Two pictures emerged for the final choice: Pauline Stafford of the trade union NATFE (l), and Andrea Wilkins, a designer (r).

Neither was Sue.

7

Intimate Relations

MARY (27): I think it would be really nice if she [Bet Lynch] found a good man who could tone her down a bit.

'I'm Worried about Benny'

What words can we use to describe our relationship with all the characters and personalities who nightly come tumbling out of our television sets into our homes, all the remote and illustrious men and women, the personalities and superstars, the heroes and villains who pop in to talk to us in such a relaxed convivial manner from that corner by the fire, the alcove by the bed, the windowsill in the kitchen? Are we to speak of them as acquaintances, friends, relations, lovers? Models with whom we can identify?

Some experts dismiss the question as absurd. How can we talk of enjoying any sort of relationship with such ephemeral images? The characters and stars of television have little contact with our own lives. Neither do they engage with our imagination. Unlike the heroes and villains of the cinema or literature, they are not grand or fantastic enough to provide models for identification or empathy. One could understand how our petty romances and ordinary anxieties might be translated into grand passions by filling them with notions derived from the lives and exploits of Gable and Bogart, Bacall and Bergman, Brando and Redford. But such transcendence, such idealisation of our own lives, is hardly likely to be accomplished by our listless daily attention to half-hour doses of Hilda Ogden, Max Bygraves and Gloria Hunniford.

But against this view runs the argument that television is by its nature far more suited to establish that peculiar sense of similarity with others which is the basis of identification. Instead of being impersonally located in an alien commercial setting it is part of the household itself: instead of presenting abnormally sized overpowering images its principal characters have heads the same size as our own, live their lives within similar families, and seem bedevilled by crises not unlike those we know ourselves. What's more, they seem to need us so much more than those superstars upon the screen: they beckon to us, whisper in our ears, nod knowingly, and almost take for granted that we are already old friends.

Although we've already raised similar questions in regard to chat-show hosts, where the very ordinariness of their skills and the assumed association between their fictional and factual lives seems to provide a special opportunity for us to feel that they somehow represent us by their presence on the screen, the issue is much more pertinent in relation to soap operas. For here, the audience has a much wider range of characters to like or love or loathe, complete galleries of heroes and villains and situations with which to empathise and identify. And whereas there may be no great social implications in large numbers of us feeling that Wogan or Aspel or Harty are somehow our televisual surrogates, there is likely to be a greater agitation within the ranks of teachers and priests and politicians, if it can be said that millions feel themselves to be as ruthless and cynical as J.R., as materialistic and exploitative as Alexis, as forlorn and drunken and pathetic as Sue Ellen.

Some groups in our society certainly seem able to take or leave soap opera, flicking the dramas on and off as the spirit takes them, missing a couple of weeks and catching up the next, commenting on the predictability of it all, precluding any emotional response of their own by erecting a large kitsch bracket around the entire period of viewing. For these people the notion of identification is absurd, the question of working out the nature of their relationship with Benny or Hilda ridiculous.

Yet others know in just as routine and obvious a way that they can easily start worrying about characters in soap operas as though their predicaments deserved the attention they might give to friends or even members of their own family:

DEB (32): You're talking about them as though they're real people.

DAWN (27): Yes, I know. Isn't it awful?

DEB: But this is it, you do, we do. They are part of your life.

JILL (38): Like my husband a little while ago, he said, 'I'm so worried about Benny [from *Crossroads*], I haven't seen him lately.' And for a moment I could see him wondering if he should go and look for him.

JEAN (44): Yes, I was on the phone a couple of months ago, I'll never forget this, talking to my friend about this person who'd died on a programme. And when I'd finished my husband said, 'Who died? What happened?' He was really concerned. When I said, 'Oh, whatsisname on whatsisname programme', he – well, he just died laughing. Because, he said, 'I really thought from the way you were talking it was a real person.'

ALICE (35): But you do get involved. I was watching *Sons and Daughters* yesterday and there was a bit where a very young wife goes out and leaves her little baby. She goes out, and suddenly it's all on its own. I'm going, '*Lyn*, please don't', 'They're going to go mad', 'Wait till thing finds out' [*all laughing*] 'He'll go mad . . . the baby . . . her husband . . . Oh, he'll go spare . . .' You know, and I thought, you silly cow, it's only a programme. *There's a camera in front of all that.*

Vulnerability

The laughter from the rest of the group which punctuates these confessions suggests that everyone present could tell a similar story, and also shows how public this relationship with beloved soap characters can be. This is not the first time that these people have talked about Benny and Fallon and Hilda as though they were real. Jean's husband and Jill's husband are both around to confirm that it's a part of normal domestic conversation.

It could be that the situations described here are those designed to bring the viewers – in this case mainly female viewers – into a close relationship with the characters on screen. What could be more resonant, closer to home, than the *Sons and Daughters* scene with the little baby left all on its own, and the possibility of the husband discovering her neglect?

This would suggest that television people are closest to us when they are at their most mundane, when they are caught up by the predicaments of everyday life. It is then that we have the strongest wish to intervene, the greatest likelihood of forgetting at least for a few moments that we have no real need to worry because 'there's a camera in front of all that'.

If this is true then we would also expect to feel closest not to the heroes of the soaps – the good kind handsome men, the caring beautiful solicitous women – but to those who are precarious or vulnerable figures, those who lead messy indeterminate lives much like our own, and who might therefore be regarded as equals.

It's certainly possible to ask a realistic question about such a classically vulnerable character as Bet Lynch in *Coronation Street* and get answers which would be difficult to separate from real advice to close friends or neighbours. Only occasionally is there any obvious recognition that the changes might come less from within her than from the scriptwriter's pen.

MAUREEN (39): I mean, in all honesty, if I was a man I wouldn't want her to be my wife, she looks too tarty.
PAT (47): Yes, she is very tarty.
ANNE (45): I wish she'd change.
MAUREEN: I don't think she can now. She's been like that too long.
PAT: The fringe on her forehead.
MAUREEN: Yes, her hairstyle is so old-fashioned, but I suppose they've got to give that impression.
MOLLY (41): She's been very unlucky.
EDNA (42): Every man she's had has more or less finished with her.
MOLLY: But that's the part she's meant to play.
JANET (32): The men use her.

MOLLY: She's been very hurt. I mean when she was with Mike Baldwin she really idolised him, didn't she?

JEAN (42): Every time a new man comes along you expect her to start getting off with him.

ANNE: Diving in.

Another group were equally certain about the need for her character to develop.

DEB (32): She's got to change her character.

CHRISTINE (31): Yes, she's got to mellow a bit with age.

DEB: Ugh, those leopardskin dresses, the long earrings.

KAREN (32): Some of the colours as well.

MARY (27): I think it would be really nice if she found a good man who could tone her down a bit.

To see if this degree of involvement held for 'vulnerable' characters in more glossy soaps, we also asked for reactions to Sue Ellen in *Dallas*. What did viewers think of her? How would they try to improve her unhappy life? At first the group talked for several minutes about her clothes, as though emphasising a lack of affinity, but as soon as historical reasons were raised for her present condition, there was a rush of understanding.

ALICE (35): I like the outfits she wears.

ELIZABETH (35): Oh no, big padded shoulders, she always wears those big padded shoulders all the time.

DEB: She walks about like this all the time. [*Gives impersonation.*]

JEAN (44): That's right, yes.

HELEN (28): She hasn't got a personality . . .

KAREN: Bit wet and wimpy.

HELEN: No, she used to be nice when she wasn't with J.R. But then she's so stupid because she can't see through him. I mean she's been on and off with him for years, and suddenly she goes back with him and she starts going back his way. And she can't see through him now. She *can't* see that he's doing anything wrong.

DAWN (27): No, she knows. [*All talk.*]

JEAN: No, we can all see that she doesn't.

DAWN: *She knows* . . . but she can't admit it.

HELEN: Yes, but she's not seeing through him like she did. She doesn't stand up to him like she used to, *she used to give him a fight* . . .

Even though this seems far less neighbourly than the attitude towards Bet Lynch, it's still remarkably intimate. As the group went on discussing Sue Ellen, the detail became finer and finer. Having started from a general discussion of her clothes and her strange way of walking, it culminated in an analysis of one corner of her mouth: it was here, more than in her rhetoric or demeanour or behaviour, that her character might best be discovered.

ELIZABETH: She's got this mouth, hasn't she? That annoying mouth.
JILL (38): Yes. There's something about her mouth, isn't there?
ELIZABETH: Yes, that's why she's so annoying. You can tell she's always going to be wet. Because of her mouth.

This also seemed to be a critical site in *Dallas* for Clive James. One of the key elements in the series was, he proposed, 'the hundred different directions she could move her mouth' (*Glued to the Box*, 1983).

This emphasis on facial features in soap opera is far from trivial. Our sense of being intimately involved in the action is enhanced by the manner in which the camera in such series allows us to ride on its back as we swoop in close to the faces of the characters – usually two at a time – who occupy the screen. So familiar is the soap-opera two-shot that quite modest changes in the distance between the faces can be of psychological and dramatic significance. And we are nearly always there at eye level – except of course for the initial high wide shot over the rooftops of *Coronation Street* (or the much higher helicopter vision of the towering skyscrapers of *Dallas*). Otherwise high (and low) shots are rare: much of the time we look at one character through another's eyes, or see one in the foreground and another a little distance away in the background. At emotional moments the 'camera circles [the] characters and brings us closer and closer to them, right up to their eyes and mouths so that we can see their tears and hear their breathing'. (Bernard Timberg in Newcomb, ed., *Television*, 1982.) It is this which makes regular viewers such experts on those facial nuances which tell us of the leading characters' frustrations, desires and triumphs:

MARIE (39): There's something around his mouth that you can see.
TRB: J.R.'s?
MARIE: Yes. And he's got a very little laugh.
LENA (38): He's got a slight twinkle in his eye . . .
MARIE: A little chuckle . . . Yes, when he does something bad, when he knows that he has.
LENA: Sort of a half smirk.
LOUISE (31): Yes, they often finish with that at the end of the episode or the scene, don't they?

Downright Baddies

Yet this additional information about how identification may be effected in soap operas takes us only a little way into understanding why some characters are more likely to touch our feelings than others. Apart from the vulnerability of Bet Lynch, and the rather less appealing insipidity of Sue Ellen, what other features excite admiration and even emulation? How do the baddies fare? Did any of the female viewers in our soap-opera groups imagine themselves as Alexis Colby, or want to live and behave like her?

> ROSALYN (31): I love all those suits that she wears in the day time, you know, and all the matching things that go with them. They are fantastic.
> KIM (29): Yes. Sometimes she dresses a little bit . . .
> JUDY (27): Over the top?
> KIM: Yes, she looks like she's just walked out of a shop window. And also her hair. Now her hair looks fabulous, but until she had that accident when she had the fire and she had to go and have it cut off, before that she always looked as though she had a wig on. It looked horrible.
> DEE (28): I think that's a wig now that she has got.
> KIM: Well, it's fabulous.

But apart from this somewhat guarded estimation of her attractiveness, nobody felt any psychological affinity with Alexis, even when we asked whether there was ever any sense of pleasure at seeing her score over other characters. Indeed in one group there was reluctance to admit to any direct sense of resemblance with characters in the glossy soap.

> TRB: Tell me who you sometimes feel like in either *Dallas* or *Dynasty*?
> CHRISTINE (31): Definitely not Kirby.
> ALICE (35): None of them, I don't think.
> CHRISTINE: None of them.
> JILL (38): No.
> TRB: You're not like any of them?
> ALICE: No, because they're so . . .
> DEB (32): They're so different.
> DAWN (27): . . . plastic, they are plastic, I mean they're all plastic people.
> DEB: You see, they haven't got any friends, not real friends, and I've got lots of friends, I mean you never really see a friend in the programme. It's always the parents, isn't it, or relatives or business associates. Never friends.

Another group settled not for any hero or villain but for 'nice, sensible' Krystle.

> TRB: Who would you most like to be like?
> ANNA (34): Krystle, I suppose.
> JACKIE (37): Yes.
> ANNA: I mean when does she ever lose her temper? And if she does it doesn't last.
> GRETA (41): She's so calm, collected. And if she does lose her temper she puts it over in a good way without any nastiness, doesn't she?
> ANNA: She's sensible.
> LENA (29): Yeah, she doesn't grit her teeth like most of the others.

EVA (38): Yes, but it's all hopeless. It's all so full of problems. She can't do anything about it all.

JACKIE: Kirby wants to shoot Alexis and . . . Alexis wants to topple Blake and . . . bring down Krystle, and . . .

ANNA: *And poor Krystle wants everyone to be friends.*

It's as though most of the identification with TV characters depends upon domesticating them – even turning them away from the scriptwriters' intentions and refusing to allow them to be as villainous as might have been wished. As John Ellis says, 'Characters in drama series . . . tend to become familiar figures, loved or excused with a tolerance which is quite remarkable: it is more than is normally extended to members of the family or to neighbours. The construction of a "real" monster in a TV series is a difficult process: this is perhaps why J. R. Ewing in *Dallas* excited such attention' (*Visible Fictions*, 1982). Our viewers certainly tempered the 'monstrous' view of J.R. with quite enough rationalisations and excuses to secure a final 'not guilty' verdict.

TRB: What do you think of J.R.?

ANNA: I hate him.

JACKIE: Well, I like him, sometimes. He comes across occasionally. When he's nice to his secretary. [*All are silent for a second.*]

ANNA: I don't think he is nice, really . . . is he?

JACKIE: He is sometimes nice to his secretary.

LENA: I can't *bear* him.

GRETA: I just think the programme would be nothing without him. They can't live without him. But it does give you that hate for him – you know – you sit there and you get all wound up.

CARMEL (27): He does love his family.

ANNA: And I should think the men like him, because they all like to think that they're like him, and it's the same with Joan Collins, I like her, because . . . she's strong.

CARMEL: Well, I definitely don't think he's as evil as she is.

For a short time in another group it began to look as though Carmel's view of Alexis as the really evil one was going to overturn the theory that television was too familial and intimate to allow for the creation of true villains.

VAL (51): I don't like her [Alexis] in the same way as I like J.R. for his scheming and all that. To me she's just evil.

MARILYN (50): Yes, very very evil.

VAL: I mean, J.R. doesn't try and say other people are nasty, he knows he's the one that's the out-and-out bleeder. He admits it.

JAN (51): And when Alexis had that fight with her boyfriend, I mean, I don't like men hitting women, I think it's a terrible thing, but I would like to have punched her one . . . [*All laugh.*]

TRB: You wanted to punch her?

JAN: Yes. When he was like giving her some stick, I thought, bloody good job.

HELEN (56): I watch, and I think, no one can be that nasty. No one. Not that evil.

PATRICIA (49): And she always says Blake's horrible, and he's this and he's that, and in fact he's so nice . . . so nice.

But one group member – Lorna – was on hand with one psychologically redeeming feature which began to turn the tide.

LORNA (40): In fact, I think she loves Blake deep down.

HELEN: She does.

PATRICIA: She doesn't.

LORNA: Oh, I think she does, she wants him, that's why she does all those things. [*Some agree*.]

JAN: She wants his company.

HELEN: She hates him for throwing him out of her house.

[*All talk*.]

LORNA: I think she'd be back there like a shot. [*A few agree*.]

And by the end of the debate, she had been brought back into relative favour by the same familial attribute which also saved J.R.:

LORNA: They both, J.R. and Alexis Colby, both love their kids. They're both family people. You have to say that.

Biography to the Rescue

Even if nothing can be found within the actual television character which might serve to reduce their villainy, there's always a further resource – the nature of the actor who plays the part. J.R. can't be wholly bad because there is something about him which belongs to the actor.

JULIA (32): I don't think it's anything that's written in the series, I just think it's probably the character. He's got an individual character, himself.

JO (35): Well, he's gone into that himself, hasn't he?

JULIA: Larry Hagman . . . that grin is his own, isn't it?

JO: And he wears a big hat now, apparently, which he never used to.

JULIA: And he's still got that look. When he's on a personality show, and he's been on *Wogan*, he's still got that arrogant look about him.

JO: I mean, nobody else could act that look.

We found repeatedly that as soon as we asked viewers to project themselves into the more fantastic elements of soap operas, into the characters of the more outrageous people, realistic details were introduced to make matters more mundane. And once the conversation ran in this direction everyone had some biographical facts to tell. This is hardly surprising, given the massive coverage of soap operas in the tabloid press, but it does seem to place a limit upon the degree of fantastic involvement which may be enjoyed with television characters. Perhaps there are some individuals who watch their TV drama series in isolation, who never read newspapers (or watch chat shows – for of course soap stars routinely turn up in this context to describe their real lives) and who are therefore able to turn J.R., Alexis and Sue Ellen into the type of mythical character who once roamed across early Hollywood screens – but it seems unlikely. (Indeed if such beings do exist they are more likely to be denizens of senior common rooms than canteens or saloon bars.)

Of course Hollywood also had its gossip magazines, but these invariably protected the myth they claimed to expose much more carefully than today's Fleet Street newshounds, and were so far behind with the rumours that they rarely had a chance of being directly related to the part being played at the local Odeon by the star in question. With television the 'inside story' can sometimes arrive almost before the scene has yet appeared, and of course the never-ending nature of soaps means that such material is there to supplement your viewing week after week after week.

ANNE (51): Joan Collins, I don't know if anyone read it, about a month or so ago, but she was saying in that Sunday magazine that comes with the *News of the World* that she found it very hard to . . . that her and Dex got on so well, it was so real, that he couldn't control himself. She said the love scenes were really close to the mark. They couldn't control themselves. It was really heavy, you know, they were not acting, but it was real. She said that it was very hard, when they said 'cut', and they couldn't.
WENDY (31): Oooh . . . [*Laughs.*]
ANNE: He could feel he was falling in love with her.

Often the gossip is considerably more 'natural' than this rather titillating revelation (which has a certain old-time Hollywood feel about it). Famous soap stars eagerly queue up to be 'normal' on television chat shows, possibly aware, as our viewers revealed, that this does nothing to reduce their appeal but provides just those domestic and biographical hooks which pull the viewer even more firmly into the drama when the next episode is shown.

TRB: Do you enjoy seeing characters like Victoria Principal on chat shows?
KIM (29): Oh, yes. It's nice to see the real person behind the part. Even she says, 'Ooh, I never look like this, you want to see me first thing in the morning.' Oh, good, you think – we're not the only ones that look awful.
TRB: But does it stop you believing in them?
KIM: No, no.
DEE (28): Once it comes on again, I'm back into that world.

'Digger' Barnes
[never seen, dead on
arrival in *Dallas*,
ex-enemy yet
comrade of Jock's,
alcoholic]

Jason Ewing (Jock's brother)
[little known of him,
he is but a memory,
having died before the
series started.
Somewhat deranged
by all accounts]

Katherine
[had an affair with
JR, but really wanted
Bobby. For her
'future' see Bobby.
Shares the same
mother but not the
same father as Cliff
and Pam. Has moved
to *Glitter*]

Cliff
[little bit deranged:
his whole existence is
tied up with outdoing
JR. Had affairs with
Afton, Sue Ellen,
Mandy; married
Jamie with ulterior
motives]

Jamie
[Jamie turned up out
of the blue claiming
part of Ewing Oil.
Cliff married her for
the oil but didn't get
it . . .]

Jack
[single man rap
produced to rep
Bobby in plot –
affair with Jenn
Wade, perhaps

Pam
[was married to
Bobby then divorced
him, became engaged
to Mark Grayson who
has since disappeared,
believed
dead-through-
suicide-as-he-had-
cancer-and-did-not-
want-to-burden-Pam-
with-it. Pam has
scoured the world's
cancer clinics looking
for him. Pam seems to
have a bleak future
ahead of her (see
Bobby). But will
Mark Grayson come
back? Adopted
Christopher]

CAMEOS

Lucy (a.k.a. 'the poison dwarf') She is a Ewing and
unlike her dad Gary, prefers to be at Southfork than
Knot's Landing. This midget was 'unlucky in love' until
she remarried her ex-husband Mitch. Liked by Miss
Ellie especially when played by Bel Geddes.

Sue Ellen Divorced, remarried and now estranged from
JR, this sometime alcoholic/mental case has had affairs
with Cliff ('very serious'), Dusty Farlow (crippled son of
Clayton) and Peter (a young camp counsellor) with whom
she lost a child in pregnancy. Will Dusty Farlow come
back into her life?

Christopher
[see Bobby]

N.B. We are here only concerned with the main
characters in *Dallas*. Hundreds more actually pop in and
out of the 'family'.

```
                              ┌───── Jock Ewing—and ─────   'Miss Ellie' Ewing ──────┐
                              │     [Big man died in air      [Widowed then
                              │     crash]                    married Clayton
                              │                               Farlow. Miss Ellie has
┌─────────────────┐          │                               been played by
Gary                         Ray                             Donna Reed since her
[Gary is not too fond        [Ray was the foreman            honeymoon, but the
of his family, except        at Southfork Ranch,             original actress
Miss Ellie, so has           but simultaneously              Barbara Bel Geddes is
started his own series,      married Donna, a                 to return, without of
Knot's Landing.              widowed                         course a 'dramatic'
Produced Lucy]               millionairess, and was          explanation]
                             found to be Jock's
│                            illegitimate son. Ray
                             and Donna have split
Lucy                         up; Donna is
[see Cameo]                  pregnant . . .]
```

Gary
[Gary is not too fond of his family, except Miss Ellie, so has started his own series, *Knot's Landing*. Produced Lucy]

Lucy
[see Cameo]

Jock Ewing—and
[Big man died in air crash]

Ray
[Ray was the foreman at Southfork Ranch, but simultaneously married Donna, a widowed millionairess, and was found to be Jock's illegitimate son. Ray and Donna have split up; Donna is pregnant . . .]

'Miss Ellie' Ewing
[Widowed then married Clayton Farlow. Miss Ellie has been played by Donna Reed since her honeymoon, but the original actress Barbara Bel Geddes is to return, without of course a 'dramatic' explanation]

Bobby
[Bobby was divorced from Pam (nee Barnes), was to marry Jenna Wade (played by Elvis Presley's ex-wife) but Jenna was forced to remarry her ex-husband the Italian kidnapper (of their daughter) Renaldo who was killed and Jenna wrongfully accused of the murder.
Bobby has been written out of *Dallas*: he died in a car accident when he saved Pam (whom he was going to marry instead of Jenna) from a car (driven by Katherine Wentworth who died behind the wheel). Bobby and Pam had previously adopted a boy who lives most of the time with her]

Christopher
[considered by some to be the ugliest child T V performer]

J.R.
[J R, the man people love to hate, married Sue Ellen (sometime alcoholic/mental case), divorced her and remarried her and is estranged from her sexually once again. J R 'shares' the same women as his arch-enemy Cliff Barnes (J R's one-time sister-in-law's brother – Sue Ellen, Afton, and Mandy. J R is a little promiscuous. J R and Sue Ellen produced John (pronounced Jaaaan) Ross]

John Ross

Alexis Colby
[once married to Blake – 'still loves him really', now married to Dex Dexter. May be taking a toy-boy lover?]

Adam Carrington
[a recently discovered 'lost son', who tried to kill Alexis, his mother. All is now forgiven. Had an affair with Kirby, and maybe with Sammy Jo. Lost a baby with Kirby. Next – a fling with Claudia]

Fallon (now deceased) Carrington
[reformed nymphomaniac who married Jeff Colby (no *real* relation to Alexis – who 'married' his uncle when he was on a life support machine). Fallon divorced Jeff, then he married Kirby; she was about to remarry him following his divorce from Kirby when she disappeared, a body was found, and 'Fallon' was buried. She is found in LA suffering from amnesia, and with a 'new face' – in fact a new actress, Emma Samms.
Fallon had an affair with the now definitely deceased Mark Jennings, Krystle's ex-husband (No. 1). Fallon and Jeff produced a child]

'little Blake'

Amanda
[English aristo-Sloane beauty, suddenly turned up, claiming to be Alexis's daughter. Alexis is none too surprised, but tried to keep from Amanda the knowledge that Blake is her father. Amanda is sleeping with her mother's husband, Dex Dexter. Married Prince Michael of Moldavia]

Blake Carrington
[charming silver-haired oil magnate and paterfamilias who discovers new children with alarming regularity: has trouble escaping the snares of his evil ex-wife Alexis]

Krystle Carrington
[formerly married to Mark Jennings, who had an affair with Alexis, and with Fallon]

baby Krystina
[Could be at risk from an angry Sammy Jo (and her friend Rita who is Krystle's 'double')]

Steven Carrington
[bisexual, recovered from near-fatal accident and put together (differently) by plastic surgeon, now married to Claudia who lost her husband Matthew (who once had an affair with Krystle) and daughter in the jungle and who once had an affair with Jeff. Has another gay lover following his affair with Luke. Steven has a son through his first marriage to Sammy Jo, a failed model]

Danny Carrington

Dominique Devereaux
[Dominique is a *black* cabaret singer-cum-millionairess, reasonably happily married, who is Blake's lost half-sister. A new white lover?]

The process is two-way, of course. You can call up biographical knowledge of J.R. to temper the fictional image, or use fictional material to supplement some tabloid revelations. In the case of Ronald Allen (David Hunter of *Crossroads*) it all adds up to a happy marriage.

> TRB: What about David Hunter?
> JUDY (27): I should imagine he and his wife, or the girl he's with, are very similar.
> ROSALYN (31): Yes.
> JUDY: She used to be in dirty films.
> ROSALYN: I know.
> FRANCES: I should imagine that's the way she lives normally.
> YVONNE (28): I should imagine he's got a very good relationship. [*Laughs.*]
> FRANCES: Very stable and very sexy.
> YVONNE: And music, I mean you often see him playing classical music and I'd put him into that category.

The balance between the fictional, the factual and the pseudo-factual (tabloid and chat-show revelation) is a tricky one. Granada Television provided quite other fictional reasons for the recent demise of Len Fairclough in *Coronation Street* than the factual appearance of the actor Peter Adamson as defendant in an indecent-assault case (in which he was found not guilty). But viewers were resigned to his departure. You could excuse J.R.'s *fictional* character by importing *biographical* details of his niceness: the process didn't really work the other way round.

> TRB: But didn't you think that once he'd been found innocent they should have kept [Len Fairclough] on the programme?
> BETTY (27): I'm not sure.
> WENDY (33): I don't think so, I think it ruined him.
> FRANCES: It's hard, 'cos you're talking about children.
> YVONNE: And the public as well.
> FRANCES: Mud sticks.
> KIM: I think they thought he did it.
> YVONNE: And even when he was not guilty they thought he should die.

The Realm of the Para-Social

There have been a number of attempts to describe the peculiarities of our relationship with television characters. But often they can seem too heroic, too escapist to match the reality. Ellul's description of an isolated idealising viewer, for example, hardly fits the people who chattered so eagerly in our groups.

> Rather than face his own phantom, he seeks . . . phantoms into which he can project himself and which permit him to live as he might have willed. For an hour or two he can cease to be himself, as his personality dissolves

and fades into the anonymous mass of spectators . . . He goes to bed with the leading lady, kills the villain, and masters life's absurdities. In short, he becomes a hero. Life suddenly has meaning. (Jacques Ellul, *The Technological Society*, 1964.)

No doubt partly in order to get away from such transcendent views, American sociologists Horton and Wohl developed a more ordinary way to describe our relationship with television characters. It allowed for a certain unreadiness to respond to much of the personal button-holing nature of television's output, but also made some provision for the development of deep involvement. They referred to our relationship to television images as *para-social*.

> Para-social relations may be governed by little or no sense of obligation, effort or responsibility on the part of the spectator. He is free to withdraw at any moment. If he remains involved, these para-social relations provide a framework within which much may be added by fantasy.
> (Donald Horton and Richard Wohl, 'Mass Communication and Para-Social Interaction', *Psychiatry*, 1956.)

This allows that TV characters may at times stand in as real persons but that this relationship can at any moment be broken. When they are 'real' to us they may take all sorts of shapes, serve quite different functions. They may be surrogate parents or spouses or lovers who help to show us how to behave and how to feel in many normal situations. 'What after all is soap opera but an interminable exploration of the contingencies to be met with in "home life"?' (Horton and Wohl, ibid.) They may be companions or friends or acquaintances who make us feel less lonely and less dissatisfied with our own existence.

In none of these cases can we talk about the TV characters as being simply the images on the screen. As we have seen they are complex multi-faceted beings composed of fiction, fact and pseudo-fact. What's more, they are at least partly brought to life not amid the scenery of *Dallas* or Denver or *Coronation Street* or the Crossroads motel but in homes and shops and bars across the country. It is in a million conversations that these characters acquire much of the density and coherence which helps translate them from flickering images into central roles in contemporary popular culture.

Any extended conversation between viewers about their favourite television characters brings out this creative aspect as well as the overlapping between real life and fiction, and between different dramas to which we've already referred. Here, for example, is one group discussing the highly charged subject of whom they are sexually attracted to in *Dallas* and *Dynasty*.

MARY (27): Jeff . . .
ALICE (35): Bobby . . .
DEB (32): Jeff and Bobby. [*All talk*.] On different nights, though.
TRB: Who would you least like to go to bed with?
DAWN (27): Oh, Adam.

JEAN (44): J.R.

GLENYS (36): J.R. and Adam.

JILL (38): Pam's brother, Cliff Barnes.

DEB: Ooh, he gives me the creeps.

DAWN: If you notice his lip, it looks as though he's had a stroke or he's drunk. I mean the way he talks gives me the creeps. If you watch his lip.

DEB: Ooh, he's horrible.

CHRISTINE (31): He sort of seems to want a bigger part really, I don't like him at all, he's trying to take over.

DEB: He's trying to be like a J.R.

From the tight close-up on Cliff Barnes's lip, and on the peculiar convergence between the actor's wish for a bigger part, and his fictional attempts to outdo J.R., the group moved on to Denver.

ALICE: I think in *Dynasty* it's that guy with the scar, the one, I can't remember the name, he was running in . . .

JEAN: Flex . . . flex . . .

DAWN: Oh, Dex. [*All agree.*]

DEB: Oh, my . . . [*Sighs.*]

KAREN (32): The one with the funny voice.

DEB: Yeah, he was having an affair with Joan Collins, and then . . .

MARY: Who had the fight with her.

ALICE: Yeah.

DAWN: Oh, I like Jeff. [*Sighs.*]

DEB: Oh, I think Jeff's lovely. [*Most agree.*]

DAWN: He reminds me of, um . . . he's an action man.

DEB: His hair, he's changed his hair.

ALICE: I like him, but he's too smooth.

GLENYS: Yes, I don't like smoothies.

But Alice hadn't finished with *Dallas* yet – in particular with Bobby, and the consistency of her devotion.

ALICE: In *Dallas* it was definitely Bobby.

ALICE: Bobby . . . ooh, Bobby was beautiful. Don't you think so?

DAWN: No, I don't.

ALICE: I even loved him in *Man from Atlantis* when he used to have funny eyes and webbed feet. [*All laugh and talk.*]

Did it worry them that the conventions of soap opera meant that there were unlikely to be any very explicit sexual scenes in which Bobby or Jeff or Dex could have properly erotic parts?

JEAN: Well, Jeff did in one programme.

JILL: He undid the buttons.

CHRISTINE: Yes, they came in the bedroom, I think she had a towel or something on, and he picked her up and . . .

HELEN (28): Was that Kirby?

CHRISTINE: Kirby yes, it was Kirby, wasn't it? She's one I can't stand.

CHRISTINE: Can't stand her eyebrows. [*Laughs.*] Like a woodcock, isn't she?

MARY: You're very observant, I don't notice these things. [*Laughs.*]

ELIZABETH (35): Oh, I do.

KAREN: They haven't got much wrong with them. *It's so sickening.*

Karen's sudden sense that it might be difficult to identify with such perfect creatures was quickly and brusquely dealt with by Jean.

JEAN: Oh, but her clothes . . . the clothes she [Kirby] wears.

DEB: She looks like she's just walked out of a home for retired matrons. They're so boring.

DAWN: But you see, she's not really like all the others.

GLENYS: No, she's the waiter's [Joseph, the butler, committed suicide] daughter. She's not supposed to be like one of those.

DAWN: She wasn't brought up like them.

DEB: Oh yes. But she should have got the class by now. That gear she wears is so weird . . . horrible.

JEAN: *I mean, you wouldn't enjoy any of it unless you could bitch about them.*

And if there was to be anything explicit it had to be properly romantic. Deb had particularly liked a Jeff and Kirby scene.

DEB: When they were just beginning to get to love each other, and they were getting married, there was a love scene which really shook me. I've never seen so much. It was about five minutes long, and the way they were looking at each other, straight in the eyes, and both naked, and he was on top of her, and kissing her and . . . [*All laugh.*]

TRB: And did you enjoy that one?

GLENYS: Oh yes . . . I thought it was so nice because you couldn't see anything. There was nothing dirty about it. It was very subtle the way it was put over.

With no obvious change of gear the group promptly switched from identification with a passionate love scene to the dispassionate discussion of what exactly you might be allowed to see in soap opera – the erotic close-up which was the counterpart of the attention paid to Sue Ellen's mouth, or Cliff's lip.

ALICE: She took off her robe the other day, didn't she?

DEB: Fallon?

DAWN: No, the other one, Sammy Jo.

ALICE: Yeah, but you only saw a little bit.

DEB: And from the back. The camera . . .

DAWN: . . . the camera went down to the crack of her botty.

8

All Right on the Night:
Tricks and Techniques

SUE (43): On *The Price is Right* there's a woman that has the same laugh week after week. . . . She goes 'Wooo-ooo-ooo'. And it's the same, exactly the same every week.

It is perfectly in keeping with television's view of itself that it should have had such a programme as London Weekend Television's *It'll Be Alright on the Night*, a compilation of blunders and mistakes which shows the artifice behind everything that usually looks so relaxed and confident. In many ways it fulfils a similar function to the chat shows, providing an opportunity for actors, presenters and 'artists' of various kinds to show the 'real' person behind the television persona. Once again, those who would argue that television fills our life with idealised and unrealisable images will have to cope with dozens of awkward examples; scene after scene in which such superheroes are seen falling off stages, tripping over carpets and forgetting their words while in full flow.

In fact, when we asked viewers to talk about what went wrong on television, about any tricks which they spotted, any production or acting or location mistakes, they failed to mention such well-publicised blunders. Several were less interested in the stars than in the audience they saw on their sets, the happy, cheering, waving audience so often in the forefront of *The Price is Right*, or the serious, carefully selected audience for *Question Time*. How far were ordinary studio audiences responding to what *we* were seeing on the screen and how much to special instructions they were receiving from elsewhere? And how on earth could you account for their enthusiasm?

JOHN (41): Somebody told me that in *The Price is Right* before they start they have a warm-up man insult the audience.
SALLY (27): I used to live in Wood Green when I was little and they used to record *Morecambe and Wise* there, and we used to go every week, because we always got free tickets, and the warm-up man was always on. He got everybody really going for as long as perhaps twenty minutes before the actual filming started.

TRB: So you think you enjoyed it more than somebody watching it at home?

SALLY: Oh, sure.

MARIAN (41): Yes, because at home you start from cold, don't you?

Even though the presence of a warm-up man explained some of the laughter and enthusiasm, Sue felt sure that there was also some 'fixing' going on. She noticed that the laughter on some programmes 'didn't come at quite the right time'. And there was often something about the length of the laughter which made you think it was either 'canned' or very organised.

SUE (43): When you hear it again and again, you tend to recognise the same laugh.

There were other clues:

SUE: On the *Price is Right* there's a woman that has the same laugh week after week, and my husband says, 'Listen, you can tell that's a recorded laugh, because when they get to a certain point she goes, "Wooo-ooo-ooo".' And it's the same, exactly the same, every week.

Donald Sinden recently described a conversation he'd had with a couple who'd been to see a performance of a comedy in which he was starring. It had not seemed to him to be a particularly good night and he asked his friends somewhat tentatively if they'd enjoyed their evening. 'Oh yes,' they insisted. 'Very much.' 'But I don't recall hearing you laugh.' 'Well, no, we wanted to lots of times but we were frightened of missing the next bit.'

The actor was inclined to explain this as one of the effects of too much television viewing. Nobody on the box could ever wait for the chuckles to die down and time his next line to soar splendidly above them. Viewers had no alternative but to suppress their laughter.

Studio laughter can of course be seen as an artificial device for creating this space. The only problem is that if it is somehow seen as inappropriate then it can stifle the very response from the home audience that it is supposed to elicit.

TRB: Why do you think they put the laughter in?

JENNY (50): Obviously they don't think it's funny enough that people are going to laugh without it.

DEREK (55): You know you've got to be encouraged to laugh. They're saying, 'Come on. This is funny. Laugh.'

JEREMY (50): Maybe it's to cover up the silences.

When domestic situation comedies are punctuated by studio laughter it is always possible to accept that they were videotaped before a live audience. The setting is sufficiently like that which one might encounter on a stage for an audience to seem appropriate. This was far from being true for all sit coms:

JIM (60): In *Last of the Summer Wine* [nostalgic Lancashire comedy], they do a lot of that, don't they, laughing.

DEREK: They laugh at something which isn't funny, sometimes.

IVY (58): That's stupid, because it's funny enough on its own without canned laughter.

JIM: Yes, and what's also strange is that the people who're laughing just couldn't be there.

JOHN (41): Yes, you're right out in the middle of the country, and you hear the laughter going on in the fields.

Ivy referred to 'canned laughter' on BBC's *Last of the Summer Wine*. Others used the phrase frequently to refer to the odd laughter sounds which punctuated television programmes. But the BBC insists that it does not use this device.

What is it then about the laughter which is causing concern – sufficient concern for the BBC to have printed a standard letter which unequivocally asserts: '*The BBC does not used canned laughter*'?

Probably it is the frequent recourse which television editors and directors (on all channels) have to 'sypher suites' – to special studios where it is possible to run through the recorded show, listen to the actual laughter which was emitted by the studio audience in response to certain jokes, and then move this 'laughter' around from place to place – building up the chuckles in one place, 'enhancing' (a favourite term) the guffaws in another. Although the prospect of a court case in which the jury was required to listen to example after example of 'laughter' is appealing, we will tread carefully and say that it would indeed be a testament to the thorough-going integrity of editors and directors if, in a studio which contained hundreds of examples of excellent laughter from other shows, they never borrowed the smallest whoop or yelp to add to the ambience of their own.

Posers and Popsters

Even when the setting for the laughter or enthusiasm is less incongruous, it's rare for the viewer to be able to see any of the attempts which are being made to manipulate it. But when the BBC carried out its own research into *Top of the Pops* as it existed before the 1985 revamp, there was some surprise in the discovery that so many people – even from the young age groups – were perfectly able to pick out the 'paid cheerleaders' and unpaid normals. The report summarised the reactions of viewers to both sets.

CHEERLEADERS Sometimes referred to as 'posers' or 'rent-a-crowd', these members of the audience are instantly recognisable due to their atypical dress and dancing styles. Their overt attempts to be sexy are incongruent with the rather androgynous appearance of many young people today and their enthusiastic, 'over-the-top' dancing is at odds with current disco and club styles.

'NORMAL' PEOPLE Most viewers think the ordinary members of the studio audience are an asset and come over well. . . . Nevertheless, it is sometimes thought that they are rather like clones and are herded about like sheep. . . . Indeed, it was felt these audience members should be given more space as they sometimes appeared to be squashed together and inhibited by the cheerleaders.

Knowing about the artificiality of *Top of the Pops* and the tricks and techniques it used was important to the viewers in our seven to nine age group and particularly to those in the fourteen to sixteen group. Farouk (15) had some mates who went to it and they'd told him that 'you keep getting pushed about by the cameraman to stand around the stage and make it look packed'.

The idea that some of the people were being paid to look enthusiastic ran against their central belief that the music, or at least some of it, was intrinsically worthwhile. They were eager to get some revenge on those they saw as traitors to their age group.

SYLVESTER (14): Real show-offs.
SEAN (15): Yes, they look really pathetic.
TRB: Why do they look so pathetic?
SYLVESTER: The clothes they wear.
FAROUK (15): Yes, the way they dance.
GARY (14): Eight different colours of paint on their face or something.
TRB: They wear funny clothes?
GARY: They look stupid.
SEAN: They can't dance.
DARREN (15): They look at the camera.
SEAN: They don't dance to the music, they just dance the way they want to dance.

As the BBC research showed, there was more ambiguity in such assertions than might at first appear. Only the younger age groups, up to twelve or thirteen, were 'allowed' to be generally enthusiastic; after that it was the accepted thing to moan about *Top of the Pops* but still watch it conscientiously. No doubt, the fact that it was the 'authoritarian' BBC, or even 'Auntie Beeb', which produced the programme added some spice to the general criticism of its technical features.

PETER (15): They've bought these new lights which are sort of cheap lights with four of them just like a circle. They keep going on and off and I think they are a waste of time. They might as well get lasers instead. It would be much better.
TRB: So do you think that's because it's the BBC?
PETER: Yes, they are trying to economise, aren't they? They are trying to make it cheaper but keep it the same but it's not. People notice the difference.

The teenagers' feeling that the programme wasn't really theirs in the same way as, say, *The Tube* (Channel 4, Tyne-Tees) gets some support from the ratings which show that two-thirds of the audience for *Top of the Pops* is made up of people over the age of twenty-five. Sean had an idea why some of them were watching.

SEAN: They're always bringing on sexy birds and that. For the dads.

The main puzzle for our fifteen- and sixteen-year-olds was the recruitment of the *Top of the Pops* 'cheerleaders'. Where could they have come from? They'd never met anyone who behaved like that in their lives. A comment on their behaviour in the *Sunday Times* (1 May 1983) suggests they may have been occupational therapists in drag: ' "Cheryl and Sandra, stick yer 'andbags under the stage there. Move forward, boy; don't be shy." The resident cheerleaders chivvy out smiles and practise clapping with hands above head as if it were rehabilitation for the afflicted.'

It looks as though it takes some time before the artificiality of acting becomes quite so evident as it did to teenagers watching *Top of the Pops*. Eight- to nine-year-olds, for example, who saw children on television commercials were inclined to believe in their naturalness. There was nothing very special about how they got to be on the screen.

TRB: So they are just ordinary people?
JANET (8): Yes, if they are passing by in the streets they could stop and ask them to be on.
BECKY (8): Yes, like those dolls that have really long hair and you can plait it. They have girls with really long hair.
TRB: So are the children in the advertisements real ordinary children?
JANET: I think they are just ordinary children and they have just been asked to do something.
TRB: What happens to them after they have been in an advertisement?
SUSAN (8): I think they get a free sample or something.
TRB: And then they go back to school?
BECKY: Yes.

Not that their own attempts to have some contact with television people had been as easy as walking down the street. They'd done what they were asked to by the people on *Blue Peter*, the BBC children's magazine programme:

BECKY: My sister sends stuff like stamps and that.
JILL (8): Yes, we collected them at school. [*Some agree.*] The infants and the juniors got a big box full so we sent those along.
TRB: To *Blue Peter*?
JILL: Yes.
BECKY: To help Ethiopia.

But attempts to make the communication two-way had been rather less successful:

> TRB: Anything else you do? Do you write letters, phone up?
> BECKY: I've tried to phone *Saturday Superstore*.
> SUSAN: Me too. I didn't get through even though there was nobody on the phone there. It wasn't engaged.
> ALEX (8): I got through the first time, but I never got to talk to the people.

And neither did it seem that nepotism helped.

> JILL: I tried it with Wham! and I couldn't get through. Then I tried it with Slade because my mum used to go to school with Jimmy Lea.
> BECKY: My mum used to go to school with Elaine Paige.
> ALEX: My mum used to live round the corner to Cliff Richard.
> MANDY (8): My mum used to go to school with nobody.

Script Time

Mandy might at least have a promising career ahead as a scriptwriter – an occupation which baffled many viewers when they considered comedians. There was a reluctance to accept that behind their favourite comedian sat another person or group of people writing out the jokes. Who did they think was the most natural of all?

> TRB: Which ones do you think will go on being funny for ever and ever?
> MARGARET (52): The Two Ronnies. [*All agree.*]
> HEATHER (49): Ronnie Barker. I think he's the particularly funny one.
> MARGARET: Yes, Ronnie Barker is good.
> NORA (57): And Russ Abbott, I think.
> MARGARET: Lenny Henry.
> TRB: They'll be funny for ever and ever?
> HELEN (52): Yes, I think so. [*All agree.*]
> MARIE (54): They're natural.
> HELEN: As long as they want to work, anyway.

So which ones wrote their own scripts?

> ALAN (50): Ronnie Corbett.
> JIM (47): Ronnie Barker does.
> ALAN: Ronnie Barker does.
> DAVID (41): On the titles, it says so at the end.
> PETER (47): Yes, but in conjunction with someone else.
> DAVID: Yes.
> PETER: Not entirely on their own.
> JIM: No.
> TRB: Who doesn't write their own scripts, do you think?
> ALAN: I wouldn't think Little and Large do.
> JIM: Little and Large don't.

If Little and Large don't write their own words, how much would they have to pay to get someone to do it for them?

> ALAN: Oh, that would cost a lot.
> JOHN (56): For the whole series?
> TRB: No, just for the one show.
> ALAN: About five hundred pounds, I should think. [*Most agree.*]

Several in the group talked about the peculiar catch-22 which meant that Little and Large's ability to pay their scriptwriter as much as £500 (our own evidence suggests the figure would be nearer £2000) allowed them to be funnier than other, more struggling comedians. How then could one ever really distinguish between comedians except in terms of 'naturalness'?

> JOHN: I think the higher up they go, the more they're able to afford scriptwriters. I suppose if you're starting off, then you've got to scratch around, haven't you? Use old jokes.
> PETER: But then again, if you're starting off, you've got to make a good impression so that's when you need scriptwriters most. When you're established, people laugh at you anyway.
> JOHN: Yes, but then, if you can afford to pay for the service, why shouldn't you?
> DAVID: But don't you think the best comedians in the end are those who do their own work?
> JOHN: Probably. Lenny Henry I can imagine doing a lot of his own work.
> DAVID: Yes, he does his own, because he's a natural comedian. I mean he doesn't have to do anything. He just has to wear that woolly hat and stand there. No scriptwriter.

Didn't he need any rehearsals? Most thought very few. But when we asked viewers, 'Which comedians need the most rehearsals to get their jokes right?' Lenny Henry did rather less well than some. The fact that Ronnie Barker was known to write his own jokes must have helped lift him to the top of this league. (The groups were given a list of ten comedians to put in order.)

'Least rehearsal' league table
1. Ronnie Barker
2. Jim Davidson
3. Russ Abbott
4. Lenny Henry
5. Ronnie Corbett
6. Bernard Manning
7. Bob Monkhouse
8. Les Dawson
9. Max Bygraves
10. Little and Large

There was still considerable respect for even those comedians who needed to buy up expensive scripts and have lengthy rehearsals to get them right. Nobody in the groups felt that they themselves would be able to tell jokes as well on television or write them for other people. This modesty was replicated in our national sample. Eighty-nine per cent declared that they would not be able to tell jokes with any success on television and 90 per cent considered that writing comedy would be beyond them.

Less reticence was evident when we asked about scripts for drama series.

TRB: Suppose you had to write a *Starsky and Hutch* [American cops-and-robbers] programme for one hour . . .

BOB (51): That's easy. He's always jumping over cars and then doing somersaults.

ALAN (42): Yes. [*Laughs.*]

BOB: A load of action at the beginning, very boring in the middle, more action at the end.

DENNIS (27): One ends up with the girl and the other one doesn't. *Simple.*

EDDIE (31): And everything's always sorted out at the end; never any untidy bits left over. Whereas in *Hill Street Blues* things do go wrong, they do die. In *Starsky and Hutch* you know the main characters are always going to survive. There's usually a situation where their life is threatened but you know it'll be all right.

PAUL (37): The hero comes through in the end.

TRB: And *Hill Street Blues* is not like that?

EDDIE: People do die there. Terrible things do happen to people. It's not all sorted out neatly.

In other scripts, the complaint wasn't so much about matters being too easily sorted out as about the speed at which it all happened.

JOE (37): If you can imagine this: in *Crossroads* we recently had the restaurant manager in a space of three weeks meet a total stranger, court her, get engaged to her, marry her. At the same time she's having an affair with somebody else in the motel.

Those who thought they could write or design scripts for the better-known soaps also had a good idea of the peculiar structure to which they'd have to conform.

PAUL: You have to have a lot of little scenes.

TRB: How long do they last?

PAUL: Oh, a minute or two.

EDDIE: Some a bit longer than a minute.

PAUL: Some . . . three minutes.

DENNIS: Yeah, I'd say roughly two and a half to three minutes.

TRB: And how many people usually appear in each of those scenes?

EDDIE: Not many.

JOHN (42): Two or three.

PAUL: Two or three or four, but you don't get a big cluster.

JOHN: No, about two or three.

PAUL: Sometimes, in *Dallas*, they're all together before they go in for a meal. But that's the only time.

JIM (41): And mainly evening. Because you never see them all together in the morning. Do you?

PAUL: No, they all come down in dribs and drabs, don't they?

EDDIE: And you never see them all sitting by the pool like a family or anything, it's always just two or three people.

DEREK (49): And there's a lot of telephoning.

PAUL: And knocking on the door.

It's difficult to imagine how many soap operas and sit coms and drama series could manage without the changes of mood and scene made possible by the telephone call or the sudden knock on the door (or some sort of doorbell: the chimes in the *Dick Van Dyke Show* became almost as familiar as the characters themselves).

The telephone has a particularly strong part to play in soaps – in those intense two- or three-person scenes that Derek earlier described.

> The telephone is used for a special kind of talk-communication with someone who is not there in one sense, present and close in another. The telephone is thus a perfect emblem of the recurrent problems of soap characters: together yet alone (in their secret feelings, thoughts and fantasies), apart yet together (in their passions, obsessions, and searches for the missing other) . . . And the telephone *in potentia* (the call that might come, the missing husband, friend, or daughter who may or may not pick up the phone) is an even more powerful ritual object in soap opera than the telephone in use.
> (Bernard Timberg in Newcomb, ed., *Television*, 1982.)

Perhaps there is a thesis to be written on the changing role of the telephone in twentieth-century drama and certainly such a piece should include at least a chapter on the plot-setting function that it performed so admirably for years on the British stage in drawing-room comedy – a function hilariously parodied by Tom Stoppard in *The Real Inspector Hound*, 1968.

> [Mrs Drudge the charlady enters; she answers the phone.]
> 'Hello, the drawing room of Lady Muldoon's country residence one morning in early spring? Hello! Who? Who did you wish to speak to? I'm afraid there is no one of that name here, this is all very mysterious and I'm sure it's leading up to something. I hope nothing is amiss for we, that is Lady Muldoon and her houseguests, are here cut off from the world, including Magnus, the wheelchair-ridden half-brother of her·ladyship's

husband Lord Albert Muldoon who ten years ago went out for a walk on the cliffs and was never seen again –'

Moving Scenery

In drawing-room comedies there was commonly a brief pause after the curtain went up, not for any dramatic purpose that it was possible to discern, but so as to allow the audience to marvel at the set and, if they were so minded, applaud it. Although there was no shortage of glowing references to the monumental scenery in such blockbusters as *Brideshead Revisted* and *Jewel in the Crown*, few viewers seemed particularly aware of the domestic set in their favourite programmes. It was just there. You'd got used to it. It was part of the background. But in *Only Fools and Horses* (a motherless-family sit com), it was a constant source of amusement – something which was intimately related to the plot and characterisation.

> KAREN (32): Oh, that room and those curtains, and the furniture. [*Laughs.*]
> ELIZABETH (35): It's like a junk room.
> TRB: What's the furniture like?
> KAREN: Oh, it's all bits from everywhere, isn't it, all odd bits and pieces.
> DEB (32): It's just how a house would be if there was no woman in it.
> HELEN (28): He puts the pizza in the oven and it comes out like a cinder.
> DEB: But they're still so close.
> JEAN (44): I think it's lovely.
> ELIZABETH: I like the way they stick together, though. You know, I think, God forbid, if ever I died and left my boys, I'd love to think that they could survive, and they could grow up to be adults, with this protection for each other. This deep love, I think, that comes across. And in *that* room.

Viewers were very glad, though, that they didn't have to stay in that room all the time; that the programme, unlike some others, took them outside into a 'public house, or a club, or the markets'. It was welcomed when it happened in other programmes.

> TRB: You quite like it when they go out of the studio?
> JAN (51): Yes, because it's different. It's a relief.
> ALEX (42): Before, when Doris Speed [Annie Walker in *Coronation Street*] was there, Fred used to take her out in the car quite a bit, didn't he, in the Rover.
> JAN: You never saw how far she went.

But not any old outside would do:

> ANDY (27): I mean, in *Dallas* they've got a 'library' shot, which is out from the gate, and you walk up to the house, and then the same bit of cloud in the sky, and that's there two or three times in any one episode.

And at least one radio programme was seen as likely to benefit from staying where it was:

> CARMEL (27): I used to think that *Woman's Hour* was like a magazine where there were little bits and all sorts of things . . .
> JACKIE (37): Yes.
> CARMEL: But it's not now. All the things that they have, they seem too long. You never get enough in that programme now.
> JEAN (38): And they shove it all round the country.

The fact that some dramas were filmed in the actual location, and others mainly studio-based with a few exteriors thrown in, aroused little interest. Perhaps in America there is some concern about the representation of Dallas or Denver or New York on television, but when there is no reality with which to compare the programmes, 'America' becomes a big set with San Francisco and LA merging into one technicolour backdrop. When it came to technical aspects of crime series, it was considered more important to make the scenes of destruction and death more realistic:

> JEZ (31): Well, you can see the pile of empty boxes, you can see the car going along, and the ramp ready for it to go over on its side. I mean, they don't even hide the fact now. [*All talk.*] They must write off these black and white police cars they've got over there, ten a series.

Meanwhile in our nine- and ten-year-old group they were longing for just the kind of spectacle which Jez was finding so contrived.

> MANDY (9): In the children's crime ones they never kill anyone . . . like on *The A-Team* [American children's adventure series], they always end up in prison or something like that.
> JOANNE (10): And all these cars get blown up but you don't ever see anyone dead or injured.
> TRB: And you do in adult ones?
> ALEXANDRA (9): Yes.
> TRB: Blood and things?
> ALEXANDRA: Yes. [*Most agree.*]

Only one small voice spoke up for the innocence of childhood – for the values of a simpler, less realistic, world.

> JESSICA (10): *Yuk!*

Acting: The Very Special Case of *Crossroads*

Television actors are hardly overlooked. Sometimes it seems that almost weekly we are treated to one of those long back-slapping programmes in which a TV personality excitedly introduces a famous TV actor who in turn excitedly presents a gold statuette of a television camera to another famous TV actor. (Cynical viewers looking for excitement on such occasions can only hope that at least one of the lucky winners will turn out to be thoroughly inebriated.)

Despite the fact that this interest in acting and the quality of individual actors is often the stuff of television reviews in the quality press, it is surprisingly absent from most of the discussion of popular television drama. Although the characters from *Dallas* and *Dynasty* and *The Thorn Birds* and *Coronation Street* and *Emmerdale Farm* and *Juliet Bravo* and *Dempsey and Makepeace* can expect to have their pride and passion, their fads and foibles exhaustively analysed, it is rare to hear anyone referred to as a 'good' or a 'poor' actor.

Indeed, only in relation to one popular programme is the quality of acting spontaneously raised, and then promptly condemned: *Crossroads*. Even those who watch regularly find it necessary to concede the existence of this central defect.

> DENISE (43): I have to admit I started watching *Crossroads* through my husband. 'For God's sake, I can't stand this programme. The acting is so crummy.' But because he was always watching, and it was when we eat, I still sort of get like, 'Well, what happened to her then?' It's a love-hate relationship with *Crossroads* and me.

Interestingly, because the acting in *Crossroads* is so energetically discussed, quite dramatic distinctions between good and bad actors are likely to be made.

> TRB: Are they all bad actors?
> JEAN (41): No.
> MARIE (44): That Glenda [mid-twenties with baby Katy-Louise through artificial insemination – married to unemployed decorator] could do with a good slap, couldn't she?
> DENISE: Mac [a black garage mechanic – deserted by wife, good sort, occasionally in trouble] I think is brilliant actually.
> MARIE: I like Mac.
> TRB: Why do you like him?
> MARIE: He's very down to earth, isn't he?
> JEAN: He plays it so naturally.
> MARIE: Yes, if there's an argument going on, he'll interrupt as though it was a proper conversation.

Actors on *Crossroads* (or at least the main ones – there have been nearly 16,000 actors in the series since 1964) have to put up with almost microscopic examination of their characterisation and delighted estimates of their incompetence. Even real foreigners may be accused of not being foreign enough.

> AUDREY (39): But Paul Ross is not very good. [Italian restaurant manager though a real-life Yugoslav, marriage of convenience, lady's man.]

JOAN (36): I don't like him.

AUDREY: I don't know whether he is foreign or not.

AUDREY: Sanjor [sic] whatever his name, Engres [sic] or something like that, that's his name.

JOAN: Yes, it's something like that.

AUDREY: His eyes look foreign. [*All laugh.*]

BETTY (40): His hair annoys me because it always looks a bit scruffy, yet the other week he had it cut and done. I noticed it straight away, it's much better now.

AUDREY: But when he talks, I don't know whether he really is a foreigner.

JOAN: It's like putting it on, in fact.

AUDREY: Yes.

JOAN: Yes, although I think he probably is foreign, I always feel he's putting his accent on.

The notion that actors may be wrestling with discordant biographical features with varying degrees of success is also invoked to explain Miranda, the Sloanish daughter of the ruthless tycoon, J. Henry Pollard.

JOAN: Miranda [office worker at the motel, engagement broken off, has turned down local doctor] – oh yes, she's very efficient.

BETTY: Efficient, and she's really upper class, isn't she?

JOAN: Yes.

BETTY: And she even throws it over when she does her acting, I think.

Everyone seems quite clear about the least successful actor on *Crossroads*: David Hunter. And he is closely followed by Barbara, his wife, who is further indicted for having 'a moveable mole' on her face. ('It really moves about. Sometimes it's here [points to chin] and sometimes here' [points to cheek].)

Not that it's very easy to nail down David Hunter's specific defects.

JOAN: Well, he does, 'er, er, er', like that sometimes I've noticed.

SUSAN: Unless that's the way he has to go. I don't know. It could be good acting.

In fact, as soon as the conversation turns to the details of bad acting by David Hunter or anyone else, it seems that the general reputation of the programme may be more important than the real skills of the actors.

TRB: How can you tell it's so bad?

MARIE: They forget their words all the time.

TRB: Do they?

JEAN: No, that's not true now, it's all changed.

Jean's insistence upon the improvement she'd read about got little attention.

MARIE: I'm sure I could do it better than they could.

And in this Marie was firmly in line with the general opinion. When we asked a national sample of viewers whether or not they thought that they could act better than those in *Crossroads*, a staggering 42 per cent said they could, even though they were considerably more modest about their chances of being able to do such other jobs as read the news (10 per cent) or tell jokes (8 per cent).

DENISE: You're waiting for the mistakes, aren't you?
JEAN: But they're not doing that anymore. They've changed all that now.
JEAN: It's just got a reputation for bad acting.
JEAN: I mean, my husband – if he's watching something, his remarks are, 'God, they must have got these actors from *Crossroads*.'

Loyal viewers are not likely to regard the 'poor' or 'crummy' acting as somehow a reason for abandoning the programme. Although such an attitude would make little sense in the context of the cinema or the theatre, it seems that bad acting in *Crossroads* can be accommodated more or less as though it were a defect in the scenery rather than something which raised serious doubts about the credibility of the entire enterprise. And, in addition, some sort of defence of the thespian failures may be mounted.

DENISE: It's live, you see.
MARIE: Yes, but I think even without the mistakes they should know what they're talking about. They should remember their lines.
TRB: Well, whose fault is it?
DENISE: It's the director.
MARIE: I mean, this is why they're taking out a lot of actors. Because they have got bad ratings. And they want the ratings to go up like *Coronation Street*. All the comedians on telly take the mickey out of *Crossroads*.

Another defence is to concentrate upon those who are labelled 'good actors'. Again there is no ambiguity. Benny is best, with Mac a close second. Benny Hawkins, in fact, is almost as much a part of contemporary folklore as Hilda Ogden: a warm-hearted, innocent, educationally subnormal boy/man – a 'real' enough figure in the series to be the recipient of many requests and invitations relating to his fictional character. (In a recent episode, a Gloucestershire girl who wrote offering to look after his pet mouse was 'adopted' by a *Daily Star* reporter who, after much searching around Birmingham pet shops for a male mouse look-alike, was disconcerted to receive a letter from the girl announcing the arrival of six baby mice.) Neither does the actor (Paul Henry) who plays Benny seem averse to promoting this link between character and reality, having spent some time commercially promoting the distinctive woollen 'Benny hat'.

Objective evidence that these people are played by superior actors is as hard to come by as evidence with which to condemn David Hunter. Nothing about the previous careers of the actors suggests a wide divergence of talent. Indeed, David Hunter (Ronnie Allen) boasts a line of successful television roles including the editor of *Compact*, the football manager in *United* and the rampantly gay

Uncle Quentin in the Comic Strip's Enid Blyton spoof, *Five Go Mad in Dorset*, as well as Old Vic roles like Mountjoy in *Henry V* and Paris in *Troilus and Cressida*. And Allen himself has no doubt that the portrayal requires some skill.

D.H. How much is David Hunter Ronnie Allen?
R.A. Remarkably little if you are talking about actual personalities, remarkably little . . . it's part of my job to make them believe that David Hunter exists, but I actually don't care whether they know that Ronnie Allen exists. In fact I always try to avoid publicity. Interviews I avoid whenever I can because I prefer to be an actor playing a part.
(Dorothy Hobson, *Crossroads*, 1982.)

Perhaps the broad distinctions between the actors are not so much related to acting ability as to the parts they play. Certainly, it was a surprise to most people to find that Paul Henry (Benny) was not quite the character he played.

MARIE: I saw him on *Bullseye* [a quiz game based on darts, hosted by Jim Bowen] and when he spoke I was so amazed because you expected him to sound all daft, but he's quite an intelligent man when he's talking normally.

If you missed the 'reality' of *Bullseye*, then what nicer way to make up for Benny's apparent mental deprivation and overall niceness than to declare him 'best actor'?

The process in relation to Mac is subtly different. As an easy-going garage mechanic he is hardly, as a fictional character, particularly deprived. Indeed, he has been remarkably free of some of the grosser misfortunes visited on other characters (death from drug addiction, accusations of rape, blackmail). But he is black. And that may be enough to ensure his extremely favoured position when viewers hand out their *Crossroads* Oscars.

What, though, are we to make of the overall concern with 'acting' in *Crossroads*? Can it really be marked off in this respect from other relatively low-budget series such as *Gems* or *Sons and Daughters*? Complaints about Crossroads acting may, at least in part, be ways of referring to the inadequacies of the characters or the plot. These are difficult objections for regular viewers to raise. They immediately invite the query 'Why watch then?' Perhaps as long as the actors are blamed, it is still possible to maintain that *Crossroads* itself is fundamentally all right. It is a heavy price for the cast (with the lucky exceptions of Benny and Mac) to have to pay.

Meanwhile the comedians, amateur as well as professional, can carry on using the programme as their favourite butt.

TRB: Can you remember past characters in *Crossroads* who were good actors?
JOANNE (37): Kath Brownlow's husband. But they killed him.
SALLY (41): But did you hear that joke . . . 'No wonder he died, it took them, what was it, from Monday to Thursday before the ambulance got there.' [*All laugh.*]

9

Audience Watching:
The Planners and the Press

MARY (27): We've still got programmes we recorded last year that we haven't looked at yet. Lined up all along the shelf.

Television Meals

Even among the small number of contemporary cinemagoers, disagreements can still break out between couples over the precise time at which they should arrive at a cinema. While one half argues that there's no point in going until 8.25 pm because that's when the main feature starts, the other will express a liking for the trailers and the adverts which makes it necessary to get there twenty minutes earlier. Older people are more inclined to the latter view, a legacy perhaps of the days when a visit to the cinema meant sitting through three to three and a half hours of entertainment which routinely included 'news', trailers, a second feature and the main film.

The scheduling of films on television still parallels the traditional cinema arrangement. Apart from the occasional Saturday or Sunday matinee and the special arrangements for Christmas and bank holidays, they are usually timed to appear at the end of the evening's viewing, after all the news and travelogues and second features have been cleared out of the way. This somehow seemed natural to our viewers when we asked them to devise a perfect schedule for an evening's viewing. Nearly everyone considered that a film – and not a television film – should complete the programme. Audience appreciation figures also suggest that a film is still regarded as the 'main dish' on television. Despite the very high ratings for soap operas, for example, they still lag behind films (most films at least) when viewers are asked to say how much they like them.

Only in our over-seventy discussion group did we find any reservations about the scheduling of this item.

EVA (72): They put films on too late.
MARIE (78): We could all grumble about that. The films start just as we're getting ready for bed: our age group are all too tired to sit and watch.

HELEN (71): Between eight and ten, that's what we want.

JESSE (72): They used to have an afternoon play, and you could iron at the same time, that took all the chores out of evenings.

Other parts of an evening's television viewing also seem to have developed a certain naturalness about them even if they were originally conceived by cynical planners anxious to maximise the ratings for their favoured programmes rather than suit the convenience of the patrons. Some viewers feel that the sort of attention required by some programmes is well suited to the time that they appear. Early evening programmes are snacks which can be nibbled at before the first proper course arrives.

JO (37): The thing is with *Crossroads*, it's good background TV. If you sat down at nine o'clock in the evening and watched it then, with full attention, it wouldn't stand up to critical . . . But at half past six you don't mind so much.

SHIRLEY (29): Well, yes, they put the *Street* on at the right time of the evening, just when people feel ready to get involved with something.

Somehow the programmes can be made to coincide neatly with an opportunity for watching rather than the other way round: it feels as though they have fitted themselves into *your* timetable. So a favourite programme may for some appear to arrive tidily after a meal; for others – equally tidily – during it.

DEREK (29): You've got to watch *Coronation Street*, though, haven't you? It's always on while tea is being dished up. It's well-timed.

It's not straining the analogy to say that many viewers treat an evening's television much like a five-course meal. Some courses can be skipped, some treated cavalierly, others given complete attention; but everybody has a pretty firm idea of the order in which they should arrive, an expectation based on years of familiar scheduling.

After the early evening soaps, for example, our viewers described the ideal as a quiz or a comedy; a mild release of tension which would take the evening round to eight o'clock. Then, an American soap or detective drama; followed by a play or documentary and the *News at Ten* (although when viewers are left to plan their own evening it was surprising how many omitted any mention of news from their schedule. Watching it was something 'you should do'). Finally, to round off the evening in fine style, at about ten thirty or eleven – a film. There was some evidence that if television couldn't provide its own film, this would be the moment when some of the viewers with videos would settle down with the rest of the family to watch the one hired from the corner shop. (The fact that film rental is now a common sideline for the local off-licence or late-night corner shop means that you are able to make the decision to hire at almost any time during the evening.)

For people who approach an evening's viewing with some idea of watching more or less all the way through (although of course rarely on the same channel), the worst feature of scheduling will be the consecutive appearance of two identical programmes – two fish courses. Derek was particularly incensed by ITV's Friday arrangement.

DEREK (57): I think they've saturated the market. It's *Dempsey and Makepeace*, followed by *The Gentle Touch* [British woman detective series]. I mean it's stupid, it's bad planning. You get to the point where you've just had enough of the same thing even though you enjoy that sort of light entertainment. When it's rammed down your throat a lot, you're bound to go off them both, whether they're good or not, because you've simply had enough. You forget which one you're watching. You keep thinking – now, which is this?

NIGEL (51): Yes, in the old days it was *Dixon of Dock Green* and that was it, whereas now there's loads of them every week.

This frequently expressed concern about the need for variety, about one's capacity to watch consecutive programmes on the same subject (or those involving the same format) makes fears about the imminent arrival of 'wall-to-wall' *Dallas* or 'kerb-to-kerb' *Coronation Street* seem unfounded. Viewers, for example, loved comedy programmes, and expressed the wish that there were more around. But when pushed a little into planning an evening, they were relatively abstemious:

TRB: How much comedy can you take?
MARILYN (50): I think the more the better.
TRB: Doesn't it reach a point where you think, not another comedy programme?
MARY (52): Yes, I agree. I wouldn't want too much of it.
JAN (51): No, I wouldn't either.
MARY: Half an hour at a time, or an hour in the evening.
JAN: A sit com and then later on – two hours later – a comedian, that's probably enough in one evening.

And there were good reasons given for this self-denial. Too many soap operas were 'draining', you couldn't manage that amount of involvement, and as Jackie pointed out, comedy perhaps needed even more careful rationing, in that it was hardly bounded by the length of the programme. Some people went on laughing at the jokes and contriving action replays. It rolled over into the rest of life:

JACKIE (37): I think with most of the comedy shows, and *The Young Ones* [anarchic sit com], the kids take bits out – my eldest son particularly. You know, we'll be in the kitchen talking and something will crop up and all of a sudden one of the kids will take over one of those personalities and it brings comedy into the home outside of the programme.

Monday 2 November 1936 *The first evening of all*	*1946*	*1955*
'The world's first public high-definition television service transmitted regularly to people in their own homes starts today, provided by the BBC from Alexandra Palace, North London.'	11 am–12.10 Demonstration film 3 pm Variety 3.30 Film 3.50–4.00 Cartoonists' Corner: Harry S. Michaelson 8.30 pm Radio Forfeits 9.15 The Murder Rap: a television thriller by Gilbert Thomas 10.15–10.25 News (sound only)	3 pm Family Affairs 3.30 In Town To-Night 4.00 Watch with Mother 5.00 Children's Television 7.25 Weather 7.30 News 7.40 Portrait of Alison (episode 3) 8.15 Television Time 9.00 Viewfinder 9.30 View Clues (crossword game) 9.45 Eric Barker in Look At It This Way 10.15 Science Review: Review of scientific films 10.30 News (sound only)
3 pm Opening of the BBC Television Service 3.15 British Movietone News 3.20–3.30 Variety, produced by Dallas Bower, with Adele Dixon, Buck and Bubbles (comedians and dancers) 9 pm Programme summary 9.05 Television comes to London 9.20 Picture Page: a magazine of topical and general interest 9.50–10.00 British Movietone News		

1965	1975	1985
9.35–10.20 am Schools	12.25 The 60, 70, 80 Show	6.00 am Ceefax
10.45–11 Watch with Mother	12.55 News	6.50–9.20 Breakfast Time
11.5–11.55 Schools	1.00 Pebble Mill	10.20 Playschool
1.25 News	1.45–2.00 Chigley	10.40 International Cricket
1.30–1.45 Watch with Mother	2.35–3.00 Schools	1.5 News After Noon
2.5–2.25 Europe – North to South: Norway's Westland	3.58 Regional News	1.35 International Cricket
5.5 Musicstand	4.00 Playschool	3.55 Mop and Sniff
5.30 Look: Ponies of the New Forest	4.25 Pixie and Dixie	4.10 Ivor the Engine
5.55 News	4.35 Jackanory	4.15 Jigsaw
6.5 Town and Around, Weather	4.50 Blue Peter	4.30 Bananaman
6.30 First Impressions	5.15 Sam and the River (a serial)	4.35 Dogtanian and the Three Muskehounds
6.55 Tonight	5.40 Magic Roundabout	4.55 John Craven's Newsround
7.30 Compact: A Testing Time	5.45 News	5.5 Blue Peter
8.00 The Bed Sit Girl: the last half inch	6.00 Nationwide	5.35 Doctor Kildare
8.25 Danny Kaye Show	6.55 Tomorrow's World	6.00 The Six O'Clock News
9.15 News	7.20 Top of the Pops	6.35 Regional News Magazines
News	8.00 The Liver Birds	7.00 EastEnders
9.25 Born Chinese (documentary)	8.30 Are You Being Served?	7.30 Tomorrow's World
10.20 Monitor: Discussion with Norman Mailer	9.00 News	7.55 Top of the Pops
11.5 Association Football	9.25 Play: The Saturday Party with Peter Barkworth	8.25 The Little and Large Show
11.35–12.5 News Summary, followed by The Changing World: an introduction to geology	10.40 Midweek	9.00 The Nine O'Clock News
	11.28 Weather	9.25 Matt Houston
		10.15 Question Time
		11.15 The Learning Machine
		11.40–11.45 Weather

Neither would 'wall-to-wall' *Dallas* – or even a modest version of such a scenario – allow for the pleasure of expectation which is so tied up with soaps and drama series. Supposing, for example, that *Dallas* immediately followed *Dynasty*?

> JO (29): It would be too much for me. Too much.
> KATHY (33): Well, you'd watch them, I suppose. You'd still watch them.
> JO: Yes, but I'd hate the rest of the week. There would be nothing to look forward to.

Alongside the sense that you could get too much comedy, or crime, or soap, were some real fears about another aspect of scheduling – the fear of being short-changed over *Dallas* when the news first came out that Thames Television had outbid the BBC for the right to show it. Newspapers might carry stories about how clever Thames had been or about their new difficulties in persuading other companies to screen it, but a lot of viewers were furious with the idea that anyone should play so fast and loose with something which was a part of their lives. *Dallas* was not a commodity which could be bartered between a few top executives: it had long ago passed into public ownership.

> SUE (31): I'm dreading *Dallas* because of the cuts. You're not going to get the hour.
> FAY (40): It's not going to be on ITV.
> SUE: Well, they said they've got the copyright. The BBC can't show it.
> FAY: No, they're not going to give it to ITV.
> KATHY (33): They're *not*?!
> FAY: No, there was a programme with Terry Wogan and he said, 'I'd like to tell all the viewers that *Dallas* is still with us.'
> SUE: But that was only the eighteen episodes they'd already bought. And after that it's going over to ITV. [*All talk.*]
> FAY: Oh, I'm sorry. I see.
> TRB: So you're going to dread that because of the adverts.
> SUE: Yes, because it's fifty minutes at the moment. Now you're going to get two adverts, which, say, takes five minutes.

It wasn't, however, the intrusion of the advertisers which alarmed Sue so much as another possibility which suddenly dawned on her – the possibility of what the planners might now decide to do:

> SUE: They might . . . because that would be a clever thing to do, wouldn't it?
> BERYL (32): Oh, no!
> TRB: *What?*
> SUE: Put *Dallas* on at the same time as *Dynasty*.
> KATHY: *Oh, they wouldn't do that, would they?*
> SUE: I think they probably would, actually.
> FAY: Oh, I don't think they'd do that, no.
> FAY: But there would be an uproar.

PHILLIPA (27): I don't think they'd care.

SUE: They'd do anything to cut each other up.

Strictly Numbers

Even if *Dallas* is now safely back with the BBC, there are other grounds for such fears. Some time ago ITV was seen as having 'launched a raid' on Terry Wogan's chat-show audience by switching its latest medical soap opera *The Practice* (14 million viewers) into direct competition. Meanwhile *Emmerdale Farm* was moved later in the evening to take on the BBC's *EastEnders*, and the BBC saw off Granada's *Albion Market* with Ronnie Barker's *Open All Hours*.

Programme planners themselves are not particularly happy to talk about this cut-throat aspect of their work – what they call 'strictly numbers scheduling' – preferring to concentrate upon the 'vertical' rather than the 'horizontal' aspect of scheduling. There are certain rules here on all channels. In general, for example, it is assumed that people will not sit down before 9 pm to watch serious documentaries. There's no hard evidence to support this idea (although it does coincide with our viewers' scheduling). It seems to be based on the rather snobbish view that the main audience for such programmes would be middle class – and that, frankly, the middle class haven't finished their dinner by then.

Another general rule is 'to follow like with *almost* like'. Not one comedy immediately after another, but – say – a situation comedy after a comedy quiz show. This maximises the 'inheritance' factor (the number who will stay with that channel to watch the next programme) but of course depends upon the availability of programmes. BBC 2 attracts an exceptionally high audience for *The Young Ones* but the lack of anything else which even remotely resembles it means that inheritance by the next programme is always very low.

The critical points for any scheduler are of course 'the junctions' – the moments when one programme ends and people punching buttons are able to hit the exact beginning of another. At such points co-operation as well as conflict may be observed. It's interesting, for example, to see that the James Burke BBC 1 series to which we referred earlier was not only a critical failure but also a ratings failure. No more evidence is needed of this than the selection by BBC 2 of a strong programme to meet the junction immediately preceding Burke's philosophical hour so that audiences who switched might at least stay with the BBC.

Programme planners claim not to be too affected by what people say they would like to watch during a typical evening. Their long experience in the ratings battles of the past has convinced them that there is a big gap between what viewers *say* and the numbers who *watch*. This is even true when it comes to highly popular programmes. Even avid fans of *Dallas* and *Dynasty* may well miss several of the episodes in any one series. This indeed is the now famous conclusion reached by Goodhardt, Ehrenberg and Collins in *The Television Audience: Patterns of Viewing*, 1980.

Only about half the people who see a repetitive programme one week see the next episode in the following week . . . The repeat-viewing level shows little change from the average level of about 55 per cent even for episodes further than one week apart. But there is some tendency for the repeat-viewing level to increase with the size of the audience.

So even though the very high figures for *Dallas* and *Dynasty* mean that more than half of those who watch one episode will be watching the next, it is still the case 'that few people see all or nearly all the episodes in any extended series'.

These findings are now somewhat dated and have been found too extreme when individual series or programmes have been examined. But there is still strong evidence that people quite dramatically overestimate the number of episodes of a series that they watch. When the IBA, for example, asked viewers about the seven-part royal historical series, *Edward and Mrs Simpson*, they discovered that 31 per cent said they had seen all seven episodes. That at least was the claim. But according to JICTAR, BARB's predecessor for ratings, the figure was really 9 per cent.

Perhaps this feeling that we've watched more than we have is a tribute to the 'backstory mechanism' of television series: their ability to fill us in on what has already happened. But it may also be connected to our strong views about the programme. If we want to enthuse publicly about it, we may feel somehow disqualified if we admit that we have missed a couple of episodes (even though, as Goodhardt et al. insist, our reasons may be perfectly good: *'failure to repeat view is generally* a matter of variable social habits rather than a reaction to programme content'). The new practice of repeating episodes on, say, the following Sunday – as with *Blott on the Landscape* (an adaptation of a Tom Sharpe farce) and the omnibus *EastEnders* – will no doubt do something to bring viewers' claims about repeat viewing more into line with reality. For *Archers* fans there was actually an additional element of suspense in the Sunday omnibus edition.

> TRB: Is that a real advantage, that you can catch up on Sunday?
> JAN (57): Oh yes.
> PATRICIA (49): But the other advantage is that you don't have to listen to it only twice: you can hear it *three* times if you want to. [*All laugh.*]
> JAN: Yes.
> PATRICIA: And if you notice, they take out a little bit from each one. And it's interesting to try and guess which bit they have missed out in the omnibus edition.

Times A'Shifting

Nasty cynical programme planners can, of course, now be thwarted by all those with video cassette recorders. And although the latest evidence is that sales of these are now beginning to fall quite dramatically (dropping from 2.2 million units in 1983 to 1.5 million units in 1984), there is no indication that they are being less employed in those homes (about 26 per cent of all TV households) which already have them. So much so that viewers felt no hesitation in blaming the BBC for not bearing such considerations in mind when they adjusted their schedules. It was almost as though the video cassettes were seen as part of the television package. Obviously television companies should adapt to them.

> SUSAN (41): What annoys me is that they never ever put programmes out on time; when you've set your video, you want them to keep to time.
> JACKIE (33): Yes, that's right.
> MO (27): They do better on ITV. Because of the advertisements.
> JANICE (31): Yes, they're very strict with their times. They'll never show the last set of a tennis match. They stop filming and schedule it for afterwards.
> MO: They've got to do that, because it's their livelihood.
> MARIAN (34): Yes, but they could do away with one advert.
> MO: But people are paying the money to have them on at that exact time. They can't change them just because of a programme.

It's been amusingly suggested by Peter Fiddick that video cassette recorders do much to reduce 'television guilt' – the uneasy feeling that one should have watched this or that worthy programme but failed to do so. If, so the theory goes, a programme is recorded, then this guilt is reduced, even though the recording is never subsequently watched. We didn't ask our viewers directly about their use of this technique but there was certainly evidence of unplayed tapes.

> MARY (27): We've still got programmes we recorded last year that we haven't looked at yet. Lined up all along the shelf.
> TRB: You find it difficult to find the time to watch these recordings?
> HELEN (28): Oh yes.
> MARY: You get up early on Sunday morning specially – but then it's *Rub-a-dub-tub* [a children's programme], so you're blown out again. *That's that*. Back on the shelf.

But Mary probably gets to watch most of the material she records off-air. Surveys carried out by AGB (Audits of Great Britain) in the period 1981–83 showed that 84 per cent is eventually viewed. In fact, in some homes, the problem with video recorders may relate more to attempts to stop certain people viewing – especially children.

> BETTY (27): There was a time I videoed various things and then I realised my six-year-old could work it himself. He'd take it out, put it in, and I'd find him watching *The A-Team*.

At least Betty recognised *The A-Team* when she saw it. Deb, on the other hand, yielded to the requests of her seven-year-old and recorded a programme she'd never seen herself:

DEB (32): Now my son kept saying to me, 'Will you video *The Young Ones?*' and I really didn't know what the programme was. And I couldn't believe it. I just merrily switched on and recorded *The Young Ones* and he was getting up before I was getting up in the morning and watching.

TRB: What is *The Young Ones?*

DEB: Well, I'd never actually watched it, but one of my daughters was off school one day and she said to me, 'Can we put the video on, *The Young Ones?*' I switched on, walked out of the room, came back and I said, 'What are you watching?' and I couldn't believe it. It was terrible. With videos, you say, 'Oh yes,' you think it's fine, *The Young Ones*. I mean it doesn't sound anything, does it, not the name. And all his friends at school are watching it so I just thought, Oh well, it's a kids' programme. But although it's on at nine o'clock it's not really a kids' programme at all. I think this is the trouble with video. It changes the times of everything.

One of the first things that viewers brought up when we discussed video recording was the importance of films. And this is re-emphasised by surveys showing that films are the most likely programmes to be recorded off-air. What's more, along with a few of the major series – *The Thorn Birds, Brideshead Revisited* – they will be stored for repeated viewing in the future. Of course, prerecorded films can also readily be hired for round about a pound a night, and no one who has seen customers walking away from rental shops with their six to eight films for the weekend (two or three for the children and the rest for mother and father) can doubt the importance of this use of the video cassette recorder. One recent study of this practice (Gray, *Women and Video*, 1985) provides some evidence that it is losing ground. Although groups of women do hire films to watch together in the afternoon, and although the occasional extended family may gather on a Sunday afternoon for 'film-time' round the video, there's no sign of this becoming a common domestic ritual.

Whether or not viewers use their video cassette recorders for time-shift or prerecorded material, it does not seem to replace the time devoted to normal television viewing. Extra time has to be found to accommodate the extra viewing. And it doesn't look as though many people relish this idea. When we asked our national sample, 'How much TV do you intend to watch in future? More/Less/About the same', 90 per cent said 'About the same'. Present trends suggest this may only be a pious hope.

Hey Barb-A-Ree-Barb

No doubt it is our guilt about the time we already devote to viewing which leads us to claim that we watch considerably less television than the national average figures suggest that we do. Members of our groups admitted readily to watching television a great deal: it was, after all, on the basis of this admission that they were recruited in the first place. But although the set might well be on for up to twenty-eight hours a week, they were, they said, not watching it for that long. And neither were their friends.

In these circumstances there is perhaps a natural bias in favour of the statistics. Their averages and trends look so precise and hard when set against the denials of a few hundred viewers. But behind those rows of figures, those rivers of statistics which pour into the offices of television and advertising executives each month, sit another group of ordinary viewers: the BARB panel. Not that it's all that easy to discover what they – or their predecessors – actually do. As we discovered, finding the details behind the statistics can be a long and confusing task.

'Is that the IBA?'

'Yes.'

'So sorry to bother you, but we're having a little difficulty understanding how you get all the actual data for your ratings. You know, the figures which say that this number of people watched a particular programme. It seems a little confusing – and, well, mysterious.'

'It's all changed.'

'What's that?'

'The basis of the figures has changed.'

'Ah.'

'You see, the first collection of figures for those watching programmes began back in 1952 when the BBC combined a head count with some qualitative research.'

'Sort of interviews?'

'Exactly. About 2250 daily interviews with people about their previous night's viewing. They varied the panel every day. In one year they'd question 800,000 people.'

'Sounds thorough – but a little primitive.'

'Quite so. That's why when ITV came along, it adopted a system pioneered in America by A. C. Nielsen Inc. of Chicago. Instead of all that interviewing you took a representative panel of 2650 homes and connected a meter to each television set, and in addition gave the viewers a diary to fill in quarter-of-an-hour periods – just as an additional check.'

'That was carried out by ITV?'

'Not ITV itself. But a company called AGB (Audits of Great Britain) for JICTAR – that's the Joint Industry Committee for Television Audience Research.'

'Of course.'

'It's all much simpler now.'

'Ah.'

'Since 1981 we've all gone BARB – that's the Broadcasters Audience Research Board, which now on behalf of *both* BBC and ITV commissions AGB – you'll remember AGB?'

'That's the Audience . . .'

'Yes, yes; they use a system called AMS – d'you want to know what that stands for?'

'Frankly, no.'

'Well, anyway, it involves 3000 households throughout the UK – that's, say, 9000 individual people – and in each home there's electronic equipment which monitors whether the set is on or off, which channel it's tuned to, and when individuals are watching.'

'How can it know that?'

'This is the cunning bit. Each individual in the household has to press a button on a handset to show when viewing starts and when it ends and all this information goes into the meter. And then in the middle of the night . . .'

'Yes?'

'A computer rings up and interrogates the meter, which tells it immediately who was watching what at each minute of the previous day.'

'What about people who don't live in homes – you know, prisons, boarding schools, ships, hospitals, the army . . . ?'

'Forget them.'

'Forget them?'

'Forget them. We only do homes. But listen, this new technique is so sophisticated that by the time all the meters were installed, in December 1984, we found that viewing figures were 25 per cent higher than we'd thought.'

'Sounds like good news.'

'Only to the programme makers. The advertisers suddenly realised they could spend less money and still reach the same number of people. All right?'

'Just one last thing. How do you know that people press their buttons conscientiously? Do they get paid for taking part?'

'Sorry – that's secret.'

'Could we have a word with one of the panel, perhaps?'

'Absolutely not. In fact, if any contact is made with them by outside individuals, they're declared "contaminated" and struck off the panel.'

'Gosh. It's just that so much seems to depend on people – quite ordinary people – remembering to press the button whenever they're watching.'

'And *stop* watching.'

'Yes. And to get everyone else in the house to press as well. Do they all have their own handset?'

'No, but each child over four has their own button on the panel. And there's one for guests who arrive.'

'I see.'

'And, oh yes, I forgot to mention that BARB is a limited company jointly owned by the BBC and ITCA. I expect you'd like to know what ITCA means. Hello? *Hello.*'

TRB: On what channel was *Brideshead Revisited*?

CARMEL (27): That was BBC.

EWA (38): ITV.

LENA (29): BBC.

ANNA (34): ITV.

JACKIE (37): ITV.

JEAN: BBC, I thought.

TRB: Does it sound as though it *should* be on BBC?

JEAN: Yes.

GRETA (41): I thought it sounded a bit like it should be BBC.

LENA: I think the BBC generally do classical serials.

TRB: And *Jewel in the Crown*?

ANNA: ITV.

EWA: BBC, I would have said.

Our ideas about television channels are important in a number of ways. It may mean that we try one channel rather than another when we first flick on the set. Once hooked on the programme that we find there, we may, after its conclusion, decide to stay with the same channel for what follows. It is something which can, of course, be encouraged by come-ons for the next programme in the form of 'suspense' and continuity announcements. ('Parts of northwest England have been without window cleaners for the last month because of a local strike. What exactly does it mean for those people who suddenly find they can no longer see their own back gardens? Find out after the break.')

This simple preference for one channel may grow into a 'channel loyalty' which not only ensures that we tune into one channel more readily than any other, but that we feel the programmes it transmits to be more 'our' sort of programme, and, what's more, are prepared to disregard any evidence which conflicts with this channel image. We think of ourselves somehow as BBC people, or Channel 4 people, or ITV people. We believe we know what their products are like.

This is what lay behind our question about *Brideshead Revisited*. For although this production was widely advertised as an ITV Granada production, although each episode was shot through with telltale commercials, it was still widely regarded as a BBC series. It wasn't only our viewers who were likely to make this mistake. Research carried out by the IBA showed that 39 per cent of viewers thought that *Brideshead Revisited* was on BBC.

This research did not ask for the reasons behind this dramatic reallocation but perhaps an important factor was the aristocratic country-house setting for the series – an upmarket ambience which is part of BBC's channel image. Of course this is not to deny the possibility that viewers decided it was a BBC programme on the basis of its technical and dramatic excellence. At least one viewer who got the channel right was able to do so precisely because of his strongly developed sense of channel image (one which allowed him to watch only one channel habitually and yet know perfectly well what was happening on the others). 'It's the first TV on ITV that I've watched. It was excellent in all aspects and very different from the usual rubbish on this channel.'

It must have been bad enough for Granada Television to see *Brideshead Revisited* sliding over to the BBC side, but they fared only slightly better when viewers were asked to allocate another Granada production, *Jewel in the Crown*. At least this time only just over a quarter considered that the BBC were responsible for the series. But worse was to come.

During the time that *Jewel in the Crown* was being transmitted, a row blew up over the BBC's decision to broadcast *The Thorn Birds*, a dramatic series starring Richard Chamberlain as a priest disturbed by the strength of his passion for Rachel Ward. This was widely referred to by critics as 'second-rate schmaltz' and 'not worthy of the BBC', who were described as having been artistically and creatively upstaged by the excellence of the Granada series.

If anyone at the BBC was embarrassed by such comparisons, then some comfort was soon on its way. Whereas 39 per cent of viewers between thirty-five and forty-four believed *The Thorn Birds* to have been on BBC, 45 per cent decided that it was on independent television. Our viewers were well in line with national trends.

> TRB: Do you remember what channel *The Thorn Birds* was on?
> JOHN (42): ITV.
> ALAN (42): ITV.
> TRB: Well, actually it was on BBC. Why do you all say ITV?
> BOB (51): Because most of the rubbish is ITV.

It's true that *Brideshead Revisited* and *The Thorn Birds* provided dramatic examples of how ready people are to reallocate programmes to bring them into line with channel image, but the tendency extends to other drama series and to quite different types of programme. For instance, 37 per cent of the IBA sample believed that you could see *University Challenge* on BBC (in fact it is Granada), while 28 per cent expected to catch *The Dukes of Hazzard* (an American comedy car-chase series) on ITV (it is BBC 1). All in all, eighteen programmes were tested in this way: in each case the percentage indicates the number of people who ascribed the programme incorrectly.

ITV PROGRAMMES	BBC PROGRAMMES
Brideshead Revisited (39%)	*The Thorn Birds* (42%)
University Challenge (37%)	*The Dukes of Hazzard* (28%)
The Far Pavilions (24%)	*Angels* (24%)
Kennedy (22%)	*Blankety Blank* (20%)
The Jewel in the Crown (21%)	*The Cleopatras* (13%)
Auf Wiedersehen, Pet (13%)	*The Borgias* (12%)
Shelley (12%)	*Top of the Pops* (7%)
Knight Rider (8%)	*Life on Earth* (5%)
Crossroads (3%)	*Panorama* (4%)

The trouble with this research is that although it suggests that the *names* of programmes may be playing a part in misleading viewers, it could always be the case that the ascriptions are being made on the basis of known *quality* – hence the persistent idea that the BBC (or ITV) makes better programmes. If then *University Challenge* is thought to be well made, it must be BBC – rather than being incorrectly allocated by a third of viewers on the basis of the 'BBC' word 'university'.

We decided to disentangle these factors by asking a somewhat larger sample (3000 compared to the IBA's 1500) to look at a number of forthcoming programme titles and say on which channels they would be appearing. In all cases the titles were completely fictional and no production plans existed (although after some news of this research was reported in an academic journal we were flattered to receive a request from one producer asking if he might indeed use one title. We will not aggravate the situation by revealing the title or the producer's provenance). Our titles and their allocation by viewers to BBC and ITV were:

	BBC	ITV
Westminster Frolics	65%	35%
San Diego	30%	70%
Understanding the Mind	85%	15%
Postman's Knock	25%	75%
The Trelawneys of Hereford	76%	24%
Laughter Unlimited	22%	78%

We had spent some time trying to devise a title which would split the vote – one which summoned up the BBC's image of establishment sobriety as much as it did ITV's friendlier, more light-hearted stereotype. In this we failed. Although *Westminster Frolics* brought viewers' ideas more closely together than any other title, it seemed that the word *Westminster* was quite enough to cancel out the promise of the *Frolics*. It went firmly to the BBC.

There was not much indication that this tendency to read off channel from title was likely to decrease in the near future. When we tried out the titles on a group made up of fourteen- and fifteen-year-olds, they subscribed even more readily to the stereotypes than the national sample.

Even when we move away from specific programmes to general types, viewers, according to IBA research, have no difficulty in deciding whether BBC or ITV would 'do the best job'.

BBC 1 thought to be better

Plays	Arts
Science & nature	Current affairs
Documentaries	Dramatic serials
Educational programmes	Sport
National news	Religious programmes

ITV thought to be better

Films from the cinema	Adventure/Police series
Entertainment/Variety	Soap operas/Serials
Comedy	Local news

But what is it about ITV or BBC which promotes these images – apart from the much repeated distinction between the serious/stuffy nature of the BBC and the light-hearted/rubbishy character of ITV? We asked our national sample to tell us how much they agreed or disagreed with a series of statements. ('Don't knows' are excluded from the percentages given.)

- *Independent television is more friendly than BBC TV.*
  (30% agree; 30% disagree)

When the BBC carried out research into why some viewers preferred ITV's *News at Ten* to the BBC's *Nine o'Clock News*, friendliness stood out as one important reason. But it didn't seem to extend to overall channel image. Viewers were equally likely to find the BBC 'friendly'.

- *BBC TV has more intelligent programmes than ITV.*
  (47% agree; 24% disagree)

Although a clear majority agreed with this statement, they were not prepared to go along with the more insidious suggestion that

- *ITV programmes are easier to understand than BBC.*
  (21% agree; 32% disagree)
- *The BBC tends to ignore ordinary people's taste.*
  (23% agree; 47% disagree)

Neither did this 'elitist' statement find any support at all, with twice as many disagreeing as agreeing.

Even when we came to those attributes which are often regarded as lying at the core of the BBC's appeal –

- *The BBC is better than ITV at maintaining British values.*
  (36% agree; 27% disagree)

- *In times of crisis the BBC is more reliable than ITV.*
  (32% agree; 32% disagree)

– there was little sign that viewers now held radically different opinions about the two channels.

All this would suggest that although there are still strongly entrenched ideas about what is a 'BBC' and what is an 'ITV' programme, these are no longer based on an 'establishment' idea of the BBC or a 'populist' notion of ITV. The BBC is more or less as 'ordinary' and 'friendly' and 'understandable' as ITV, whereas ITV is just as 'reliable in a crisis' and nearly as 'good at maintaining British values' as the BBC. What remains is the tendency to ascribe most serious-minded programmes to the BBC – irrespective of their origin.

What is most interesting, however, is that this apparently conveys no information about channel loyalty. For the latest IBA research suggests that people have now accommodated the existence of four television channels by becoming utterly feckless. They will happily seek out the programmes they want to see on any of the four channels without any sense that Channel 4 or ITV is not for them. The notion that there might be 'races' of BBC 2 or ITV people is no longer tenable. Of course, some may declare themselves to be Channel 4 watchers or BBC 2 types but their viewing habits provide no support for such protestations of allegiance. There are two very small exceptions to all this: a section of the 'unskilled working class' still show an 'undiscriminating' loyalty to ITV, but there are signs that this is declining. (A source other than the IBA believes that it will be accelerated by the growing availability of remote-controlled television and the channel having these facilities.) Finally there is some evidence that older people are slightly more reluctant to tune to Channel 4.

This readiness to move between channels does not, of course, mean that we spend the same proportion of time with each one. But even here there are signs that the 'minority' channels of BBC 2 and Channel 4 are beginning to become regular parts of our viewing pattern. Whereas in the period January to April 1983, Channel 4 only took 3.9 per cent of viewing, and BBC 2 10.9 per cent, in January to April 1985 the figures were 7.5 per cent and 11.1 per cent respectively. This means that together they have raised their share of viewing from 15 per cent to nearly 20 per cent.

A More Distant Image

As something of an antidote to all this 'ordinariness' and 'friendliness' which viewers appeared to perceive on television channels, there is the interesting case of Radio Three. Regular listeners to this minority station (mainly middle class, male, over fifty-five and resident in the southeast) often seem able to regard the very lack of close association between the presenters and themselves as a reason for feeling closely identified with the output. In these circumstances it becomes a compliment to be able to say of the broadcasters:

> 'They are not really there at all.'
> 'You could just imagine them in some little turret somewhere with just their record player.'
> 'Just a teeny bit unworldly . . . my husband describes them as a mermaid in a sea cave . . . it's lovely.'

It's not surprising that some of the less regular listeners find the whole thing too distant and anonymous for their taste.

> The type of voice is very similar to what's used on BBC TV if somebody's died . . . Always solemn . . . And the pauses at the end of the thing. You always get a great long pause so people can go 'Mmm, wasn't that good' or something.
> (BBC Audience Research, Special Report, *Radio 3*, May 1984.)

Radio Times, September 28, 1923.

THE RADIO TIMES

THE OFFICIAL ORGAN OF THE B.B.C.

Vol. 1. No. 1.   [Registered at the G.P.O. as a Newspaper.]   EVERY FRIDAY.   Two Pence.

OFFICIAL PROGRAMMES
OF
THE BRITISH BROADCASTING COMPANY.

For the Week Commencing
SUNDAY, SEPTEMBER 30th.

LONDON	CARDIFF
BIRMINGHAM	NEWCASTLE
MANCHESTER	GLASGOW

SPECIAL CONTENTS:

LORD GAINFORD'S MESSAGE TO LISTENERS.

P. P. ECKERSLEY ON "SIMULTANEOUS BROADCASTING."

A SONG OF ANCIENT CHINA.

GOSSIP ABOUT ARTISTES.

WIRELESS HUMOUR.

THE "UNCLES'" CORNER.

LETTERS FROM LISTENERS.

WHAT'S IN THE AIR?

By ARTHUR R. BURROWS, Director of Programmes.

HULLO, EVERYONE!
We will now give you *The Radio Times*. The good *new* times. The Bradshaw of Broadcasting.

May you never be late for your favourite wave-train.

Speed 186,000 miles per second; five-hour non-stops.

Family season ticket: First Class, 10s. per year.

*   *   *   *

[*All this, presumably, is "by the way": not "In the Air."*—EDITOR.]

*   *   *   *

So I am instructed to write about programmes and not "talk like an Uncle"!

*   *   *   *

Let me tell you all about our plans.

Wait, though! I—I'm just a little bit uneasy. My predecessor in the broadcasting business made a mistake of this character with painful consequences.

You probably remember the incident.

A Company, with distinguished Directors, having lofty ambitions, established a power-station at Westminster. Despite quite a stirring programme there were no oscillations, owing to Government intervention. The Director (Guido Fawkes) and his colleagues somehow lost their heads, and the long-anticipated report failed to materialize.

When WE broadcast Parliament—and it's bound to happen this century or next—the process will be a more dignified one than that planned in 1605. The fate of the culprits may be another matter.

*   *   *   *

Perhaps, after all, it is by stepping clear of the pitfalls of ancient and modern history that British broadcasting has got so far without any serious mishap. (Touch wood!)

*   *   *   *

Do you know that from November 14th last year until now, with only six out of eight projected stations in operation, and despite opposition from some of the "Big Noises" in the entertainment industry, we have shaken the ether of Great Britain for approximately 8,000 hours and have transmitted roughly 1,700 distinct evening programmes. How this ether-shaking process has been carried through so uninterruptedly is for my unrepentant colleague, Captain Eckersley, to tell (possibly with Morse and reactive obligato). The fact remains that if our plans for the next twelve months go through, even in their present basic form, we shall add to this record 2,500 other distinct programmes, consisting of 16,500 hours of ever-changing musical, dramatic, and instructive entertainment.

[Photo]   "Faulkner & Benfield.   Mr. ARTHUR R. BURROWS.

*   *   *   *

Two thousand five hundred distinct programmes!

[*Perhaps it IS as well that your comments are inaudible.*]

And some folk pressing for a six-hour day!

*   *   *   *

Have you ever played jigsaw?

At 2, Savoy Hill, London, W.C.2, is the biggest jigsaw puzzle yet invented, railway time-tables *not* excepted. It goes by the name of simultaneous broadcasting, a process which comes into existence so far as our musical programmes are concerned on Monday next, October 1st. For some weeks now the writer and others of the same Department, all in varying states of mental distress, have pored over this latest brain-teaser, trying to coax a refractory twiddly-bit into some time-space for which it was never intended.

(Continued in column 3, page 2)

The front page of the Radio Times, *28 September 1923 – the first issue included an item entitled 'Gossip about artistes'.*

Still, if some respite is needed from the buttonholing intimacy of much television and popular radio, from the persistent enthusiasm about forthcoming events, the energetic transformation of the ordinary and contingent into the extraordinary and meaningful, then Radio Three might be the answer. Certainly there is no sign that it is likely to be deflected from its task by the mere opportunity to sensationalise. As one regular listener prophetically caricatured their style:

> 'World War III has just broken out and after the next programme we'll be going into more detail.'

Gathering the TV News

Apart from the statisticians and schedulers, there is another large group of professionals who monitor the slightest shifts in the audience's loyalty to personality, programme and channel – the television press corps.

> MAUREEN (39): I read it all up in the papers . . . like on a Monday they have a little block in the paper that tells you all that's going to happen with every soap opera.
> MOLLY (41): I get the paper so I know exactly what's going to happen to all the people and what the story's going to be about that week.

It has been said that the tabloid newspapers are fleas upon the back of television, that their remorseless daily articles about each and every aspect of soap-opera plots, their inside stories on TV personalities, their gossip about the love life of the latest hero or villain, is all secondary to what occurs on the screen. But increasingly the relationship seems more symbiotic than parasitic. The close correlation between the readership of the popular dailies and the viewers of popular television, the greater devotion of television companies to hand-outs and tip-offs, and the immediate assumption by stars and personalities that their biographies should be in the public domain, mean that many television programmes can now be fully comprehended only by those who have mugged up on their past. Our knowledge about the characters is critical to our understanding. As Charlotte Brunsdon says (in Masterman, ed., *Television Mythologies*, 1984): '. . . these stories of "real-life" run as a kind of sub-text, or parallel soap to the one we watch on television. This sub-text is not kept separate when watching. The knowledge that you have about particular characters "in real life" feeds into and inflects the pleasure of soap watching.'

The same ebb and flow between fiction and reality characterises the tabloid treatment of soap stars. In the top example overleaf, it is genuinely difficult to know which domain is being described, as we shift between 'real' love and real mothers, and real husbands and their fictional equivalents. Even at the end of it, we're still not quite certain if Linda Gray is criticising Larry Hagman's sexual abilities (particularly as a picture caption declares: 'no super stud'). In this sense, of course, it is probably ideal copy.

★★★★★★★★★★★★★★★★★★★★★★★★★★★★★★★★

SOAP SECRETS WITH GEOFF BAKER

BED - HOPPING JR is not the super stud he thinks he is.

Who says so ? The girl who should know—Linda Gray, who plays his wife Sue Ellen in Dallas.

She says that if she was really married to the Texas oil baron, he wouldn't be man enough for her.

Strength

Lovely Linda explains that any husband who plays about with other women as much as JR wouldn't have enough strength left to keep her happy.

"I'm a very physical person," she adds. "I need lots of love from a man.

"A guy like JR wouldn't provide anywhere near enough for my liking."

☐ INCIDENTALLY, I hear JR will soon have **TWO** mums in Dallas.

(Daily Star, 29 April 1985)

JR's not man enough for me, says Sue Ellen

For in addition to Miss Ellie, it's whispered that Larry Hagman's real mother — actress Mary Martin — will be joining the cast.

Mary, 71, was once tipped to land the part of Miss Ellie.

She didn't get it, but I hear she has now won another part and will be acting alongside her son in scenes to come.

JR ... no super stud

WISE UP ON THE SOAPS

★ BRIAN and Gail are happily back together again, but they have one big problem.

How do they tell Ivy they won't be living with her any more in **Coronation Street (ITV, today and Wed, 7.30pm)?** Meanwhile Vera Duckworth's silver lurex dress is set to wow the town hall dance.

CROSSROADS (ITV, times and days vary). Barbara Hunter confronts husband David as he loses heavily in the casino. Joe MacDonald takes over at the garage when Harry

One snag for Gail

Maguire leaves after his son's death. **EMMERDALE FARM (ITV, times and days vary).** Jackie Merrick is recovering from his motorbike accident, but Alan Turner still feels local hostility. Storyline varies in London and Anglia.

EASTENDERS (BBC 1, Tues and Thurs 7pm, repeat Sun 2pm). Temporary barman Lofty discovers that pretty Sharon has been making anonymous phone calls to Sue.

THE PRACTICE (ITV, Fri 7pm, Sun 7.15 pm). Janis Jones is rushed to hospital on the back of her boyfriend's motorbike when her baby is on the way. **BROOKSIDE (Channel 4, today and Tues 8pm, repeat Sat 5.05pm).** Terry is becoming even more jealous of girlfriend Michelle's relationship with her smoothie dance teacher. **DALLAS (BBC 1, Wed 8.10pm).** Pam and Sue Ellen's new-found friendship is cemented when they fly off to Hong Kong together. **DYNASTY:** Postponed due to next Saturday's Eurovision Song Contest.

(Sun, 29 April 1985)

172

Alexis on the defensive...!

DYNASTY: Alexis dismissed her defence lawyers to plead her own case and was found . . . guilty of first degree murder. Steven was called to testify that he saw her push Mark to his death. Dominique came to the rescue of Denver Carrington.

DALLAS : Pam felt she could trust no-one until she was offered an unexpected helping hand by Sue Ellen. JR in a bid to win the Ewing Oil war, tried to sell off his assets secretly.

EMMERDALE FARM : Seth Armstrong opened the NY Estates Social Club. Alan Turner was made distinctly unwelcome. Tom Merrick has outstayed his welcome at Emmerdale.

CORONATION STREET : Brian and Gail were reconciled. Kevin Webster agreed to repair Terry's car in return for partnership in the removal business. Vera Duckworth was looking for a design for a dress that would 'make Joan Collins look like a lollipop lady'.

THE PRACTICE: Chemical works owner Jack McClelland faced criticism from victims of the explosion including attacks from its blinded hero. Fifteen-year-old Janice Jones had her baby and adopted teenager Nick Armstrong met his natural mother.

CROSSROADS : Barbara told Jill her marriage is probably finished. Kevin confessed he had been sacked as trainee salesman. Paul told Miranda he was thinking about applying for a job in Torquay.

BROOKSIDE : Heather and Tom Curzon spent their weekend in Portugal. Damon gave up his career as a gorilla and Pat ran into opposition over his kissogram service.

EASTENDERS : With Den on holiday, Angie enlisted Ethel's skills to start her pub lunch scheme. Doctor Legg asked Debbie to lead the campaign against demolition. Pauline was worried about the disappearance of their teenage son, Mark.

THE ARCHERS : Tony Archer caught Brian and Caroline in a passionate embrace and spread the rumour that they were having an affair. Phil was outraged by a potted palm and Eddie Grundy sang his new record, Clarrie, at the Goat and Nightgown Country and Western evening.

(*Daily Mail*, 29 April 1985)

CORONATION STREET: Gail and Brian got together again and resolved to set up a home of their own. Kevin was tempted to repair the Duckworth car by the offer of a partnership in the moving business with Terry and Curly, and Ivy agreed she would like to see more of George Wardle.

CROSSROADS: Barbara felt her marriage to David was at an end, but made a final effort and persuaded him to stop his obsessive gambling. The funeral of Pete Maguire went ahead. Glenda told out-of-work Kevin she was willing to make a fresh start in Canada.

BROOKSIDE: The

(Daily Star, 29 April 1985)

naughty - night - nurse kissogram enraged Sandra. Harold took legal advice about Edna's bet and was told he could object to the renewal of the bookie's licence. Heather grew closer to Tom in Portugal, but was upset when he said he had no time to fall in love.

EMMERDALE FARM: Jackie turned the corner to recovery. Even though the police have no case against Alan Turner, he was cold-shouldered by the villagers. Amos worried about the threat of beer sales at the new social club, and Jack gave Matt the go-ahead for the new lamb shelter.

EASTENDERS: The campaign against demoli-

tion of part of the square got a mixed reception from the residents. The Fowlers were desperately worried about the disappearance of their teenage son Mark.

THE PRACTICE: Roy Hodder, hero of the chemical explosion, faced blindness. His wife demanded that the factory should not be rebuilt. Schoolgirl Janis Jones gave birth, but her mother still refused to let her keep the baby.

DALLAS: Sue Ellen kicked J.R. where it hurts most when he tried to make love to her against her wishes. But it hurt him even more when evidence which he thought proved Ewing Oil belonged only to the family turned out to strengthen Cliff and Jamie's case. Pam supected that Cliff was behind the Mark plot.

DYNASTY: Steven told the court he saw his mother push Mark off the balcony. But Krystle cast doubt on her guilt. Alexis (Joan Collins) sacked her lawyers and faced the verdict alone. Jeff was still obsessed with the memory of Fallon. Alexis was found guilty.

GEMS: Financial problems at the company began to upset the staff, and Stephen and Alan pinned their hopes on

ALEXIS . . . verdict

help from the bank manager.

SONS & DAUGHTERS (Granada): Patricia fought to save her marriage.

SONS & DAUGHTERS (Thames): Back from overseas, Jennifer began to make her presence felt.

ISAURA THE SLAVE GIRL (new Channel Four soap): Isaura decided to fight for her freedom, and tried to find out who her parents were.

And for radio fans . . .

THE ARCHERS: Elizabeth made more expensive purchases for the new bathroom, and Shula was annoyed when the boss's nephew began to throw his weight about at work. Tony told his mother that Caroline and Brian were having an affair.

We decided to collect all the material about television which appared in the tabloid press – *Daily Mail, Daily Express, Daily Mirror, Sun, Daily Star* – and their Sunday equivalents for the seven days from Saturday 27 April to Friday 3 May 1985.

Most of the material fell into four broad categories.

STARS (31 articles)
– personal and family background of the stars
– rise and fall of the stars
– love life of performers
– scandal (crime, divorce, money problems of the stars)
– stars on stars

PROGRAMME DETAILS (26 articles)
– soap content controversy and plot
– programme revamps (new hostesses, new studios, new formats)
– background to programmes
– TV mistakes

TELEVISION COMMENTARY (106 articles)
- previews/reviews
- soap updates
- battle of the ratings
- programme enthusiasm and programme abuse

'EDITORIALS' (11 editorials)
- editorial comments on TV
- social effects and the impact of TV

(See below for detailed examples.)

THE STARS

'EastEnder Mark in Shock Sacking'

'Teenage *EastEnders* star David Scarboro has been sacked from telly's newest soap opera . . . Scarboro said he was sacked after he accidentally missed a day's filming' (*Sun*, 27 April 1985)

'Sultry Selina Scott is being treated like something akin to royalty down at the Beeb these days . . she's one of the few remaining jewels in the BBC's rather tarnished crown . . . so the message inside the corporation is clear, "what Selina wants, Selina gets". . .' (*Sunday People*, 28 April 1985)

'Sexy Joan Collins may quit *Dynasty* for an even bitchier role in a new soap series . . . as Helene Juno, the ruthless boss of the world's biggest magazine empire . . . in *Sins*' (*Sunday Mirror*, 28 April 1985)

'TV personality Anna Ford, who expects her second child this week, is to give women advice on birth control, in a radio programme' (*Daily Mirror*, 1 May 1985)

'A storm erupted yesterday over a "rogue" computer that revealed details of the £350,000 a year the BBC pays Terry Wogan' (*Sun*, 3 May 1985)

'Texan beauty Deborah Shelton is fed up with the ogling she is getting in *Dallas*. She considered it an insult and says: "I don't want to be that 'pretty lady', as they call me. I'm an actress." The incredibly pretty Deborah, who plays Mandy Winger, says even her husband, composer Shuki Levy, scoffs at her acting talent' (*Daily Star*, 29 April 1985)

THE PROGRAMMES

'Fury over Gay Sex in Dynasty'

'A gay sexpert has been hired by TV's *Dynasty* – to make sure homosexual scenes are true to life. His job is to advise on a gay affair involving the soap opera's heart throb Steven Carrington' (*Sun*, 1 May 1985)

'The bill . . . for libelling Harley Street slimming expert Dr Sidney Gee – already an astronomical £1.2 million – soared even higher yesterday when two doctors paid him £25,000 agreed damages. They were the medical experts who provided information for the Esther Rantzen *That's Life!* programme which branded Dr Gee "a profiteering, unscrupulous quack". . .' (*Daily Express*, 3 May 1985)

'The mammoth £8 million BBC TV Shakespeare project comes to a close tonight with Anna Calder-Marshall hideously deformed and Eileen Atkins eating her own sons in a pie . . . The BBC has spared no fake blood in bringing *Titus* to the screen, creating painful memories for Anna Calder-Marshall, whose hands and fingers were strapped tightly to splints to represent stumps for hours at a time' (*Daily Express*, 27 April 1985)

COMMENTS AND CRITICISMS

'War of the Blockbusters'

'Cheque-waving TV bosses have gone on a blockbuster spending spree in the latest battle of the ratings war. Top men from the BBC and ITV tried furiously to outbid each other as America put its latest smashes up for sale at last week's TV festival . . . BBC led the way by snapping up *Kane and Abel*, the powerful novel by master story-teller Jeffrey Archer' (*Sunday Mirror*, 28 April 1985)

'*Goldfinger*, the 20-year-old James Bond film starring Sean Connery, attracted 17 million viewers when it was shown on ITV – but it was still beaten into second place in the ratings by *Coronation Street*' (*Daily Mail*, 29 April 1985)

'The new BBC-1 *Saturday Night Out* gives us a glimpse of the beautiful people who infest London nightlife. A pretty repulsive lot they are, too. They've got coloured hair, wear clothes which have been dipped in gloss paint, and it is difficult to tell the men and women apart' (*Daily Express*, 2 May 1985)

'*Bleak House* (BBC-2, 9.10) If Charles Dickens hadn't existed then television would have had to invent him. His novels and characters translate so well that they might have been written especially for the medium. The Beeb's latest effort is sheer delight' (*Daily Mirror*, 1 May 1985)

'The money must be good, that's all I can say. There he is, Terry Wogan on BBC-1, stretched as tight as his old rugby player's jockstrap over three regular spots a week. Faced night after night with the trashy glitter and spluttering glare of all those pop people ninnies and aging showbiz personalities . . . our Terry battles bravely on' (*Daily Mirror*, 2 May 1985)

EDITORIALS

'Robin Hood Slammed'

'Mary Whitehouse went into battle against Robin Hood yesterday . . . She said: "the transmission, during the early evening, of *Robin of Sherwood*, dealing as it does with Satanism and even the apparent raising of Robin from the dead . . . has, not least because of its extensive violence, given rise to a very great deal of concern". . .' (*Sunday Express*, 28 April 1985)

'If you thought the adventures of Dr Who and his time machine was kids' stuff, think again. Clean-up-TV campaigner Mary Whitehouse . . . says the popular children's sci-fi series is getting too violent' (*Sunday People*, 28 April 1985)

TRB: Does all this mass of information about plots and stars spoil the programmes for you?

Yes. [Some]

KAREN (32): Oh, *The Thorn Birds* . . . they did that in the paper and I didn't want to read it, but because it was there, I just wanted to read about what was going to happen next.

DAWN (27): Well, don't tell me. I haven't watched the video yet.

TRB: If they write about what's going to happen next in *Dallas* or *Dynasty*, does that spoil it?

DAWN: Well, we know what's going to happen anyway. In a way.

DEB (32): Well, I think we've got a good idea.

MARY (27): The papers always put it across in such a way that they're not spoiling it for you as much as saying how good it's going to be.

DEB: They want you to keep on watching, so they give you little hints.

It may even be, as Charlotte Brunsdon suggests, that 'wondering what's going to happen next' is not the only way to describe the fascination of soaps for their addicts. 'For the soap fan, one of the moments of pleasure is when you can say "Oh, I *knew* that was going to happen". But this is not quite the same feeling as the attendant fascination of *how* it is going to happen . . . The viewer has to juggle all the different sorts of knowledge to get it right.'

There was certainly general recognition among viewers that the newspapers and television programmes were often hand in glove.

TRB: Where do you think they get those bits of juicy information?

MARY (37): Leaks, deliberate leaks.

Giving It All Away

In Britain, at least *forty* journalists are employed as full-time television reporters on the tabloid papers, a number which increases from time to time as other feature writers and stringers join their ranks. Keith Little was anxious to insist that his work involved much more than sitting around waiting for tips and leaks.

I knocked out, the other day, a list of twenty-six programmes that I knew were being made at the moment, programmes that we should be looking at at some point for spreads or major features or whatever. I mean it's not a hand-to-mouth thing.

But at least part of the planning has to be directed towards thwarting one's opponents in the field.

There is a system between quite a lot of TV writers. If they go to a preview and a particular star is there, and she says something that might make a big feature and say it's on a Wednesday, there's quite a lot of them who would have an agreement – a 'gang-bang system' – where they'll not use it until they're *all* going to use it . . . this Saturday, or whatever. My attitude is, and an attitude of a few of us, is *fuck that*. I'm employed to get stories before other people, so I'm never party to that kind of agreement.

Was he as unscrupulous with the *plots* of soap operas? Were there any occasions where he'd keep developments to himself?

You try and find out as much as you can. Storylines, that's dodgy, sometimes you do give it away, sometimes you don't. It tends to be leaks with *Coronation Street*; if you know something you tend to give it away . . . because it's so secretive and so popular.

But were there differences between the companies or the programme staff over deliberate leaks? And if there was a no-leak policy, who broke it?

I don't think Granada ever gives deliberate 'leaks'. What happens is that because lots of newspapers have moles, i.e. either production staff or members of the cast who are in the pocket of some newspaper, they tend to leak it that way. When the *News of the World* did a thing on Bet Lynch – she was going to become the new landlady of the Rovers – they went apoplectic over that because that was going to be a big storyline. And they went bananas over the press coverage of the Ken–Deirdre–Mike affair, absolutely screwy over it. They were getting quite abusive . . . 'Why are you ruining people's enjoyment?' We were saying, 'Well, you're making the bloody show, you are engendering the story, writing this storyline, we're only reacting to it.'

When Mavis's wedding to Victor [in the *Street*] was called off, the *Sun* blew that and they went absolutely bananas. *Crossroads* got very angry with me when I revealed they were going to have a junkie in the plot. There's a kind of sanctimoniousness about the soaps you don't get in other TV departments. They had this heroin addict which we found out about and I did a piece and called him a junkie. They objected to us calling him a junkie. What they were saying was, 'You're presenting a wrong image, we're trying to show that heroin does this and that.' We revealed the wedding of Adam Chance to Jill [in *Crossroads*], we actually got pictures of that . . . they went bananas about that . . . We had our own mole and *Crossroads*' problem was when they did any funerals or weddings or christenings they always used the same church – near Redditch – so we just put two and two together, knew they were filming, knew it was probably likely to be this one, so we just whizzed down to the church and there they all were. But they hire minders. They were physically preventing us from going into the church. But we were saying, 'Get stuffed, the church is public.' We were saying, 'We're going to get the bloody police here.' And it was getting out of control. When they were doing the burning of Noele Gordon there was a similar thing . . . they not only hired private security, they hired private security *with dogs*. That was at an airfield outside Stratford-on-Avon where they built this set all in secret. I know because I crawled through fields on my knees with a duffle coat the wrong way round my head to get through the brambles . . . the hood was there across my face, because the photographer I was with, who was about fifty-eight, refused to do it. So I took his Nikon and went through this field and got the picture of the set. I was then chased halfway across this airfield by these people with dogs. And after all that they phone up your editor and complain, saying you're ruining people's enjoyment. *It's not true.* When the burning of the motel happened, everyone in Britain knew they were going to burn the motel – everyone [tabloids] had done it – the viewing figures for that night's episode was about four million higher. Yet we all knew what was going to happen, we'd all done photographs, we'd even got photographs of the place going up . . .

It was the viewers, however, who foretold the rest. For although the Crossroads motel did indeed burn to the ground on Wednesday 4 November 1981, by Wednesday 11 November, viewers knew that all their pleas had been answered. Meg Mortimer was safe. She had been saved from the fire and the plot allowed her to sail safely to Australia. Not even the valiant beduffled Keith Little could have accomplished that.

10

How Do You View?

TRB: Can you remember the first time you saw a television?

ALICE (77): Yes.

HELEN (70): It was tiny.

ALICE: There was a neighbour near us, and we used to go and peep in the window when she had it on, we used to crouch by the window . . .

EVA (78): I can remember coming home from work one day and my mother said, 'There's been an announcement on the wireless that they've got a thing out called television, and you can see what's going on in the next room.' She said, 'You're not going to have a bit of privacy, your neighbours are going to see what's going on.' I never forgot it. I was sixteen at the time.

TRB: And when the television came?

EVA: We were amazed. All the lights would go out, we'd all sit in rows . . . and you daren't speak in case you missed a word. In the interval somebody would put the kettle on.

ETHEL (79): I can remember when television first came out everybody had television chairs, television trays, television lights.

JESSE (72): It ruled your life for a year or two. It absorbed everything and you believed everything . . .

ETHEL: Yes, but we don't now.

HELEN: Now, we take it all with a pinch of salt.

Cold Blank Screens

If it becomes known that you're writing about television, you're likely, on more than one occasion, to be asked whether you're 'for' or 'against'. 'Television' for some is still apparently a coherent single object about which it is possible to have strong views.

Neither is this tendency confined to casual acquaintances. Contemporary experts on the subject still feel able to talk about what happens to us when we watch television, as though the experience is unidimensional:

Not unlike drugs or alcohol, the television experience allows the participant to blot out the real world and enter into a pleasurable and passive mental state. The worries and anxieties of reality are as effectively deferred by becoming absorbed in a television programme as by going on a 'trip' induced by drugs or alcohol. And just as alcoholics are only vaguely aware of their addiction, feeling that they control their drinking more than they really do . . . people similarly overestimate their control over television watching.

This is not the type of effect which critics of television are likely to regard themselves as falling prey to in their own controlled viewing. Maria Winn, the author of *The Plug-in Drug*, 1985, from which the above analysis comes, describes the basis of one family's immunity. 'We read a lot, talk a lot, listen to music. Once in a while we'll rent a set for a special occasion like the Watergate hearings.'

That is hardly the type of viewer we've been listening to in the rest of this book. The people in our discussion groups, in many of BBC and IBA research projects, and in our national sample, were by definition all regular members of the television audience. And their viewing was by no means confined to *The South Bank Show* (an arts programme) or *Panorama* (current affairs) or *Arena* (arts) – or indeed the Watergate hearings – but was firmly rooted in the most popular television programmes: cops and robbers, soap operas, game shows, light entertainment, drama series, chat shows, and the news. Very few people in our sample decided how many hours of television they would watch in advance, or went through the *Radio Times* or *TV Times* ringing the programmes they intended to view. For many, television had become as much a feature of their houses as the electricity supply.

> JOHN (42): As soon as I walk in my house in the evening at four-thirty, the TV's on, it doesn't go off till about eleven or twelve.
> TRB: Is it the same for all of you?
> JOHN: Even the kids put it on. If they go out they don't bother turning it off.
> ALAN (42): That's right, yes . . .
> JIM (41): I think it's a permanent thing, isn't it, if you turn the light on, you might as well turn the TV on . . .
> PAUL (37): Yes.
> JIM: *Might as well be on the same switch, really.*

For others there was something almost unnatural about having a set which wasn't on:

> MARIE (54): I'm not proud of the fact, but I find it very cold when it's off, cold, yes. I feel that it should be on . . .
> TRB: You mean because of the atmosphere?
> MARIE: That's right, yes . . .
> JOAN (51): It's like the old coal fire. It's like having a coal fire with the light bulb off. I mean, a television without pictures – a blank screen like that.

Just as artificial coal fires can happily burn away untended in the corner of the room, so a television can burn on into the night even – in one case – when there is no one around who might possibly be warmed by it:

TRB: But how do you actually feel when it breaks down?

NORA (57): Well, you're lost, aren't you?

HELEN (52): There's a big gap without television on in our house. I feel as if there's somebody missing . . .

TRB: Somebody missing?

HELEN: Yes, because I mean we're never without it. There's probably television on at home now even if there's nobody in.

JOAN: Is there? [*Laughs.*]

HELEN: Oh yes.

All this is a long way from the silent rows of people sitting in semi-darkness on their television chairs. Today's television may be lucky to win itself a glance from people who are busy rushing past it on their way to other business:

NATALIE (37): Yes, I have it on most of the day even if I'm not watching it.

JOANNA (32): Yes, it's usually on but whether you actually stop and watch it . . .

JILL (31): We have it on but we don't sit watching it. We turn it on first thing in the morning when we come down and it's on till late at night. I'm out in the garden, doing the gardening, going back and forth – I'm not watching telly all the time – it's just there and it's on.

It's a common technique in market research to ask people to personalise products – to imagine what kind of person a bottle of Smirnoff vodka, a tub of Stork margarine or a tin of Castrol might be, if they were to come to life and stroll into the living room. Some viewers in our discussion groups did not need to be prompted into this way of regarding their television. It already was some sort of individual:

PAT (47): It's another person living in your house all the time, isn't it? It's like having an extra person there.

JUDITH (40): It's a *lot* of people in your house, isn't it, really? A lot of different people.

Although occasionally this 'person' was seen as a demanding or even disgruntled relative – a nagging granny or granddad in the corner imperiously demanding some attention, the usual description was 'friend'.

ANNE (45): It's a friend, really.

TRB: A friend?

PAT: Yeah.

JUDITH: A companion.

JANET (32): *Yes.* [*All:*] Television is company.

EDNA (42): I like to hear it in the background. It gives the home a bit of warmth.

MOLLY (41): It seems to bring a room to life.

JEAN (42): I hate silence.

MOLLY: If the television's off it's a dead room, but if the television's on, the room seems lively. [*Others agree.*]

EDNA: It's like, in the morning I used to put the radio on, and now there's breakfast television. I don't sit and watch it, but I put it on and I walk round the house and I listen to it like I used to listen to the radio.

MOLLY: The house is too dead without it on. It's too quiet.

For one of the people in one of our old person's groups – and probably for many others, to judge from some of the correspondence we've already quoted from Dorothy Hobson's *Crossroads* – this companionship was not merely a background 'warmth', it was something without which life became very difficult.

EVA (72): I was going to say that I'm in all day and it's company for me.

ETHEL (79): I've got a nerve condition and I've got to have something in the house.

EVA: It's a friend to a lot of people.

ETHEL: I can't be on my own indoors, otherwise I've got to have the doors and windows open. But if the television's on, it's all right.

ALICE (77): It's psychological.

ROSE (74): I used to know a lady, and when anyone had a drink on the television she'd go and get herself one and drink with them. [*All laugh.*] 'If he's going to have one, I'll have one with him.'

A Sense of Guilt

If we restricted ourselves to such comments about the experience of television, its companionability, the sheer pleasure in its presence, then our argument would be as one-sided as those who declare that television is simply 'addictive', palpably 'mind-numbing', or pure 'escapism'. Television experience is various. Even behind the clear statements about its ability to combat loneliness lie doubts about using it for this purpose:

JAN (51): It's just some company. I'm not very good without it. I hate loneliness. Some women can stay indoors and set to and do the windows. But I just get very lonely.

There was never any suggestion that watching television might ever increase your sense of loneliness, that the sight of so much glamour and wealth and show-biz cheerfulness on the screen might remind you of your own lack of friends or social life. When we asked our national sample if 'Watching TV can make you feel lonely' only 7 per cent were prepared to agree.

What it certainly did make people feel was 'guilty': the word, or its equivalent, cropped up over and over again in the groups. Sometimes people felt guilty because they sensed that television was interfering with their social life:

SHARON (35): You feel guilty, particularly when you're trying to listen to friends and you're half trying to watch telly at the same time.

DEBBIE (29): Yes. With some friends you can say, 'Come in and shut up a minute while I must watch this.' But others you can't.

Some caught worried glimpses of their dependence upon it, how much it was needed as an escort as they moved about the house.

MARY (35): I've got my telly upstairs on wheels, in a little box, and we wheel it into each other's rooms.

DOT (37): Terrible, really.

MARY: I either wheel it into my room, or the kids have it in their room. Yes, it's terrible really.

And some had begun to feel that it might be interfering with their whole existence.

JOAN (51): I am embarrassed. I am ashamed to admit I sit there and watch so much television.

TRB: Why?

JOAN: Because I feel that I should be doing more with my time and my life.

Television programme planners somewhat cynically recognise the presence of this volume of guilt in the terms they use to describe people's readiness to watch more television (say, breakfast or afternoon television). They talk of people requiring 'permission to view' and point enthusiastically to the increase in afternoon viewing as being related to the development of breakfast television. Once, so the argument goes, people feel that they have denied themselves *some* television by deciding not to watch at breakfast time (and in fact total viewing figures for that period are relatively stable at 3.5 million) then this helps to give them 'permission' to watch in the afternoon (when viewing now accounts for 30 per cent of all daily viewing).

What people feel most guilty about is the loss of 'time': the idea that there are other things they should be doing which are somehow more worthwhile, but nevertheless not any longer so attractive:

The fact that they don't read and don't plant their garden or sew or crochet or play games or have conversations means that those activities are no longer as desirable as television viewing. In a way the lives of heavy viewers are as imbalanced by their television 'habit' as a drug addict's or an alcoholic's. (Winn, op. cit.)

But there are some difficulties with this position. For a start our national sample showed that only a minority (28 per cent) believed that television 'stopped them from doing interesting things'. It was common to find people who had at least some activities organised around it:

> VICKY (27): I couldn't sit and watch the telly doing nothing, I have to do something.

Television reduced the drudgery of some household chores:

> CLAIRE (29): I like watching telly while I'm doing ironing – it makes ironing less boring.

And it could hardly be called a 'waste of time' when you could point to a new cardigan at the end of the week:

> JUDY (23): Yes, I watch television, and I can knit at the same time, you see. So I never think I'm wasting my time, if I sit and knit watching it.

There was the same pattern of general agreement followed by particular disagreements when we asked if television was a 'conversation killer'. Des's account of what happened in his home nicely illustrated the idea of 'talking' taking a clear second place to 'viewing'.

> DES (34): I'm married, got two daughters, one is four, the other fourteen months. Television is always on in the evening. That's not to say it's always watched. *We lapse off into conversation sometimes.*

But gradually the matter became more complicated.

> JAN (36): I *can* talk, I don't get hooked. I watch it regularly but I don't get hooked. I'm not sort of entranced by it, I'll talk to people in the room at the same time, and there can be loads of noise going on, but I'm still watching the storyline.

Sometimes the conversation revolves around the programme itself:

> SALLY (41): My husband's very sarcastic. 'Oh, come on, boys, mummy's watching her programme', 'I don't know what you want to watch that load of rubbish for,' he'll say, and he'll lie on the settee and I'll look at him now and again and he is sort of grinning and saying things. I know he's watching it, but he's taking the mickey out of it all the same, especially *Crossroads*. He thinks *Crossroads* is the worst thing ever.

It may also be directly prompted by it:

> TRB: Do you regard television as a 'conversation killer'?
> ANDY (25): I think it's a pain in a lot of ways.
> MARK (28): But then sometimes, I think it creates conversation, depending on what you're watching.
> GEORGE (31): It does, I suppose . . . [*All talk.*]

MARK: I mean, we've quite often sat and watched something, and we've turned it off and we've sat and discussed what we've watched.

There was still the persistent idea, though, that there must have been more conversation before the television arrived. Husband and wife must have sat and talked to each other. Only George wanted to disagree. And he found some support.

GEORGE: You go on about the art of conversation, but I don't care. Unless you've got an exceptional marriage, after fifteen or twenty years, you have a look at husband and wife going into a pub, and they sit on their own, you can tell the husband-and-wife couples. There's the old man over there looking one way and she's looking the other.
GEOFF (32): They don't talk to each other . . .
MARTIN (37): . . . they don't talk to each other. *Right?*

Ask the Family

Maybe television is not always the cause of silence between elderly married couples. But many of our viewers were middle-aged, and shared their house with children, and it is this very *familial* aspect of television which worries other experts. The set is somehow thought to stand between children and parents; it interferes with the hundreds of little encounters and conversations which are the essence of childhood, which help to bind the family together. Children, so this argument goes, are no longer inclined to listen to parents when more attractive tutors and models can be tuned to on their television sets.

MARIAN (37): The majority of us have got kids and if you go up to the kids and say, 'Right, go and do so and so, go and tidy your room', it's 'Let me watch this, let me see the end of this.' 'Your tea's ready, come and have it downstairs.' 'No, I want to watch this.' The kids' lives and therefore your lives are controlled by the telly.

And it is this parental reluctance to go into battle against the television, this abdication of their role of controller, which is thought likely by some to have such serious consequences:

In its effect on family relationships, in its facilitation of parental withdrawal from an active role in the socialization of their children, and in its replacement of family rituals and special events, television has played an important role in the disintegration of the American family. (Winn, op. cit.)

Some parents certainly sounded as though they had thrown up their hands in the face of their children's demands.

TRB: But it's your television set, you can turn it off.
VAL (51): But it's not your television, it's the family's, isn't it?
TRB: Who switches it on?

MARY (37): The kids, the minute they walk in from school.
JO (36): The children turn it on when they come home from school.

Not that it has to stay on. Some fight back:

MOLLY (41): I use it for punishment, 'Any more fights and off goes the television', and I mean it. Out comes the plug, and they can't believe it. They really don't know what to do with themselves.
JANET (39): Oh, it's depressing.
MOLLY: It *is* depressing. [*All laugh.*]

Molly's laughter, though, seemed to point more towards the universal experience of kids and parents rather than to the particular problems created by television. And Jane remembered at least one programme which positively brought all the family together:

JANE (43): That *Fools and Horses* – it's the only thing that keeps the whole of my family, from the youngest to the oldest, really amused. Everybody says, 'Oh, it's *Fools and Horses* tonight.'
DEB (39): Yes, they all come downstairs. And there's no fighting.
JANE: Everybody watches that, you know.
MOLLY: Yes, I've turned it off when friends have come around but they say, 'Oh please, let's just have it on for half an hour.'

The children themselves are also pretty good at noticing how their own programmes attract other members of the family. There they are happily settling down in the late afternoon and all of a sudden there's Dad or Mum nudging up beside them.

MANDY (10): My dad likes all the cartoons and he watches them. [*Some agree.*]
REBECCA (9): My dad likes *Tom and Jerry*. [*Some agree.*]
MARY (10): My dad always watches sport in the afternoons and when *Tom and Jerry* comes on he wakes up.
GAIL (9): My mum likes everything except *Dogtanian* [cartoon series].
REBECCA: Whenever my dad's got a holiday the same as everyone else he starts watching *Sesame Street*.
TRB: Do you think it's funny that your dad watches it?
REBECCA: Yes.
SUSAN (9): He's too old. My dad's about forty-six or something like that.
GAIL: It's for little kids.
REBECCA: My nan is nearly sixty and she watches *Button Moon* [a children's programme].

There are plenty of other dads and mums and nans watching children's television (see chart). So many, indeed, that you wonder if the production staff take them into account. ('Charles, I'm a teeny bit worried about the present

Adults watching children's programmes
Figures are for audiences as percentages of age groups

		4–9 yrs	9–15 yrs	over 55s
8.30 am	*Wide Awake Club*	12.5 491,000	6.8 332,000	1.4 186,000
3.42 pm	*Cartoon Time*	2.5 98,000	.3 17,000	3.5 471,000
4.01 pm	*Thomas the Tank Engine*	21.0 826,000	4.7 236,000	7.5 1,015,000
4.11 pm	*Wacky Races*	11.2 442,000	5.2 258,000	2.4 321,000
4.12 pm	*SuperTed*	12.2 482,000	4.8 239,000	2.4 321,000
5.0 pm	*Dangermouse*	26.1 1,027,000	13.9 692,000	10.9 1,473,000
5.05 pm	*Blue Peter*	18.8 742,000	12.8 636,000	9.6 1,296,000
5.15 pm	*Blockbusters*	10.3 406,000	13.3 662,000	31.1 4,212,000
5.17 pm	*Crackerjack*	28.9 1,139,000	15.1 749,000	6.8 922,000
6.0 pm	*The A-Team*	36.6 1,441,000	26.6 1,322,000	24.8 3,358,000

series of *Dangermouse*. Nice high ratings, of course, but we must remember that nearly half our audience *is* over fifty-five. And although I don't want it to look as though we're leaning over backwards, but any chance at all, d'you think, of an occasional reference to, say, Vera Lynn or Tommy Handley, or Stanley Matthews? *Just a thought, you understand.*')

While their parents somewhat indiscriminately soak up *Dogtanian*, *Tom and Jerry* and *Sesame Street*, the children are busy making sharp distinctions:

JAYNE (10): I like *Street Hawk*.
SALLY (10): *Knight Rider*.
SUSAN (9): *The A-Team*.
TRB: Why do you like *Knight Rider*?
SALLY: I like the car. [*Some agree.*]
TRB: And *The A-Team*, you like that?
SUSAN: Yes. [*Most agree.*]
TRB: What's good about it?
SUSAN: It's got a lot of action.
MARY (10): I like Murdoch. [*Most agree.*]

SUSAN: He has this sock and he draws a dog face on it and keeps talking to it.

MARY: Yes, he's really stupid.

SUSAN: He's in a mental home now.

GAIL (9): They always send Face to get him out of the mental home.

JAYNE: I like *The Young Ones*. [*Some agree.*]

TRB: And what would you say the most boring children's programme is?

SALLY: *Button Moon*.

MARY: I like it. [*Some agree.*]

SALLY: People are all made out of spoons and sponges and things.

GAIL: Out of things in the kitchen.

MANDY (10): I think the most boring thing is *Playschool*.

GAIL: No, *Rainbow*.

SUSAN: Oh, I like that. [*Some agree.*]

TRB: Why don't you like *Rainbow*?

GAIL: I think it's a bit young.

MARY: So you don't have to watch it if you don't like it.

GAIL: Zippy and George have only got one arm.

JAYNE: It's funny.

MANDY: No, they have got two *arms*, it's just that they have only got three *fingers*.

GAIL: They have only got one *arm*.

Even four- and five-year-olds at a northern primary school who were asked by their teacher to say why they liked some programmes more than others seemed to be well on the way to developing firm favourites:

'I don't like *Playschool* because they do stupid things and just play.' (Paul, 5)

'I like *Street Hawk* because the motor bike goes fast and does skids and jumps.' (Lisa, 5)

'I like *Knight Rider* because it jumps so it's good.' (Graeme, 5)

'It's football that I don't like because they hurt their knees.' (Nicola, 5)

'*Tom and Jerry* – it's good 'cos I like it, 'cos Tom always catches Jerry.' (Steven, 5)

'I like *Bananaman* [young children's cartoon] best because he can fight the baddies best.' (Ian, 4)

'I like *The Incredible Hulk* [an adventure series] because he goes green and angry.' (Robert, 5)

'I like *Dracula Returned From His Grave* and I watched it, that is my best programme.' (Katie, 5)

It's the presence of *Dracula* in that list – the clear indication that four- and five-year-olds are watching adult programmes – which still caused much concern, especially among our older groups.

Knightrider: *'I like it 'cos it's electric and it goes fast.'* (Derry, aged 5)

'Films are boring.' (Lee, aged 5)   Football: *'I don't like that.'* (Lee, aged 5)

ALICE (77): There was a little boy committed murder several years ago because he used to look at Westerns and they get up and they're on next week, aren't they, and he killed this child and he thought that child was going to get up and play . . . come back again . . . he didn't realise that death really meant death.

Our particular group of nine- and ten-year-olds didn't seem, though, to be having it all their own way.

> TRB: What programmes don't your parents like you to watch?
> ALEX (9): They don't like me watching rude films. [*All agree.*]
> JESSICA (9): Or horror films.
> ALEX: And those where they always get into bed naked and everything.
> TRB: They don't like you watching that?
> ALEX: No.
> TRB: Do you like watching those kinds of films?
> ALEX: Yes. [*Laughing.*] They are quite good actually.
> TRB: What's good about them?
> ALEX: They are just good; they have got more action in them.
> TRB: Which others do your parents stop you watching?
> SAMMY (10): My mum doesn't like me watching *The Young Ones* but she lets my brother tape it sometimes.
> ANNE (9): Because these things are on too late, that's why they don't let us.
> ALEX: My mum doesn't let me watch it because it's got too much swearing in it.
> TRB: What time do you have to stop watching?
> ALEX: My dad normally makes me turn my light off at nine but I never do. I close my door instead and they don't see.
> JESSICA: I normally stop watching at the time I go to bed about ten past eight.
> SAMMY: I go to bed at eight or half past or nine. When my dad has gone down I start reading a book.
> NICOLE (10): I read in bed for ages.
> JOANNE (9): I go at nine and I shut the door, put the light on and read.
> TRB: Do your parents ever watch programmes with you?
> ALEX: Yes. [*All agree.*]
> TRB: Which ones?
> JESSICA: *Dr Kildare* [an American hospital soap].
> JOANNE: That's boring. [*Some agree.*]

In 1982 Peter Fiddick asked the BBC's Broadcasting Research Department to find out if children watched as much television as their elders. He was able to conclude:

> *They do not.* The amount of television viewing, averaged across the entire population (except the under-fours), was 17 hours 28 minutes per week (17:28 hours). But among children, aged 4–15 years, the figure is 11:32 hours, with boys watching 50 minutes more than that, and girls 55 minutes less. Such figures scarcely suggest a picture of a generation addicted to the screen, regardless of what they watch. (*Listener*, 4 November 1982.)

But the latest figures are less reassuring (at least to those concerned about the matter). In one week in 1985 the new average for the entire population had risen to 24 hours 27 minutes a week, while that for the 4–15-year-old had moved up to 22 hours 10 minutes. These figures are based on a typical week in March 1985, whereas Fiddick's week in 1982 was in September. This, however, would typically only mean that they needed to be adjusted downwards by approximately one hour. Neither does this affect the most significant development: the narrowing of the gaps between 'child hours' and 'adult hours'.

There is still perhaps some comfort to be found in the list of adult programmes which children choose to watch. In 1982 Fiddick was able to write:

> When we look at the children's Top Ten among all programmes on all channels, it must be regarded, by anyone who is not against the box in principle, as a list sinister only in its blandness. They show an appetite for comedy. Of the ten, half are primarily laughter shows: *Game for a Laugh*, *Benny Hill*, *The Two Ronnies*, *The Monkees*, *Tom, Dick and Harriet*. Only two, *Blue Peter* and *The Monkees*, were shown at teatime, but only two finished as late as 9 pm. One of the others is the thoroughly wholesome *Wildlife on One*, another the generally acceptable *Coronation Street*. *Top of the Pops* is not violent and not shockingly sexy. (Ibid.)

In 1985, comedy still triumphs, along with magic and general fun. The *Lenny Henry Show*, *Paul Daniels Magic Show*, *Game for a Laugh*, *Punchlines* and *Top of the Pops* are high up in the top ten with *Grange Hill*, *Dangermouse* and *The A-Team* not far behind.

A Seat in the Stalls

So many people, including children of all ages, talked about the television simply flickering away in the background without anyone paying too much attention to it that it seemed worthwhile to ask about the times when viewing became more concentrated – when a favourite programme came on. Was there anything they did to make the occasion stand out from all the casual intermittent half-hearted looking?

SARAH (31): Lighting is important. If it was a really good serial, I'd turn the light off and have the little light on [*some agree*] but for anything like cops and robbers I'd never dream of turning out the main light.
TRB: So why turn the light out?
SARAH: A bit more atmosphere. [*All agree.*]
ZOE (34): And then just as you're nicely settled the phone goes. [*Laughs.*]
JANET (37): Our phone's in the kitchen, which is a real pain because in the afternoons when my friends from work want to get hold of me, they ring up and I'm always in the middle of *The Sullivans* [Australian soap opera] or

General Hospital [soap opera based on hospital] or *Country Practice* [an Australian medical series] and I think, Oh God. I go out there and they chat and chat and chat and I'm missing it all. If I leave my little boy in there, when I come back I say, 'What happened? *What happened?*' and he says, 'Not a lot' – and that's all you get. *Nothing.*

And when you've got the lighting right, and perhaps the phone off the hook, then all that's needed is to get into the ideal viewing position. Just as there used to be such strong preferences for front stalls or back stalls or circle in the cinema, so getting this part right can make a big difference to the enjoyment of the programme.

> ZOE: I like to have my feet up when I'm watching it, and really relax.
> JANET: I sit myself down by the radiator, and I've burnt my back . . .
> [*Laughs.*] Really, I've had to go to the doctor, I've burnt my complete back because I've sat on the floor, the radiator's there [*points*], the television is there [*points*].

And it seemed that habits (of a less self-destructive kind) developed early.

> TRB: When you watch something special on TV, where do you sit?
> NICOLE (10): I sit on our mat right close to the TV.
> JESSICA (9): I sit on the chair with my feet curled up or lay out on the mat really close to the TV. Or curl up on the mat or sit down like this on the mat, or lie down on the armchair with the footrest, lie down on the settee, sit up straight on the settee.
> SAMMY (10): I sit on the settee. [*Some agree.*]
> ALEX (9): I sit near the fire.
> KATE (10): I sit on my dad's lap.
> SUSAN (9): I sit all sorts of ways.
> JESSICA: In the morning I lay on my mat near the fire.
> TRB: Do you all have your special places?
> ALEX: Yes. [*Some agree.*]
> JESSICA: My dad calls the mat we've got my home.
> TRB: Has anyone else got a little home of their own?
> JOANNE (9): On the settee at the very edge near the armchair.

More and more it's not so much a question of deciding on lighting and seating arrangements, but also on the room in which to watch. Already there are eight million homes with two or more sets, and falling asleep in bed watching the television is well on its way to becoming a night-time ritual: one which might already be replacing other, more familiar ones:

> PAUL (37): We treated ourselves for Christmas. One for our bedroom. And to be honest, by the time I've got to bed and watched it for a few minutes I've crashed out. I can't really remember seeing a whole . . .

ALAN (42): No wonder there's more sex on television than there is in the home. [*Laughing together.*]

PAUL: I tell you what . . . I was thinking of putting mirrors up on the ceiling, tell you why, so I can watch the wife have a headache.

Strangely, although extra sets can disperse people around the house, there are times – *Only Fools and Horses* regularly supplies a good half an hour – when the family like to celebrate their togetherness:

JIM (41): She's got a colour in her bedroom. There's a black-and-white one upstairs, but the main one we've got in our lounge and we sit there as a family, because when we sit down, my wife says, 'Leave that, that's enough tonight. Sit down.' And I sit down and . . . we sit down as a family. We're not all scattered round the house because the dog gets so confused, she don't know where to go because we're not all together, but once we're all in the room, she plonks herself down and we sit there as a family.

Daddies can even be persuaded to leave their studies on such occasions:

MOLLY (41): My husband tends to sit in the other room and study and it will only be when the news comes on and *Only Fools and Horses*. I mean then my little boy runs in and says, 'Daddy, Daddy, *Only Fools and Horses* are on.' That's it, *whoosh*, he'll be straight in, then he'll sit at the other end of the settee.

Alice left it till late in the discussion to introduce another variable, something which doesn't really have a cinematic parallel:

ALICE (35): I must admit I tend to get closer to the television depending what the programme is, if it's *Dallas* I tend to get nearer to the television. [*All roar.*] I like to see what they are wearing.

And did she adjust her position for other programmes?

ALICE: Funnily enough it's true really, you do, I know I sit properly and watch the news. It's daft, isn't it, but I don't lounge around to watch the news. [*All really laugh.*] It's stupid when you think about it.

Giving up TV

There is no way in which this wide range of attitudes towards the place of the television in the home can be brought into close alignment with those 'anti-television' arguments which stress the threat it poses – for the family, the consequences for society of its creation of a 'passive' mass, the likely effects of children's exposure to so many hours of 'adult' viewing.

On the one hand, it was clear that many viewers shared some of the experts' anxieties: most were prepared to admit to some 'guilt' about watching –

particularly when the question of 'wasted time' was in the foreground. And neither were many very happy about the part that television played in their children's lives.

Against this, there was a general rejection of the notion that television made you 'passive'. It might well be used at times for relaxation, but on other occasions it was as likely to promote conversation as inhibit it.

Given these contradictions, it was not surprising to find that, emotionally, most viewers were equally able to wish that they watched less television, and simultaneously to give every indication of enjoying much of what they saw. In one discussion group, for example, Molly and Pauline had both spent some time expressing their concern about how television had come to dominate their lives and giving examples of their 'addiction':

PAULINE (44): When *Sons and Daughters* is on, if the phone rings, I don't answer that or the door.
MOLLY (35): I work round my whole schedule in the evening, dinner time until six thirty, six thirty till seven, in half an hour to get the kids sorted out, ready for *Coronation Street*.

But then, when they were asked about why it was they persisted in behaviour which seemed to upset them so much, they changed tack and defended their favourite habit.

TRB: So you feel you definitely watch too much telly?
DOREEN (42): Yes, I do.
MOLLY: But why should you? It's not bad for you, is it?
PAULINE: It's silly feeling worried, because if you sat down and read a book you wouldn't feel as though you had to do something else, would you?

But what exactly *would* you do if the television set was no longer there? Would the time be quickly filled with activities which were more intrinsically satisfying, would social relations improve, families grow closer, 'passivity' decrease? There is some evidence for all these effects. In *The Plug-in Drug* Marie Winn reports on three before and after experiments in which 'no television' periods of up to a month were characterised by:

More interaction between parents and children.
A more peaceful atmosphere in the home.
A greater feeling of closeness as a family.
More help by children in the household.
More outdoor play.

On the debit side were regrets at missing favourite programmes, the children's difficulties in getting on with others who still had TV, and the parents no longer being able to use 'no television' as a disciplinary threat.

Despite what looked like such a clear balance in favour of no TV, none of the participants in these experiments chose to *continue* living without television.

'A psychologist asked to give an opinion [on this] suggests that while [the parents] thought they *ought* to engage in the activities they took up during the no-television period . . . these didn't fulfil the needs that television viewing did.' Unfortunately Marie Winn does not consider that such 'needs' might also be positive, but instead regards such recidivism on the part of the no-television subjects as evidence of self-deception: 'What are the needs that television fulfils? The need for passivity, for self-annihilation, for regression to a state of dependence . . . surely habitual television viewing serves few needs more auspicious than these.' This attitude seems to rely on the assumption that television is displacing other valuable activities – a viewpoint nicely caricatured by Chris Dunkley:

> It is an absurd upper-middle-class fantasy to imagine that if only people could be induced to turn their televisions off they would all start reading Solzhenitsyn and going to Covent Garden or attending lectures on the Late Renaissance. Most people deprived of their television pick up the *Sun* or listen to Radio 1. It is sometimes suggested that in the days before television 'took over' there was a golden age when families clustered around the piano and made their own entertainment; when voters participated in public meetings instead of being fed predigested political messages by the telly; when the railwayman and the factory worker rushed out after supper to attend WEA lectures and scampered home to read H. G. Wells. No doubt there were people like that. Yet even the crudest analysis suggests that the figures for people 'doing their own thing' – whether jogging or gardening, attending evening classes or ballroom dancing – have gone up during the television age and not down.
>
> (Chris Dunkley, *Television Today and Tomorrow*, 1985.)

England, too, has had its experiments in television abstinence, the most notable of which was one carried out in the isolated Devon village of Peter Tavy in 1984. In this case the television was voluntarily switched off in a total of forty-two households – only three out of which did not manage to keep it in that condition for the entire week of the experiment. It all made very good copy for the *Daily Mirror* which organised the campaign – *Villagers resist the lure of Coronation Street on Day One of the big Mirror test* – but the amount of publicity generated by the exercise meant that the villagers' reactions to their self-denial were hardly likely to be typical. Nevertheless withdrawal did seem to produce certain mood changes. Some villagers were clearly lonelier, others became more active, thoughtful and reflective. But in line with the American studies, this did not produce any desire to continue in that condition. At the end of the week, 87 per cent of the group interviewed said they believed people would break the law to see TV programmes if prohibition was introduced, and 35 per cent admitted they would be among those who did.

Anyone for Monopoly?

We tried a rather different angle. As it was the concern with time and wasting time which dominated people's thoughts about their present viewing habits, we asked all the members of our groups to remember (or in the case of the younger groups, to guess) what people did with their time before television:

MARK (47): They had larger families. [*All really laugh.*]
JOHN (41): They must have amused each other.
HELEN (37): But people were more friendly, though, more sociable.
BOB (33): People used to visit more, families got together more.
HELEN: Where we tend to do our entertaining at weekends, I can remember when I was a little girl all getting round my grandma's piano during the week.
DEREK (35): A few years ago when there were power cuts, I quite enjoyed myself, we talked more, we played cards, you know.

Playing cards and board games, in particular Monopoly, seemed to be a common picture of pre-television evenings. There was also some general idea of people 'making their own entertainment' and this was often thought to be 'musical' in some way:

TRB: What did people do with their spare time before television?
HALEY (31): Made their own entertainment.
TRB: How? What did they do?
MARY (35): Played card games and that sort of thing. Monopoly.
JOAN (40): Played instruments.
SUE (34): Well, it depends on what class you're talking about. The working class didn't.
JOAN: The old joanna in the old sitting room.

Nearly everyone felt that there must have been more communication between people at such times, even if only around the card table.

TRB: Do you think that people spoke to each other more?
JOAN: Yes, definitely. [*Others agree.*]
MARY: You communicated, played games, Monopoly . . .

They were less ready to admit that there was any *present* lack of conversation:

TRB: So you talk less to your husbands now?
MARY: No, you talk about the programmes. Talk about different things.

The group of nine-year-old girls were as keen as their parents on filling up all that pre-television spare time with games. And what's more, they had an authoritative source of information for this assertion:

TRB: Before TV was invented, what do you think people did?
ALEXANDRA (9): Listened to the radio. [*Most agree.*]

SUSAN (9): Played games.

REBECCA (9): When TV wasn't invented they had only just invented radio.

TRB: And before radio was invented?

SUSAN: Played games.

REBECCA: *We watched how they used to live on television and they showed that.*

GAIL (9): They went to school and worked a lot and didn't have much time to rest . . .

But, of course, we did have two groups in which there was a very clear memory of life before television. Some of these elderly people also remembered different forms of entertainment:

EVA (72): I came from a big family. We used to play cards.

ETHEL (79): And we played darts.

HELEN (70): We used to sit and talk. Have visitors in.

JESSE (72): Musical evenings.

What was also remembered, though, was something which had been lacking in younger people's memories – work.

ALICE (77): We used to do a lot of knitting. A lot of sewing.

JESSE: Darning.

ALICE: Darning socks.

A man did remember mending shoes in the evening but it was the women whose evenings seemed full of tasks:

HELEN: I was ironing shirts mostly.

VERA (69): I used to do embroidery.

JESSE: Make more things.

ALICE: We grew up to make things.

ETHEL: Mend.

JESSE: You didn't just buy frocks, just like that.

And then there was the radio – the wireless. They were still young enough to remember the effects of this technological advance on their own grandparents.

VERA: My granddad was about seventy-five and my brothers made him a wireless set and put it in a cabinet. That was the first time my granddad had ever heard a man speak on the wireless, and he turned round to my brother and he said, 'Tell that bloke to talk slower. I can't understand what he's saying.'

TRB: Did you used to sit and listen to the radio as a family?

VERA: Yes . . . on Saturday night, *In Town Tonight*, that was lovely . . . *Bells across the Meadow* . . .

HELEN: The orchestras that used to come on.

JESSE: The first wireless I ever saw was when I was in London, I was eleven, I'd never seen one before, when they had the crystal set . . .

But there wasn't much sign that these happy memories of the radio made much difference to their present lives. Indeed, if anything, they were the most television-minded groups of all.

TRB: Do any of you prefer the radio?
ALICE: No. [*All agree.*]
ROSE (74): I listen to the six o'clock news on the radio 'cos I wake up at five-thirty, and it's surprising how the news changes from six to eight.
TRB: Do any of you listen to *The Archers*?
AGNES (77): No.
JESSE: No.
ROSE: Is that still on?
ALICE: I thought it had faded away . . .

'Nothing is Lacking'

Undoubtedly, though, the radio is still a powerful identity resource for specific groups of people. No loyalty to television channel or programme seems quite to outdo the dedication of the elderly male intellectual to Radio Three, the delight taken in Radio Four by sections of the metropolitan middle class, the unstinting affection of groups of young people for the latest pirate station (Solar and K Jazz in London, Radio Nova in Liverpool and North Wales).

ANNE (51): With television, you feel that everybody knows the television. They can all see it. But the radio is very much more personal.

But these are still minority groups. Radio Three audiences are frequently almost too small to measure: somewhere between 50,000 and 250,000. Radio Four's most popular programmes, *Today* and *The Archers* (*Omnibus Edition*), attract 1.2 million and 850,000 respectively; while underneath the inflated claims of stations like Solar and JFM lie listening figures of between 100,000 and 200,000. (European pirates like Laser claim much higher figures.) In some of these cases – Radio Three, K Jazz – the highly specialised nature of the output more or less limits the possibility for growth. But elsewhere there was no sign among our viewers that they might cope with any of their television 'guilt' by swinging back to radio. Many already used it to fill in the intervals between television:

HELEN (37): We always listen to radio first thing in the morning, funny enough.
DEREK (35): Yes, we do.
JOHN (41): We always have the radio on first thing, from the time we wake up until the time everybody goes out.
GLENDA (28): We haven't got into breakfast television.
JOHN: No, we don't watch it yet.
HELEN: It's the only time we listen to the radio. After that it's television.

There's always a radio at hand. They positively litter our homes. A third of the households in the UK have four or more. (So many, it seems, that some of us have forgotten exactly where they all are: 4 million household sets never get played at all.) Out on the road there are another 11 million car radios, and any number of pedestrian radios ranging from tiny personal Walkmans, three inches by four, to vast ghetto blasters measuring two and a half feet across.

'Like clocks and watches, the old co-exist beside the new; the valve radio with the expensive Japanese stereo tuner; the faithful fifteen-year-old "tranny" with the portable stereo radio cassette recorder.' (Justin Gutmann, in BBC, 1985.) With so many radios around, the whole house can become a sound studio:

> JULIE (42): I used to carry my radio with me from room to room, up and down the stairs. So I've got one up now and two down and if I am doing something in the kitchen and I go upstairs, I immediately put the one upstairs on as well and I've got it in stereo then all over the house.

For most people radio is now only an accompaniment. You justify listening by explaining that you were simultaneously doing other things. It is not so much intrinsic merit as convenience which is stressed. This means that those who are 'merely' listening to the radio (much in the way that millions sat grouped around their sets for *Saturday Night Theatre* before the arrival of television) are likely to feel guilty: 'The idea of sitting down and listening is generally considered strange and unacceptable.' (From BBC Audience Research Special Report, *Radio 3*, May 1984.)

And when it does happen, it becomes something to comment upon: 'Well, one day last week I sat in the kitchen and was listening to the end of something on *Woman's Hour* and I actually sat down to listen to it.' (Female/Bristol/Regular.)

Such was the sense of guilt aroused by not treating radio in a subordinate fashion, that Radio Three listeners were amused and relieved to learn that others had sinned in the same way as themselves: 'Somebody called and looked through the window, quite appalled . . . she was very surprised I was actually sitting down just listening, because I don't think a lot of people do.' (Female/Bristol/ Regular.)

'I really got caught at the beginning of this week. I was listening to Radio Three and doing my visits. I couldn't bear to do my visits until at least one movement in this concerto was played – so I was driving round the block.' (Female/Doctor/Bristol/Regular.)

But although this research project on Radio Three engendered a little group solidarity, the solitary nature of much radio listening makes it unsuitable as a topic for general discussion. The days when everyone in the class had heard last night's *Goon Show* and was anxious to imitate every one of its protagonists are well past. Nowadays only *The Archers* seem to stimulate such enthusiasm:

TRB: Do you think it is daft to talk about *The Archers* as if they were real people?

WENDY (31): No.

HELEN (37): Everybody who ever listens to *The Archers* always talks about them as though they are real people. I've never met anybody who doesn't.

ANNE (51): When the baby was born, I went up there and said, 'She's had it.' 'What are you talking about, "*She's had it*"?' When she had William. When my friend went to Australia a few years ago, I taped it for five weeks for her . . . when she came back she had five hours of *The Archers* to listen to. I can't imagine anyone videoing *Crossroads* for five weeks.

HELEN: Well, nothing much would happen in five weeks. [*Laughter.*]

Radio soaps do perhaps have another advantage over television. Characters can more easily be replaced.

ANNE: Grace Archer died about twenty years ago. She died really . . . I mean in the story she died. She didn't die really, not in real life. And Walter Gabriel died in real life and they had to replace him.

MARK (47): And the character of Dan Archer had to be replaced.

ANNE: He's been replaced about three times, though, Dan Archer. It does take a long time to get used to the new voice.

MARK: I don't know if it's a good idea or not. I think it's sometimes best to kill them off.

DEREK (35): Paul Johnson [from *The Archers*] a few years ago . . . he died in a motor accident.

JOHN (41): He died in real life and now they've replaced him with someone else.

But there was not much enthusiasm for those radio actors who decided to take a leaf out of television's book and start capitalising upon the success of their fictional personas.

HELEN: Someone gave me a book on *The Archers*, and it ruined it all for me, because I know exactly what they all look like. Somebody showed me this stupid book of the real men on and I was shocked because I didn't picture them like that.

WENDY: I don't want to see what they look like. I live with my dreams.

HELEN: It does spoil it.

Radio fiction could be disturbed a little – but only if the listener was allowed to call the tune:

GLENDA (28): I love to listen to plays on the radio and imagine how they've gone about getting the sound effects. You know, you hear somebody walking across a gravel path and you imagine this tray of gravel and somebody is standing there going like this to make the noise.

BOB (33): I think it stretches your imagination listening to something on the radio, more than watching television. It's done for you, isn't it? You just look at it, oh, yes, fine.

ANNE (51): You can imagine how the people look. And they always look different to everybody, don't they?

We don't any longer have to 'find time' for radio, we largely make it operate alongside our existing timetables, allowing it to wake with us at seven in the morning, follow us through breakfast, and then perhaps accompany us in our cars as a mobile newspaper on the way to work. It is a perfect servant.

Television, by contrast, still fails to know its place. Time has to be found for watching, time which is thought to be stolen from other activities and lost for ever. It is this aspect which causes most concern to the viewer: it is something which others have related to the broadest questions about how we choose to live our entire lives.

> One of the most important tasks of the human being is that of dividing up his time. He has to use it according to what is best for his nature and his aims in life. For most people nowadays this only concerns their so-called free time. Here they are not only allowed, they are also *forced* to decide what they will do; whether they will play, walk, sleep, be sociable, drink or read. And even here we find a general tendency to eliminate that choice by drawing up a plan, for example, that . . . delegates everything, even the joys of love, to their fixed times in the week.
> (Rudolf Arnheim, *Radio*, 1936.)

And now there is the new technological temptation in the corner of the room, which must also be programmed. 'It even decides the moment . . . of going to bed.' Everybody still has the choice to switch off, but 'what is significant is that he does not want it. If you don't need to choose, you don't choose. If you can be passive you lose your activity.' (Ibid.)

The only consolation to be found in this indictment of the human tendency to fall into programmed ways of life and passivity under the influence of modern media is that it was written in 1936 and concerned the ills – *of wireless*.

11

Varieties of Experience

Even though our research into the views of the television audience is relatively comprehensive compared to the existing body of knowledge, it is still based upon limited numbers, and upon verbal reports of people's behaviour, rather than upon direct observation.

But what we have heard in the preceding chapters does at least suggest that certain common assumptions about television viewing are in need of revision.

It is difficult, for example, in the face of so much humour and imagination about the contents of television, to regard the viewing experience as somehow incompatible with creativity. Over and over again in these discussion groups we found people with an ability to improvise around the themes and characters of television which gave the lie to any idea that they merely absorbed, then reproduced, whatever television chose to throw at them.

Similarly, 'passivity' is an odd term to describe the manner in which so many of these people watched their screens. In the early days of television, it may have been true that the flickering box in the darkened room could actually 'entrance' its audience: nowadays this hardly fits any description of its use. But neither should we go to the opposite extreme and declare that people hardly watch it at all: that it flickers away unattended in the corner while they get on with making tea, hoovering the carpet and completing their aerobic workouts. Sometimes it is watched with great intensity and emotional involvement (quite enough to produce tears of sorrow or hours of joy): at other moments, with an irreverent concern (in which actors and plot readily become mere laughing matters). In both cases it is likely to be a subject for conversation and comment among those present either during or after the specific programme. And whatever may have been the case in the past, nowadays, with at least four channels available and a prerecorded film for hire a few hundred yards down the road, choice is likely to be continually exercised: something which shows up dramatically in the figures which indicate that channel loyalty is now (except in name) largely a thing of the past.

Although 'television conversations' may often be about the comings and goings of fictional characters or 'personalities', they provide ways of talking about a great many other features of the world: sex, sin, retribution and death.

Indeed, as we said earlier, in some cases it seems that television drama has only properly occurred, been thoroughly realised, when the plots and the moral messages they contain have been discussed and interpreted and re-dramatised in the company of friends or mere acquaintances. This may seem an elaborate way of talking about the national concern with, say, the breakdown of Ken and Deirdre's marriage, but there is an imbalance here to correct: too often such matters are treated far *less* seriously than they deserve.

This social aspect of television also acquired some support from our national sample. Whereas only 18 per cent agreed with the statement that 'television has made me more interested in myself', 70 per cent felt that it had made them 'more interested in other people'.

Surely, though, television in the home interferes with the close relationship between parents and children, even if only by surrounding the child with more attractive images and models than those of home and hearth? Viewers did express worries about this: they found it difficult to stop their children watching, worried about their dependence on it.

But set against this was the evident pleasure which was derived from the family viewing of certain programmes (*Only Fools and Horses* seems established at the moment as such a family favourite) and the indications of how frequently parents (and grandparents) join children to watch less adult programmes. Neither does the dramatic decline in television viewing as children get older (the weekly average falls from 23½ hours per week for eight- to eleven-year-olds to 16 hours per week for sixteen- to twenty-four-year-olds) suggest that the experience of heavy viewing in childhood is ever addictive enough to offset the traditional temptations of adolescence.

What is more, few children regard television uncritically. Even the four- and five-year-old children in our sample were able to produce a long list of programmes they disliked, and among the fourteen- and fifteen-year-olds there was a very strong tendency to regard everything but *The Young Ones* as 'boring'.

Television does not emerge from our discussions as a very 'heroic' medium. Although some characters may be temporarily idealised, the appearance of the actor who played them on the *Wogan* show next evening, or news about their toupee the following Sunday in the *Sunday People*, does much to bring them down to earth. The strongest identifications are with those who make a virtue of their 'normality' – the 'ordinary' chat-show hosts – those 'celebrities' who are somehow thought to be playing no one but themselves. Even the attractions of the more 'escapist' programmes depend upon that slightly knowing suspension of disbelief which positively increases the enjoyment but hardly seems likely to encourage identification.

We have said relatively little about the 'quality' of the popular programmes which form the subject matter of most of this book, only suggesting in places that there was more to some programmes than critics sometimes allowed: that game and quiz shows, for example, were concerned with considerably more than materialism and greed, that soap operas could perhaps only be fully understood by those who were also privy to their history and the tabloid material which elaborated their characters, that the success of chat shows might have much to do with the pleasure of watching 'mere' talk; that significant distinctions were drawn between the 'expert' and 'personalities'. This is not to say that various popular programmes are 'good' or 'bad', but that they are chosen for different reasons. The great danger of talking about 'mass entertainment' or 'prime-time' viewing or 'the taste of the majority' is the assumption that the programmes which might fall under this heading are somehow all of a piece. This is far from the truth. Not only do the formats and subject matter vary greatly, but there are many different forms of appreciation: the quiet afternoon pleasure derived from *Sons and Daughters*, the gregarious family laughter of *Only Fools and Horses*, the knowing identification with Ewings and Carringtons, the sense of fellow-feeling during *Wogan*, the defensive irreverence felt towards *Crossroads*, the gentle sadness so often evoked by *Coronation Street*.

Only a few people in this world may remain for ever immune to such mild distractions, gentle pleasures and sheer delights. Some of our viewers thought even that a pity.

JANET (32): They never watch television in *Dynasty*, do they?

ANNE (45): No, you never see them sitting round the set.

MOLLY (41): Well, they haven't got time, I suppose. Far too much to do.

TRB: If they did watch television, what do you think they'd watch?

PAT (47): *Coronation Street*? Just imagine Blake and Krystle sitting there watching it all.

JEAN (42): They'd probably think that's how people in England really live. [*All laugh.*]

PAT: Sitting there listening to the music and looking at all those rooftops.

MOLLY: Oh yes. [*All shout together.*] *And the cat!*

Bibliography

Books and articles

Arnheim, Rudolf (1936) *Radio*, Faber and Faber, London.

Barthes, Roland (1973) *Mythologies*, Granada, London.

Bogart, Leo (1980) 'Television News as Entertainment', pp. 209–50, in Tannenbaum, ed. (1980).

Boorstin, Daniel J. (1961) *The Image*, Weidenfeld and Nicolson, London.

British Broadcasting Corporation Data (1985) *Annual Review of BBC Broadcasting Research Findings*, BBC, London.

Brunsdon, Charlotte (1984) 'Writing about Soap Opera', pp. 82–7, in Masterman, ed. (1984).

Brunt, Rosalind (1984) 'What's My Line?', pp. 21–8, in Masterman, ed. (1984).

Buckman, Peter (1984) *All for Love: A Study in Soap Opera*, Secker and Warburg, London.

Burns, Elizabeth (1972) *Theatricality*, Longman, London.

Buscombe, Ed (1984) 'Disembodied Voices and Familiar Faces: Television Continuity', pp. 128–31, in Masterman, ed. (1984).

Conrad, Peter (1982) *Television: The Medium and its Manners*, Routledge and Kegan Paul, London.

Dunkley, Christopher (1985) *Television Today and Tomorrow*, Penguin, Harmondsworth.

Dyer, Richard, et al., eds. (1981) *Coronation Street*, BFI, London.

Dyer, Richard (1981) Introduction, pp. 1–8, in Dyer et al., eds. (1981).

Ellis, John (1982) *Visible Fictions*, Routledge and Kegan Paul, London.

Ellul, Jacques (1964, orig. 1954) *The Technological Society*, Vintage Books, New York.

Enzensberger, Hans Magnus (1970) 'Constituents of a Theory of the Media', pp. 99–116, in McQuail, ed. (1979).

Fantoni, Barry and Melly, George (1980) *The Media Mob*, Collins, London.

Farber, Leslie H. (1976) *Lying, Despair, etc.*, Basic Books, New York.

Fearing, Franklin (1947) 'Influence of the Movies on Attitudes and Behaviour', pp. 119–34, in McQuail, ed. (1979).

Ferguson, Marilyn (1984) *The Aquarian Conspiracy*, Routledge and Kegan Paul, London.

Gallagher, Jock (1981) 'The Archers' Story I', pp. 15–46, in Smethurst, ed. (1981).

Gans, Herbert J. (1980) 'The Audience for Television – and in Television Research', pp. 55–82, in Withey and Abeles, eds. (1980).

Goodhardt, G. J., Ehrenberg, A. S. C., and Collins, M. A. (1980) *The Television Audience: Patterns of Viewing*, Gower, Aldershot.

Gray, Ann (1985) *Women and Video*, unpublished Ph.D. thesis, University of York.

Gutmann, Justin (1985) 'Radio Sets 1983', pp. 50–60, in BBC (1985).

Harty, Russell (1982) 'Shadow Across the Screen', pp. 130–39, in Wenham, ed. (1982).

Hobson, Dorothy (1982) *Crossroads: The Drama of a Soap Opera*, Methuen, London.

Hoggart, Richard (1958) *The Uses of Literacy*, Penguin, Harmondsworth.

Hoggart, Richard (1982) *An English Temper*, Chatto and Windus, London.

Horton, Donald and Wohl, R. Richard (1956) 'Mass Communication and Para-Social Interaction', *Psychiatry*, Vol. 19, pp. 215–29.

James, Clive (1981) *Visions Before Midnight*, Pan, London.

James, Clive (1981a) *The Crystal Bucket*, Pan, London.

James, Clive (1983) *Glued to the Box*, Pan, London.

Jordan, Marion (1981) 'Realism and Convention', pp. 27–40, in Dyer et al., eds. (1981).

Jordan, Marion (1981a) 'Character Types and the Individual', pp. 67–81, in Dyer et al., eds. (1981).

Kershaw, H. V. (1981) *The Street Where I Live*, Granada, London.

Lasch, Christopher (1978) *The Culture of Narcissism*, W. W. Norton, New York.

Lealand, Geoffrey (1984) *American Television Programmes on British Screens*, Broadcasting Research Unit, London.

Lewis, Bill (1984) 'TV Games: People as Performers', pp. 42–5, in Masterman, ed. (1984).

Lewis, Martyn (1984) *'And Finally'*, Century Publishing, London.

Longley, Andrew (1985) *The Making of 'The Living Planet'*, George Allen and Unwin, London.

McQuail, Dennis, ed. (1979) *Sociology of Mass Communications*, Penguin, Harmondsworth.

McQuail, Dennis, Blumler, Jay G., and Brown, J. R. (1972) 'The Television Audience: a revised perspective', pp. 135–65, in McQuail, ed. (1979).

Mander, Jerry (1980) *Four Arguments for the Elimination of Television*, Harvester, Brighton.

Masterman, Len, ed. (1984) *Television Mythologies*, Comedia Publishing, London.

Mayer, J. P. (1948) *British Cinemas and their Audiences*, Dennis Dobson, London.

Menaker, Daniel (1982) 'Art and Artifice in Network News', pp. 240–46, in Newcomb, ed. (1982).

Moorfoot, Rex (1982) *Television in the Eighties: The Total Equation*, BBC, London.

Newcomb, Horace, ed. (1982, third edition) *Television: The Critical View*, Oxford University Press, New York.

Newcomb, Horace (1982a) 'Texas: A giant state of mind', pp. 167–74, in Newcomb, ed. (1982).

Newcomb, Horace (1982b) 'Toward a Television Aesthetic', pp. 478–94, in Newcomb, ed. (1982).

Parkin, Anthony (1981) 'Fitting in the Farming', pp. 177–93, in Smethurst, ed. (1981).

Passingham, Kenneth (1984) *The Guinness Book of TV Facts and Feats*, Guiness Superlatives, London.

Scheff, Thomas S. and Scheele, Stephen C. (1980) 'Humour and Catharsis: The Effect of Comedy on Audiences', pp. 165–82, in Tannenbaum, ed. (1980).

Self, David (1984) *Television Drama: An Introduction*, Macmillan, London.

Sennett, Richard (1977) *The Fall of Public Man*, Cambridge University Press, Cambridge.

Smethurst, William, ed. (1981) *The Archers: The First Thirty Years*, New English Library, London.

Stoppard, Tom (1968) *The Real Inspector Hound*, Faber and Faber, London.

Tannenbaum, Percy H., ed. (1980) *The Entertainment Functions of Television*, Lawrence Erlbaum, New Jersey.

Thorburn, Daniel (1982) 'Television Melodrama', pp. 529–46, in Newcomb, ed. (1982).

Timberg, Bernard (1982) 'The Rhetoric of the Camera in Television Soap Opera', pp. 132–47, in Newcomb, ed. (1982).

Towler, Robert (1984) 'The Problem of Channel Image', *Airwaves* (IBA Quarterly), pp. 22–3.

Tudor, Andrew (1974) *Image and Influence: Studies in the Sociology of Film*, George Allen and Unwin, London.

Wenham, Brian, ed. (1982) *The Third Age of Broadcasting*, Faber and Faber, London.

Wheen, Francis (1985) *Television*, Century Publishing, London.

Williams, Raymond (1974) *Television: Technology and Cultural Form*, Fontana, London.

Williams, Raymond (1975) *Drama in a Dramatized Society: An Inaugural Lecture*, Cambridge University Press, Cambridge.

Wilson, Elizabeth (1984) 'All in the Family: Russell Grant on Breakfast Television', pp. 7–9, in Masterman, ed. (1984).

Winn, Marie (orig. 1977, revised edition 1985) *The Plug-in Drug*, Penguin, Harmondsworth.

Withey, Stephen B. and Abeles, Ronald P., eds. (1980) *Television and Social Behaviour: Beyond Violence and Children*, Lawrence Erlbaum, New Jersey.

Wood, Michael (1975) *America in the Movies*, Basic Books, New York.

Zillman, Dolf (1980) 'Anatomy of Suspense', pp. 133–64, in Tannenbaum, ed. (1980).

(i) BBC Audience Research, Special Reports

Why Listen?, February 1980, LR/80/28.

Viewing 'Midday News', October 1981, VR/81/324.

'Newsnight': viewing, non-viewing, and opinions, February 1982, VR/82/28.

Evaluating 'So you want to stop smoking', Interim Report, September 1982, SP 82/04.81/16.

The 'Play it Safe!' Child Accident Prevention Campaign. Research to evaluate its impact, Volume 1: Results, November 1982, SP 82/05.81/23.

The Nine O'Clock News, December 1982, SP 82/15.

BBC's Computer Literacy Project – an evaluation – summary, January 1983, SP 82/22, 81/55.

'So you want to stop smoking' – Results of a follow-up one year later, April 1983, SP 83/15.81/16.

That's Life! (Viewers' reactions), May 1983, SP 83.20/83.10.

What on Earth?, December 1983.

Young People and Music with special reference to 'Top of the Pops', January 1984, SP 83/57/83/51.

Quizzes – what makes a good television quiz programme?, April 1984, SP 84/20/83/86.4.

Radio 3, group discussions, May 1984, SP 84/33/83/99.

Songs of Praise, December 1984, SP 84/64/84/07.

'Threads' and 'On the Eighth Day', December 1984, SP 85/02/84/51.

(ii) IBA Audience Research Department Reports

Lonely People and the Media, March 1978.

The Role of Wrestling as a Public Spectacle – audience attitudes to wrestling as portrayed on television, November 1978.

Edward and Mrs Simpson – explorations of the significance of the series for the public, March 1979.

Attitudes towards an absent service – public opinions, during the ITV strike, on aspects of ITV and of BBC 2, November 1979.

The Appreciation and Viewing of Drama Programmes, June 1979.

Offence and Defence in the Home – some reasons for viewers' reactions to bad language on television, February 1980.

Fiction and Depiction – attitudes to fifteen television series, and the novels from which they were made, April 1980.

Audience Reaction to the 'Communion' programme, July 1980.

Brideshead Revisited – a flawed and final masterpiece of major TV series production?, March 1982.

The Psychological and Economic Value of TV – a pointer from Peter Tavy, April 1984.

Irvine, S. H., Irvine, M., Auburn, M., and Auburn, T., *Peter Tavy Turns Off*, Report to the IBA Research Department, March 1984.

Index